ETHICAL ISSUI
SECURITY AND SURVEILLANCE
RESEARCH

ADVANCES IN RESEARCH ETHICS AND INTEGRITY

Series Editor: Dr Ron Iphofen, *FAcSS, Independent Consultant, France*

Recent volumes:

Volume 1: Finding Common Ground: Consensus in Research Ethics Across the Social Sciences, Edited by *Ron Iphofen*
Volume 2: The Ethics of Online Research, Edited by *Kandy Woodfield*
Volume 3: Virtue Ethics in the Conduct and Governance of Social Science Research, Edited by *Nathan Emmerich*
Volume 4: Ethics and Integrity in Health and Life Sciences Research, Edited by *Zvonimir Koporc*
Volume 5: Ethics and Integrity in Visual Research Methods, Edited by *Savannah Dodd*
Volume 6: Indigenous Research Ethics, Edited by *Lily George, Juan Tauri and Lindsey Te Ata o Tu MacDonald*
Volume 7: Ethics and Integrity in Research with Children and Young People, Edited by *Grace Spencer*

Editorial Advisory Group

Professor Robert Dingwall, *FAcSS, Dingwayy Enterprises Ltd and Nottingham Trent University, UK*
Dr Nathan Emmerich, *Institute of Ethics, Dublin City University and Queens University Belfast, UK*
Professor Mark Israel, *University of Western Australia, Australia*
Dr Janet Lewis, AcSS, *Former Research Director, Joseph Rowntree Foundation, UK*
Professor John Oates, FAcSS, *Open University, UK*
Associate Professor Martin Tolich, *University of Otago, New Zealand*

ADVANCES IN RESEARCH ETHICS AND INTEGRITY
VOLUME 8

ETHICAL ISSUES IN COVERT, SECURITY AND SURVEILLANCE RESEARCH

EDITED BY

RON IPHOFEN
Independent Consultant, France

AND

DÓNAL O'MATHÚNA
The Ohio State University, USA

United Kingdom – North America – Japan
India – Malaysia – China

Emerald Publishing Limited
Howard House, Wagon Lane, Bingley BD16 1WA, UK

First edition 2022

Reprints and permissions service
Contact: permissions@emeraldinsight.com

British Library Cataloguing in Publication Data
A catalogue record for this book is available from the British Library

ISBN: 978-1-80262-414-4 (Print)
ISBN: 978-1-80262-411-3 (Online)
ISBN: 978-1-80262-413-7 (Epub)

ISSN: 2398-6018 (Series)

Printed and bound by CPI Group (UK) Ltd, Croydon, CR0 4YY

CONTENTS

ABOUT THE EDITORS

Ron Iphofen, FAcSS (British), is an Independent Consultant based in France with international recognition for expertise on research ethics and professional standards in research. Since 2008, he has presented at over 200 national and international events for universities, government, research institutes and the European Commission (EC) and European Research Council (ERC). He has served in the Universities Sector of the Association for Research Ethics UK. He has acted as consultant, adviser and/or delivered training on research ethics for the Scottish Executive, UK Government Social Research, National Disability Authority (Ireland), National Centre for Social Research, Social Research Association, Audit Commission, Food Standards Agency, Ministry of Justice, BIG Lottery, Local Authorities' Consortium, UK Research Integrity Office, Skills Development Scotland, ANR (French Research Funding agency), SSRC (Canada) and many others. His primary consultative activity at present is for the EC Ethics Unit, Directorate General for Science and Innovation, the Research Executive Agency and the ERC.

Dónal O'Mathúna (Irish) is Associate Professor at The Ohio State University, USA, in the College of Nursing and the Center for Bioethics in the College of Medicine. He is the Director of the Cochrane Affiliate at Ohio State's Helene Fuld Health Trust National Institute for Evidence-based Practice in Nursing and Healthcare, and a member of the Executive Committee of the Cochrane US Network, which reflects his long-standing involvement with Cochrane, a major producer of reliable health evidence. His interests in bioethics focus on ethical issues in humanitarian settings, disasters and pandemics. He is Visiting Professor of Ethics in the European Masters in Disaster Medicine, Università del Piemonte Orientale, Italy. He has led funded research projects into humanitarian research ethics, and has contributed to ethics initiatives and guidelines with the World Health Organization, United Nations International Children's Emergency Fund and other international agencies. He has co-edited three volumes addressing various ethical issues in disasters, and has authored numerous peer-reviewed articles.

ABOUT THE CONTRIBUTORS

Hartmut Aden is a Lawyer and Political Scientist. He is Professor of German and European Public Law, Public Policy and Public Administration at the Berlin School of Economics and Law/Hochschule für Wirtschaft und Recht (HWR Berlin), Vice President for Research of HWR Berlin and member of the Berlin Institute for Safety and Security Research (FÖPS Berlin). He is the founding Academic Director of the MA Programme in International Security Management established in 2018.

Alfonso Alfonsi has more than 35 years of experience at international level in social research, training, evaluation and scientific networking. His expertise includes urban development, poverty and social exclusion, religion and modernisation, science ethics and science policies, social and cultural change and socialisation of scientific and technological research. He works as an Expert for organisations of the UN system (such as United Nations Department of Economic and Social Affairs, HABITAT, WORLD BANK and United Nations Development Programme), for the European Union and for Italian bodies (such as Ministry of Foreign Affairs, National Research Council, Lazio Regional Government and Puglia Regional Government). In this framework, he has directed and/or participated in several research projects in Europe, Africa and Asia.

He serves as Science Ethics Expert for the European Commission, by participating in expert groups and evaluation panels (in Seventh Framework Programme and in HORIZON 2020 frameworks).

He participated as an expert in UN high level encounters and other international partnerships, contributing in the drafting of position papers and in the formulation of policy documents and manifestos. He has coordinated international multi-stakeholder networks for development, such as the Network on Services for the Urban Poor of the Water Supply and Sanitation Collaborative Council or the UN-Habitat International Forum of Researchers on Human Settlements.

Maresa Berliri is a Sociologist who has participated in several research projects focussed on the relations between science and society; Responsible Research and Innovation in research performing organisations; social subjectivity on the web and privacy protection; internet governance and digital transition; active citizenship and relations between states and citizens; women in political, scientific and entrepreneurial organisations; and in poverty and social exclusion. Among these projects, it is worth highlighting: CONSENT (consumer sentiment regarding privacy on user generated content service in the digital economy), MAPPING (managing alternatives for privacy, property and internet governance) and RESPECT (rules, expectations and security through privacy enhanced convenient technologies). She is currently involved in some H2020 Projects including: PRO-RES (PROmoting integrity in the use of RESearch results) and RESBIOS (RESponsible research and innovation grounding practices in BIOSciencies).

Marina Da Bormida is an R&I Lawyer and Ethics Expert in Italy. She obtained her degree in Law and PhD degree in Legal Issues of the Information Society. She specialised in legal, ethical and societal themes related to information and communication technology research and technological developments in the framework of R&D national and European projects in a wide range of domains (e.g. Big Data, Artificial Intelligence, digital lifestyle, Internet of Things, Factories of the Future and Smart Manufacturing, Cloud Computing, Smart Contracts and Blockchain), with consolidated experience and long-term scientific collaboration with well-known research institutions.

Dr Darren Ellis is a chartered Psychologist, Senior Lecturer at the University of East London and Course Leader of the Psychosocial Community Work programme. He is co-author *of Emotion in the Digital Age: Technologies, Data and Psychosocial Life* (Routledge, 2020) for Routledge's Studies in Science, Technology and Society Series and *Social Psychology of Emotion* (Sage, 2015). He co-edited *After lockdown, Opening Up: Psychosocial Transformations in the Wake of Covid-19* (Palgrave, 2021) for Palgrave's Studies in the Psychosocial and *Affect and Social Media: Emotion, Mediation, Anxiety and Contagion* (Rowman and Littlefield, 2018) for Rowman and Littlefield's Radical Cultural Studies Series. He has published articles on a wide range of topics including surveillance studies, for example: 'Stop and Search: Disproportionality, Discretion and Generalisations' (2010, *Police Journal*), 'The Affective Atmospheres of Surveillance' (2013, *Theory and Psychology*) and 'Techno-securitisation of Everyday Life and Cultures of Surveillance—Apatheia' (2020, *Science as Culture*).

David J. Harper is Professor of Clinical Psychology and Programme Director (Academic) of the Professional Doctorate in Clinical Psychology at the University of East London, UK. He has co-authored and co-edited a number of books including *Psychology, Mental Health and Distress* (Red Globe Press, 2013), *Qualitative Research Methods in Mental Health and Psychotherapy* (Wiley, 2012) and *Deconstructing Psychopathology* (Sage, 1995). He has published journal articles and book chapters on public understandings of surveillance, discourses of paranoia, conspiracy and surveillance in clinical and popular cultures and the history of psychological and psychiatric involvement in national security interrogations.

Richard Kirkham is an Administrative Justice Lawyer whose main research area of interest is on redress mechanisms in the administrative justice system and judicial review. His recent publications include *Executive Decision-making and the Courts: Revisiting the Origins of Modern Judicial Review* (Hart Publishing, 2021, edited with T. T. Arvind, Daithí Mac Síthigh and Lindsay Stirton), *A Manifesto for Ombudsman Reform* (Palgrave MacMillan, 2020, edited with C. Gill) and *The*

Oxford Handbook of Administrative Justice (OUP, Forthcoming, edited with M. Hertogh, R. Thomas and J. Tomlinson).

Simon E. Kolstoe, is a Reader in Bioethics at the University of Portsmouth, and chair of the UK's Ministry of Defence Research Ethics Committee (MODREC). Following a PhD in Biochemistry and ten years conducting Medical Research, his academic and research interests are now focussed on how Ethics, Governance and Integrity processes impact the reliability and effectiveness of medical and human participant research. He also chairs research ethics committees for the UK Health Security Agency and Health Research Authority.

Kevin Macnish is Digital Ethics Consulting Manager with Sopra Steria. A former Analyst and Manager at the UK Government Communications Headquarters (GCHQ) and the the US Government Department of Defense (US DOD), he gained his PhD in Digital Ethics from the University of Leeds in 2013. He has been interviewed by BBC national television and radio and has spoken at both the House of Commons and the House of Lords in relation to digital ethics. Prior to joining Sopra Steria, he was Assistant Professor in Ethics and IT in the Philosophy Department at the University of Twente where his research and consultancy work focussed on the ethics of privacy, artificial intelligence and cybersecurity. He published *The Ethics of Surveillance: An Introduction* (Routledge, 2018) and *Big Data and Democracy* (Edinburgh University Press, 2020). He has published more than 30 academic articles and chapters in his areas of interest, including the chapter on cybersecurity ethics in the forthcoming *Handbook on Digital Ethics* (Oxford University Press) and is a frequent speaker at international trade and academic conferences. He is an independent Ethics Expert for the European Commission, visiting PhD Supervisor at the University of Twente and a member of the International Association of Privacy Professionals' Research Advisory Board.

Marco Marzano is Professor of Sociology of Organizations at the University of Bergamo, Italy. His research focusses on religion, Catholicism, cancer, illness narrative and organisation theory. In terms of methodological approaches, he is interested in ethnography, qualitative research, investigative methods and covert research. He has a strong interest in social research ethics. He is the author of numerous international publications in different languages (English, German, Italian and soon Polish and French) and he has been a visiting professor at many universities in different countries around the world (from the UK to the USA, from Brazil to Argentina, from the Czech Republic to Romania). He has participated in numerous international conferences, sometimes as a keynote speaker.

Daniel Paul is a Security Risk Management Consultant, with a specialism in crisis management and security for high-risk environments. He started out his career in the British Army before briefly working a project manager for the humanitarian sector. It was here he realised he had a passion for keeping others safe and moved into the security management field. He completed his PhD in 2019, where he studied the role of knowledge management in keeping humanitarian workers safe when working in dangerous environments. His PhD provided a knowledge management framework for eliciting and sharing security specific information within organisations in order to improve security risk management systems. He also holds a Bachelors in International Security and Disaster Management. Alongside consultancy work, he lectures at Coventry University in Disaster Management. He runs modules in disaster preparedness, humanitarian essentials and lectures on the topics of security management, disaster response and risk management.

Paul Spicker is a writer and commentator on Social Policy. His published work includes 20 books, several shorter works and over 100 academic papers. His studies of housing and welfare rights developed from his early career; since then, his research has included studies related to benefit delivery systems, the care of old people, psychiatric patients, housing management and local anti-poverty strategy. He is a consultant on social welfare in practice, and has done work for a range of agencies at local, national and international levels. After teaching at Nottingham Trent University and the University of Dundee, he held the Grampian Chair of Public Policy at Robert Gordon University (RGU) from 2001 to 2015, and was Director of its Centre for Public Policy and Management. He is now an Emeritus Professor of RGU.

Alex Stedmon, CSci CPsychol CErgHF AFBPsS FCIEHF FRSA, is a Professor of Human Factors specialising in security and defence. He has also been elected as President of the Chartered Institute of Ergonomics and Human Factors (2022) and been awarded a Royal Academy of Engineering Visiting Professor role in the Psychology Department at Cardiff University. He previously worked for the Ministry of Defence before a move into academia where his research focussed on human factors issues of technology use and contextual methods for investigating public safety in various security environments. He was a Technical Lead on a Strategic Security Project in the run up to the London Olympics and has conducted pioneering research in deception, safeguarding public spaces and novel collaborative networks for security. He has contributed to winning over £33million of research funding to date and has over 230 mainly peer-reviewed publications. He was the lead Editor of the first book on *Counter-terrorism and Hostile Intent: Human Factors Theory and Application* (Ashgate Publishing Limited, 2015). During his university career, he was chair of various ethics committees and Deputy Director of Ethics for the Faculty of Engineering at Coventry University. In 2019, he retired from academia to work as a consultant for various international clients and conduct expert witness roles for the courts.

Mark Taylor is an Associate Professor in Health Law and Regulation at Melbourne Law School and Deputy Director of the research group HeLEX, which focusses on the legal and regulatory frameworks governing new health technologies. His own research is focussed on the regulation of personal information with emphasis on health and genetic data. He seeks to develop a concept of privacy that is capable of reconciling individual and community (privacy) interests with a broader (public) interest in access, use and management of personal health information.

Ian Tucker is Professor of Health and Social Psychology at The University of East London. His research interests include mental health, emotion and affect, digital media and surveillance. He has published empirical and theoretical work on care and recovery in a range of environments for mental health support, digital peer support in mental health and surveillance. He is currently working on a UKRI MARCH Network+ project exploring the impact of digital platforms in relation to 'community assets' (e.g. arts and creative communities) and experiences of mental ill-health. He is co-author of *Social Psychology of Emotion* (Sage, 2020) and *Emotion in the Digital Age: Technologies, Data and Psychosocial Life* (Routledge, 2020), for Routledge's Studies in Science, Technology and Society Series.

ABOUT THE SERIES EDITOR

Ron Iphofen, FAcSS, is Executive Editor of the Emerald book series *Advances in Research Ethics and Integrity* and edited Volume 1 in the series, *Finding Common Ground: Consensus in Research Ethics Across the Social Sciences* (2017). He is an Independent Research Consultant, a Fellow of the UK Academy of Social Sciences, the Higher Education Academy and the Royal Society of Medicine. Since retiring as Director of Postgraduate Studies in the School of Healthcare Sciences, Bangor University, his major activity has been as an Adviser to the European Commission (EC) and its agencies, the European Research Council (ERC) and the Research Executive Agency on both the Seventh Framework Programme and the Horizon 2020. His consultancy work has covered a range of research agencies (in government and independent) across Europe. He was Vice Chair of the UK Social Research Association (SRA), updated their Ethics Guidelines and now convenes the SRA's Research Ethics Forum. He was Scientific Consultant on the EC RESPECT project – establishing pan-European standards in the social sciences and chaired the Ethics and Societal Impact Advisory Group for another EC-funded European Demonstration Project on mass transit security (SECUR-ED). He has advised the UK Research Integrity Office, the National Disability Authority of the Irish Ministry of Justice, the UK Parliamentary Office of Science and Technology, the Scottish Executive, UK Government Social Research, National Centre for Social Research, the Audit Commission, the Food Standards Agency, the Ministry of Justice, the BIG Lottery, a UK Local Authorities' Consortium, Skills Development Scotland, Agence Nationale de la Recherche (ANR the French Research Funding agency) among many others. He was founding Executive Editor of the Emerald gerontology journal *Quality in Ageing and Older Adults*. He published *Ethical Decision Making in Social Research: A Practical Guide* (Palgrave Macmillan, 2009 and 2011) and coedited with Martin Tolich *The SAGE Handbook of Qualitative Research Ethics* (Sage, 2018). He is currently leading a new €2.8M European Commission-funded project (PRO-RES) that aims at promoting ethics and integrity in all non-medical research (2018–2021).

SERIES PREFACE

Ron Iphofen (Series Editor)

This book series, *Advances in Research Ethics and Integrity*, grew out of foundational work with a group of Fellows of the UK Academy of Social Sciences who
were all concerned to ensure that lessons learned from previous work were built
upon and improved in the interests of the production of robust research practices of high quality. Duplication or unnecessary repetitions of earlier research
and ignorance of existing work were seen as hindrances to research progress.
Individual researchers, research professions and society all suffer in having to
pay the costs in time, energy and money of delayed progress and superfluous
repetitions. There is little excuse for failure to build on existing knowledge and
practice given modern search technologies unless selfish 'domain protectionism'
leads researchers to ignore existing work and seek credit for innovations already
accomplished. Our concern was to aid well-motivated researchers to quickly discover existing progress made in ethical research in terms of topic, method and/or
discipline and to move on with their own work more productively and to discover
the best, most effective means to disseminate their own findings so that other
researchers could, in turn, contribute to research progress.

It is true that there is a plethora of ethics codes and guidelines with researchers
left to themselves to judge those more appropriate to their proposed activity. The
same questions are repeatedly asked on discussion forums about how to proceed
when similar long-standing problems in the field are being confronted afresh by
novice researchers. Researchers and members of ethics review boards alike are
faced with selecting the most appropriate codes or guidelines for their current
purpose, eliding differences and similarities in a labyrinth of uncertainty. It is
no wonder that novice researchers can despair in their search for guidance and
experienced researchers may be tempted by the 'checklist mentality' that appears
to characterise a meeting of formalised ethics requirements and permit their con-
science-free pursuit of a cherished programme of research.

If risks of harm to the public and to researchers are to be kept to a mini-
mum and if professional standards in the conduct of scientific research are to be
maintained, the more that fundamental understandings of ethical behaviour in
research are shared the better. If progress is made in one sphere everyone gains
from it being generally acknowledged and understood. If foundational work is
conducted everyone gains from being able to build on and develop further that
work.

Nor can it be assumed that formal ethics review committees are able to resolve the dilemmas or meet the challenges involved. Enough has been written about such review bodies to make their limitations clear. Crucially, they cannot follow researchers into the field to monitor their every action; they cannot anticipate all of the emergent ethical dilemmas nor, even, follow through to the publication of findings. There is no adequate penalty for neglect through incompetence, nor worse, for conscious omissions of evidence. We have to rely upon the virtues of the individual researcher alongside the skills of journal reviewers and funding agency evaluators. We need to constantly monitor scientific integrity at the corporate and at the individual level. These are issues of quality as well as morality.

Within the research ethics field new problems, issues and concerns and new ways of collecting data continue to emerge regularly. This should not be surprising as social, economic and technological change necessitate constant re-evaluation of research conduct. Standard approaches to research ethics such as valid informed consent, inclusion/exclusion criteria, vulnerable subjects and covert studies need to be re-considered as developing social contexts and methodological innovation, interdisciplinary research and economic pressures pose new challenges to convention. Innovations in technology and method challenge our understanding of 'the public' and 'the private'. Researchers need to think even more clearly about the balance of harm and benefit to their subjects, to themselves and to society. This series proposes to address such new and continuing challenges for both funders, research managers, research ethics committees and researchers in the field as they emerge. The concerns and interests are global and well recognised by researchers and commissioners alike around the world but with varying commitments at both the procedural and the practical levels. This series is designed to suggest realistic solutions to these challenges – this practical angle is the *unique selling proposition* for the series. Each volume will raise and address the key issues in the debates, but also strive to suggest ways forward that maintain the key ethical concerns of respect for human rights and dignity, while sustaining pragmatic guidance for future research developments. A series such as this aims to offer practical help and guidance in actual research engagements as well as meeting the often varied and challenging demands of research ethics review. The approach will not be one of abstract moral philosophy; instead it will seek to help researchers think through the potential harms and benefits of their work in the proposal stage and assist their reflection of the big ethical moments that they face in the field often when there may be no one to advise them in terms of their societal impact and acceptance.

While the research community can be highly imaginative both in the fields of study and methodological innovation, the structures of management and funding, and the pressure to publish to fulfil league table quotas can pressure researchers into errors of judgement that have personal and professional consequences. The series aims to adopt an approach that promotes good practice and sets principles, values and standards that serve as models to aid successful research outcomes. There is clear international appeal as commissioners and researchers alike share a vested interest in the global promotion of professional virtues that lead to the public acceptability of good research. In an increasingly global world in research terms, there is little point in applying too localised a morality, nor one that implies a solely Western hegemony of values. If standards 'matter', it seems evident that they should 'matter' to and for all. Only then can the growth of interdisciplinary and multi-national projects be accomplished effectively and with a shared concern for potential harms and benefits. While a diversity of experience and local interests is acknowledged, there are existing, proven models of good practice which can help research practitioners in emergent nations build their policies and processes to suit their own circumstances. We need to see that consensus positions effectively guide the work of scientists across the globe and secure minimal participant harm and maximum societal benefit – and, additionally, that instances of fraudulence, corruption and dishonesty in science decrease as a consequence.

Perhaps some forms of truly independent formal ethics scrutiny can help maintain the integrity of research professions in an era of enhanced concerns over data security, privacy and human rights legislation. But it is essential to guard against rigid conformity to what can become administrative procedures. The consistency we seek to assist researchers in understanding what constitutes 'proper behaviour' does not imply uniformity. Having principles does not lead inexorably to an adherence to principlism. Indeed, sincerely held principles can be in conflict in differing contexts. No one practice is necessarily the best approach in all circumstances. But if researchers are aware of the range of possible ways in which their work can be accomplished ethically and with integrity, they can be free to apply the approach that works or is necessary in their setting. Guides to 'good' ways of doing things should not be taken as the 'only' way of proceeding. A rigidity in outlook does no favours to methodological innovation, nor to the research subjects or participants that they are supposed to protect. If there were to be any principles that should be rigidly adhered to they should include flexibility, open-mindedness, the recognition of the range of challenging situations to be met in the field – principles that in essence amount to a sense of proportionality. And these principles should apply equally to researchers and ethics reviewers alike. To accomplish that requires ethics reviewers to think afresh about each new research proposal, to detach from pre-formed opinions and prejudices, while still learning from and applying the lessons of the past. Principles such as these must also apply to funding and commissioning agencies, to research institutions and to professional associations and their learned societies. Our integrity as researchers demands that we recognise that the rights of our funders and research participants and/or subjects are to be valued alongside our cherished research goals and seek to embody such principles in the research process from the outset. This series will strive to seek just how that might be accomplished in the best interests of all.

ACKNOWLEDGEMENTS

This open access collection was made possible and commissioned under the auspices of the EU-funded PRO-RES Project. PRO-RES is a European Commission-funded project aiming to PROmote ethics and integrity in non-medical RESearch by building an evidence-supported guidance framework for all non-medical sciences and humanities disciplines adopting social science methodologies. The project received funding from the European Union's Horizon 2020 research and innovation programme under Grant Agreement No. 788352. The editors are consortium partners and the authors for the chapters represent a range of stakeholders committed to the aims of the project – including other consortium partners. The editors wish to express their gratitude for the care and commitment demonstrated by the authors to this collection in addressing the sensitive and complex ethical issues raised in this research arena.

INTRODUCTION: ETHICAL ISSUES IN COVERT, SECURITY AND SURVEILLANCE RESEARCH

Ron Iphofen and Dónal O'Mathúna

ABSTRACT

In light of the many crises and catastrophes faced in the modern world, policymakers frequently make claims to be 'following the science' or being 'governed by the data'. Yet, conflict based on inequalities continue to fuel dissatisfaction with the decisions and actions of authorities. Research into public security may require surveillance and covert observations, all of which are subject to major ethical challenges. Any neat distinction between covert and overt research is difficult to maintain given the variety of definitions used for all the terms addressed here. Covert research may be ethically justified and is not necessarily deceptive. In any case, deception may be ethical if engaged in for the 'right' reasons. Modern research sites and innovative research methods may enhance opportunities for covert work. In all surveillance and covert work, care must be taken about how consent is managed, how observed subjects are protected and harm to all involved minimised in all situations.

Keywords: Ethical surveillance; covert research; participant observation; security research; dual use; research ethics review

Ethical Issues in Covert, Security and Surveillance Research
Advances in Research Ethics and Integrity, Volume 8, 1–8
ISSN: 2398-6018/doi:10.1108/S2398-601820210000008001

INTRODUCTION

A series of major significant events and catastrophes have stimulated the developed world to better realise the widely different interpretations of what capitalist, liberal democracies see as progress: from 9/11, the Arab Spring, mass migrations from conflict-ridden regions of the world, to the COVID-19 pandemic, various events have led to growing pressure to make sense of their causes and consequences. Policymakers look to 'science' to supply the answers, and claim they are 'following the science' when making decisions and policies. However, sometimes complex issues are thought through hastily, the studies used to inform policies are not carefully evaluated in terms of their methods or ethics, and policies are introduced with a degree of confidence not justified by the 'science.' When such policies turn out to be ineffective, the blame gets diverted to the researchers.

The scientific method and its application to the understanding of humanity and our environment has improved the human living condition significantly, but such improvements are not enjoyed by all. Inequality creates conflict which can lead to everything from distrust to despair, or in the face of overwhelming military dominance, can fuel radicalism and the continued development of terrorism by disaffected groups. Continuing research in the areas of defence, security and surveillance is critical to understand conflict, but carrying out such research raises distinct methodological and ethical challenges. Occasionally, the best research must be 'covert' or risk missing the key elements that account for events that are not willingly disclosed by those with malicious or nefarious intent, or by those who cannot risk becoming participants.

The notion of covert research has long held challenges for ethics reviewers. Part of the problem lies with precisely what is meant by 'covert'. If it simply refers to 'hidden' information relating to the research, then pretty much all research contains covert elements since only the active researcher, in the field or in the laboratory, knows everything that is going on and, in any case, it might not be in the interests of funders, co-researchers or research subjects to be told everything that is contained in or required of a research engagement. To do so might compromise the method and/or the research design without bringing any clear ethical advantage nor minimising any risks of harm to all involved (Iphofen, 2011).

Amongst some observers, another view exists that some inherently unethical research procedures exist, and covert observation is one of them. Such procedures can range from making observations of human behaviour in public places, or lurking on social media to observe how people manage their online relationships, to actively participating in a group or community without identifying oneself as a 'researcher'. This view of covert observation is seen by some as particularly problematic since it appears to necessarily imply deception since those being observed are not directly informed of the observation. Part of the problem here is with what one means by deception. We would argue that the term deception is used for a range of activities, not just telling a lie. It can involve an act or statement which misleads, or hides the truth, or promotes a belief, concept or an idea that is explicitly known not to be true (a lie). Deception can involve dissimulation, propaganda and sleight of hand, as well as distraction, camouflage or concealment, and deception can occur without being viewed as ethically problematic. For example, most commercial advertising is understood to be deceptive in the sense of manipulating the attractiveness of products and/or services in order to promote sales. We, the consumers, know that and vary in the ways in which we permit ourselves to be deceived by advertising. Yet, if the advertising stated that the product was available for £100, and nowhere sold it for less than £1,000, we would feel deceived in a way in which we would say was wrong because clearly false information was provided.

In a similar way, forms of 'deception' are vital to achieving research goals even whilst other forms are unethical. The research 'gold standard' of the double blind randomised controlled trial for drug therapies relies upon deliberate self-deception in terms of permitting the knowing concealment of the potentially 'active' substance and the application of a placebo. It is well known that part of the efficacy of a placebo for some subjects relies on the participants 'deceiving themselves' into believing they are, in fact, receiving the active substance. In other research, letting people know they are being observed might result in an alteration of their behaviour and prevent their 'true', or authentic natural behaviour, from being studied. Some research can involve a component of deception where, for example, participants are told they will be interviewed about a certain topic and audio visually recorded to help analyse the interview. This topic is part of the research study, but during every interview, a second researcher regularly gets phone messages and replies to them. Participants are not informed that the research had a second aim to analyse people's reactions to others responding to text messages during interviews. This is a form of deception, though the researchers do not explicitly lie to the participants.

If a research proposal is subject to ethics appraisal of some sort (a research ethics committee (REC) or institutional review board (IRB)) it may be the case that some members regard covert observation or deception as inherently unethical. If that were true, much of early social science would have been ruled out and many specific schools of thought (e.g. Chicago sociology and Stanford psychology) would have been proscribed. Even if no REC scrutiny is required of a research action, it remains the responsibility of the professional researcher to find the best way to protect their subjects, and themselves, when conducting research that has any degree of covert or deceptive elements within it.

Extensive opportunities for covert observation have emerged with the appearance of online social media which have given rise to new forms of community and personal identity for people which pose real challenges to the key ethical research principles of consenting, voluntary participation and vulnerability. At the same time, such media have given rise to innovative methodological approaches for researchers – in terms of access to a massive range of both qualitative and quantitative data and, as a result, our understanding of public and private space has become more complicated.

BEING COVERT

Being covert in essence means that some, if not all, information is withheld about the fact that some research or 'evidence-gathering' activity is occurring. Taking such an approach requires ensuring an appropriate balance exists and has been justified between methodological requirements and the ethical responsibility to protect the subject from undue interference. If there are really strong methodological reasons for covert observation, and a study would be worthless without it, it could be justified – as long as there are no undue consequences for those under observation. Several of the chapters in this collection offer suggestions and examples about when this might be justifiable. Typically, this is done by concealing the identities of those being observed and the site of the study. The subject *may* be protected by ensuring that it would be impossible for anyone to find out who the subject of study is and where the study is being conducted. If such 'protection' and the 'value' of the study (to society and, possibly, even to the individuals/group under study) outweighs any conceivable harm – the ethical justification is strengthened. But neither full protection nor full lack of intrusion can be guaranteed and the notion of what constitutes 'harm' can vary greatly between individuals. These justifications are complex, and people will differ in their overall assessments of the arguments.

For both covert and any form of surveillance research a conventional solution is to somehow signal to those who might be affected that the work is being carried out – such as notices in public venues or social media sites, or, for studies in workplaces, notices sent to all staff likely to be present. Inevitably, this compromises the research design to some degree: the subjects might behave differently as a consequence of knowing that they might be observed; the sample selection might be compromised as all the subjects might not have seen the research notices and may behave differently; the reliability of the evidence gathered might thus be interfered with; and, more problematically, this approach might not even secure valid informed consent. There would be no evidence, other than the notice, that the population/subjects were truly informed. People could say they had not seen the notice and, if they hear about it subsequently, could get upset about being observed. There would then have to be a grievance procedure for redress of any perceived harm – once again compromising the methodology.

One thing that is agreed upon is the need to secure the consent of the owners of the premises, site and/or organisation in which the study is to occur. Insurance indemnity issues will be involved for sure. This has become a particular bone of contention in social media studies where it is argued that 'the expectation of privacy' is illusory and by no means protected by any statements of terms and conditions (see Woodfield, 2018). Some suggest that there should be little concern about observations in public places for a range of reasons: people are observing each other anyway; we sit in café terraces and 'watch the world go by', and people do not complain. Whether we make notes about what we see, or write about and publish our observations, is of secondary concern. If people are unhappy about how they are described, and their identities revealed, the only thing they can do is to take it to law. Journalists and novelists are less bothered about this sort of behaviour than professional researchers. One could argue that the researcher's motives are likely to be more 'pure' – whatever that means!

RESTRICTING INFORMED CONSENT

Situations occur when information about the full nature of a study may have to be restricted in order to comply with a specific research design. This is particularly likely to occur with covert participant observational studies or ethnographic field research in which the researcher's role is not fully disclosed – also known as immersive field-work. To seek consent from 'subjects' or site owners in such a situation would nullify the research method and the rationale for its adoption. But any exemptions to seeking consent must be detailed together with an explanation of why they have occurred. Thus, there may be broad methodological justifications and more specific, strategic reasons to do with the safety of researchers and/or research subjects quite apart from securing the research design. Incomplete disclosure may be justified if it entailed minimal risks to the subjects, if some way of debriefing them could be made available, and, perhaps, if there were a way to provide for the appropriate dissemination of findings to subjects. In fact, it may be the case that subjects could suffer from 'information overload' if they are told too much. After all they are not the professionals whose careers are dependent upon satisfactory outcomes. Even some form of retrospective consent could be sought to allay fears.

Observational studies in which the participants are not and never will be made aware that they are being observed offer the best examples of exceptions to fully informed consent. There have been many such 'classic' ethnographic studies in the history of social science research and they usually cover the fringe areas of society – criminality, social deviance, the sex industry, terrorist groups and religious cults. In a classic text, Moser and Kalton (1971) described observation as '… the classic method of scientific enquiry' (p. 244) and expressed surprise at the relatively infrequent use of observational methods by social scientists when one reflects that '… they are literally surrounded by their subject matter'. Their only ethical concern was that:

> The method must be suitable for investigating the problem in which the social scientist is interested; it must be appropriate to the populations and samples he [*sic*] wishes to study; and it should be reasonably reliable and objective. (Moser & Kalton, 1971, p. 244)

They do caution about the potential for bias since it depends upon the observer's recording skills and their interpretations of the meanings or intentions behind the behaviour:

> [...] observers are so much part of their subject matter that they may fail to see it objectively; … their vision may be distorted by what they are used to seeing or what they expect to see; and … they may find it hard to present a report in which observation is satisfactorily distinguished from inference and interpretation. (Moser & Kalton, 1971, p. 253)

COVERT STUDIES

Sidhir Venkatesh claims that he could not have conducted his research on hustlers, prostitutes and drug dealers in any detail if they had been aware of his status as a researcher. His analysis of a drug dealing gang's accounts demonstrated how it adopted a business model successfully employed by many other modern businesses. He explains that conventional research instruments such as question-naires and interview schedules would be entirely inappropriate and ineffective in such situations and would not help researchers trying to learn about the lives of poor and marginalised communities. He saw that just as his research subjects were 'hustling' for money, drugs, sexual favours and so on, he was also hustling for the data that he saw as vital to his research goals. He had to become imagina-tive, devious and, therefore, covert in gaining information – otherwise he would be seen as an agent of the authorities and a threat to his respondents' access to services (Venkatesh, 2008).

It is vital that during the ethics appraisal process – via RECs or IRBs – the use of deception that is necessarily an element of covert research and/or surveil-lance should not be necessarily ruled out as inherently morally unacceptable. The question facing an ethics committee should not be: 'Is deception wrong?' To answer that in the affirmative would be to deny practices that are central to human civilisation – politics, economics and, indeed, normal social interaction. Rather the committee should ask: 'Would the form of deception proposed or implied here harm the research participants, the researchers and/or society in general in any way?' This is not an easy question to answer since the harms would have to be balanced against the benefits accruing to all of those constitu-ent groups if the research was conducted successfully. As Robert Rosenhal has pointed out:

> [...] the ... researcher whose study might reduce violence or racism or sexism, but who refuses to do the study because it involves deception, has not solved an ethical problem but only traded it in for another. (cited in Bok, 1979, p. 192)

Another key question about deception has to do with whether or not it dam-ages the trust the general public (and so future potential research participants) have in researchers. If deception leads to an undermining of trust, and so a reluc-tance to participate in research, this is a risk to the success of future research projects (Bok, 1979, p. 205 *et seq.*). The benefits to society of future research are thereby jeopardised by the 'contamination of the field'.

> Thus, we are always confronted with a conflict of values. If we regard the acquisition of knowl-edge about human behaviour as a positive value, and if an experiment using deception constitutes a significant contribution to such knowledge which could not be very well achieved by other means, then we cannot unequivocally rule out this experiment. The question for us is not simply whether it does or does not use deception, but whether the amount and types of deception are justified by the significance of the study and the una-vailability of alternative (that is, deception-free) procedures. (Kelman, 1967 in Bynner & Stribley, 1979, p. 190)

Another way of addressing this is to consider it alongside the issues of consent and vulnerability. Thus, if the form of deception proposed in a research pro-ject minimises the research subjects' capacity to consent and makes them more vulnerable to harm without substantially contributing to societal benefit then it becomes harder to ethically justify it going ahead. It is a complex question – but one that cannot be dealt with simply by suggesting that deception in research is inherently wrong.

INTRUSIVENESS

Finally, ethics review committees often ask whether a piece of research is likely to be excessively intrusive and so 'disturbing' the subjects' normal life routines. Of course, all research is to some extent intrusive, but that intrusiveness is variable – dependent upon how much of the respondents' time, energy and so on it takes up and, not to be forgotten, how intrusive the subsequent reporting of findings might be. Intrusiveness also needs to be balanced against the concerns addressed above – thus, ironically, the more covert a piece of research, the less intrusive in ordinary lives it is likely to be. It might become more intrusive depending upon how and where research findings are published – but that merely raises another set of ethical concerns.

In practical terms, then, to maintain the dignity and personhood of research subjects one would have to anticipate the potential limitations to their participation in research and adjust methodologies accordingly. So, perhaps paradoxically, given the condemnation of covert research in some circles, it could be argued that observation could be the least intrusive way of researching aspects of the lives of vulnerable people since it is less likely to challenge them emotionally and physically. A range of naturalistic observation methods could be employed for which in some cases they need not be made aware and, in others, might be positively enjoyed (Clark, 2007). In qualitative research, in particular it may be impossible to maintain a neat distinction between covert and overt research. Again, as Murphy and Dingwall (2001, chapter 23) have explained, settings are often more complex and changeable than can be anticipated.

THIS VOLUME

Drawing on an international authorship, this volume strives to address these key and often overlapping issues that become entangled in so many contemporary research ethics challenges. The volume begins with a general overview of the ethical issues with surveillance research, before considering the benefits and challenges of handling Big Data and how this affects concepts of privacy. This is seen as important to provide security in an increasingly insecure society, especially in relation to state intervention and monitoring, but such research must be conducted responsibly to avoid fuelling further distrust. The theme of privacy in civil society is considered in Chapter 3 in relation to the issues facing researchers seeking consent to conduct research using surveillance or covert or deceptive methods. Chapter 4 explores covert research in greater depth, exploring reasons for and against the use of various forms of covert methods. Chapter 5 examines a trend within research to explore correlation rather than causation, which raises a number of ethical issues, particularly in the context of Big Data, the focus of a number of subsequent chapters. Chapter 6 examines claims that ethical issues with Big Data are addressed through anonymisation, and points to the need for an ethical framework to ensure data are collected and used appropriately. Chapter 7 switches focus to examine ethical concerns with state authorities using health-related data for non-health purposes, and the implications of this for researchers using such data. Chapter 8 turns to examine data protection in a German context given its distinct historical experience with state authorities surveilling citizens for the purposes of oppression. The ethical issues with dual use research are examined in Chapter 9, especially when research results have the potential to be used for military purposes. Chapter 10 explores ethical tensions between community-based and systems-based (or organisational) approaches to address security concerns amongst humanitarian workers. Chapter 11 continues the focus on security research and examines the challenges of collecting data using various research methods in ways that protect participants from security breaches. The final chapter provides two concise lists of recommendations for research involving surveillance, covert and deceptive methods. One set of guidance is provided for reviewers of such research, and another set for policymakers. We offer these as a concise summary of the in-depth discussions and analyses provided throughout the volume by this group of internationally esteemed and respected authors.

REFERENCES

Bok, S. (1979). *Lying: Moral choice in public and private life*. New York, NY: Vintage Books.

Clark, A. (2007). *Making observations: The potential of observation methods for gerontology*. London: Centre for Policy on Ageing.

Iphofen, R. (2011). *Ethical decision making in social research: A practical guide* (pp.8, 36, 41, 45–46, 79 et seq). London: Palgrave Macmillan.

Iphofen, R. (2011/2013). *Research ethics in ethnography/anthropology* (DG Research and Innovation). Brussels: European Commission.

Kelman, H. C. (1967). Human use of human subjects: The problem of deception in social psychological experiments. *Psychological Bulletin, 67*, 1–11. Republished in Bynner, J., & Stribley, K. M. (1979). *Social research: Principles and procedures*. London: Longman.

Moser, C. A., & Kalton, G. (1971). *Survey methods in social investigation* (2nd ed.). Aldershot: Ashgate (2001 reprint) (first published 1958).

Murphy, E., & Dingwall, R. (2001). The ethics of ethnography. In P. Atkinson, A. Coffey, S. Delamont, J. Lofland, & L. Lofland (Eds.), *Handbook of ethnography* (pp. 339–351). London: Sage.

Venkatesh, S. (2008). *Gang leader for a day*. London: Allen Lane.

Woodfield, K. (2018). *The ethics of online research* (Advances in Research Ethics and Integrity, Vol. 2). Bingley: Emerald Publishing Limited.

CHAPTER 1

SURVEILLANCE ETHICS: AN INTRODUCTION TO AN INTRODUCTION

Kevin Macnish

ABSTRACT

This short chapter is an introduction to my 2018 book: The Ethics of Surveillance: An Introduction *(Macnish, 2018). It is provided at the start of this PRO-RES collection of essays because it anticipates and supplements the range of issues covered in this collection and lays out some of the fundamental considerations necessary to ensure if surveillance must be conducted, it will be done as ethically as possible.*

When is surveillance justified? We can largely agree that there are cases in which surveillance seems, at least prima facie, *to be morally correct: police tracking a suspected mass murderer, domestic state security tracking a spy network, or a spouse uncovering partner's infidelity. At the same time, there are other cases in which surveillance seems clearly not to be justified: the mass surveillance practices of the East German Stasi, an employer watching over an employee to ensure that they do not spend too long in the toilet, or a voyeur watching the subject of his lust undress night after night.*

As an introductory text, my book does not seek to provide a list of necessary and sufficient conditions for ethical surveillance. What it does provide is an overview of the current thinking in surveillance ethics, looking at a range of proposed arguments about these questions, and how those arguments might

Ethical Issues in Covert, Security and Surveillance Research
Advances in Research Ethics and Integrity, Volume 8, 9–16
ISSN: 2398-6018/doi:10.1108/S2398-601820210000008002

play out in a variety of applied settings. It hence provides a useful and accessible volume for policymakers wishing to rapidly get up to speed on developments in surveillance and the accompanying ethical discussions.

Keywords: Surveillance; ethics; privacy; espionage; security; public sector

INTRODUCTION

My book is divided into two parts. The first part provides an historical overview of ethical engagement with practices of surveillance, before turning to the more philosophical issues which serve as a foundation to discussions on surveillance ethics. The second part moves on to a survey of different applied situations in which surveillance raises persistent challenges in the twenty-first century. Each chapter includes case studies throughout and ends with a bulleted summary and questions for discussion. I shall take each in turn in this introductory summary.

SECTION ONE

The opening chapter on the history of thought on surveillance ethics begins with reflecting on how to define the term. Several definitions have been proposed, but most, such as those by David Lyon (2007) or the Surveillance Studies Network 2006 report for the UK Information Commissioner's Office (Ball, Lyon, Murakami Wood, Norris, & Raab, 2006), contain a sense of purpose within the definition (such as care, control, and entitlement). This leads to the challenge that an act which appears to be surveillance would not in fact be such if the purpose lay outside the list of purposes provided. Without denying the value of a definition, the preferred approach is to opt for a working definition which equates surveillance with monitoring but leaves it there. From here, the chapter progresses to consider discussions of surveillance in ancient, medieval, and modern times. This historical review ranges from biblical commands through the introduction of eavesdropping laws to the development of spy satellites in the Cold War. More recently still has been the radically transformative introductions of the internet and CCTV. Finally, the chapter considers contributions to ethical reflections on surveillance from both western and non-western traditions.

The second chapter turns to the wrongs of surveillance, most obviously wrongs related to privacy (which receives due attention) but also non-privacy wrongs which may be overlooked in public discourse. These include impacts on trust, chilling effects (the muting of democratically legitimate activities for fear of persecution, heightened by surveillance), power and control, bureaucratic error and false positives, and social sorting (the division of societal groups through surveillance techniques). It closes with a philosophical reflection on the implications of so-called harmless surveillance. Here it picks up on a paper by Tony Doyle (2009), imagining an alien light years from Earth and hence unable to have an impact on our lives. This is brought into a more applied setting when considering historical research into the dead, such as exhuming the body of Richard III or breaking the cypher used by Samuel Pepys in writing his diary.

The final chapter of the first part outlines key ethical issues in surveillance. The first such issue surrounds questions of consent, noting that most ethical issues surrounding surveillance concern non-consensual surveillance. However, these are, importantly, not the only ethical issues, and the chapter looks in some depth at ethical problems which may arise from consensual surveillance, picking up on the work of Alan Wertheimer (1999, 2006) to look at questions of coercion and exploitation in apparently consensual acts of surveillance. The more substantial part of the chapter is dedicated to non-consensual surveillance, though. Here several issues are discussed, including the cause and context of the surveillance; the authority for the surveillance and attendant issues of paternalism; proportionality and necessity; and discrimination and deterrence. The final section turns to two populist arguments and thoroughly dismisses both: the suggestion that, 'if you have done nothing wrong then you should have nothing to hide', and the politician's canard that we need to make a trade-off between privacy and security, which is always raised during times of heightened insecurity. Neither of these positions turns out to be convincing on reflection.

SECTION TWO

With the foundational theoretical work in place, the book moves to the applied section. This second section looks at ethical questions pertaining to a variety of contexts, starting with state surveillance (espionage, security, policing, and social welfare), before considering corporate practices (espionage, commerce, journalism, private investigation, and workplace surveillance), and finally two broader topics: surveillance in public places and surveillance of the very old and the very young. Of the applied areas under consideration in the book, the ethics of espionage has perhaps the greatest philosophical engagement, followed by policing. Areas, such as private investigation and surveillance of the young, have received comparatively little attention to date, making many of these chapters unique as introductions.

The ethics of espionage is one area, though, which does have a long history, and one which intertwines with that of surveillance for obvious reasons. That espionage is not tantamount to surveillance can be seen through tactics such as 'turning' agents or torturing suspects, neither of which could be considered monitoring (Macnish, 2016). However, a clear overlap exists between the practices which has only grown through the twentieth century boom in signals intelligence, which is essentially a form of industrial-scale surveillance. This history provides an opportunity to reflect on different ethical approaches to the ethics of espionage, from deontological and consequentialist frameworks through to reciprocal approaches and those, including my own, which favour appeal to the just war tradition for guidance (see, e.g. Bellaby, 2014; Macnish, 2014; Omand, 2012; Quinlan, 2007). Further issues which merit discussion include the so-called

Coventry Dilemma, in which a leader must decide whether to allow a city to be obliterated to mask the fact that they are reading the enemy's communications, and the question as to whether it is acceptable to spy on allies and civilians.

The following chapter on state security picks up on the ethics of monitoring civilians, shifting the focus from the civilians in another state to those in one's own state. Where this might be justified in cases where state security has evidence that a civilian is involved in acts which are seriously detrimental to the life of the state (e.g. terrorism), the question remains as to how to find this evidence in the first place. This turns the conversation to issues of mass surveillance and the potential justification which may be sought in the doctrine of double effect. Several problems are raised with this appeal, though, and so an alternative approach in appealing to apparently less privacy-invasive data analytics is brought into the spotlight. Again there are problems here, though, including the collection of data about those known to have done nothing to merit surveillance and the general bluntness of the approach. The chapter closes with a review of ethical challenges with encryption, which rarely seems far from the headlines, and corporate involvement in state security practices.

The chapter on policing follows naturally from that on state security, and also picks up on the challenges of uncovering the evidence necessary to justify targeting surveillance on a particular individual or group. One such solution is that of undercover policing, itself a form of surveillance but one which is more targeted than mass surveillance. This, though, as has become apparent in the UK following a string of scandals, is also highly controversial as police have targeted groups of no apparent threat to the state and officers fathered children with activists before disappearing from their lives, an act seemingly condoned by their commanding officers (Nathan, 2017). The relatively recent introduction of body worn cameras is considered before a final, somewhat more philosophical debate is introduced as to whether total surveillance by the state ever could be justified, and if so under what conditions. Would, for example, and notwithstanding the earlier challenge to a simplistic dichotomy between security and privacy, the guarantee of a genuinely crime-free society justify the surveillance of every aspect of our lives? I suspect not.

Social welfare is one of the subjects which traditionally receives far less attention from scholars than those of the preceding chapters. Yet it is an area steeped in surveillance practices, from the taking of censuses to the provision of health and social care at the expense of the state. Those who seek such care are subject to far greater levels of state surveillance than their more fortunate fellow citizens. This surveillance may be variously justified as care for the needy or detection of the greedy, depending on whom the appeal is made to. Whether either of these justifications really holds, though, is a different matter. What of public duties to share data for the general good? This has hit home particularly in the wake of COVID-19 where infection rates can be traced and people suspected of infection can be alerted to self-quarantine, thanks to surveillance through mobile phone applications. However, does one have a duty to download and use such an app (Klar & Lanzerath, 2020)? Is refusal to do so a civil right or a breaking of the social contract?

Surveillance in the private, as opposed to the public, sphere tends to be far less regulated and, as a result, far more ethically complex in its execution. This is particularly so in the case of corporate espionage, which may range from stealing items from bins outside a company's headquarters to paying for privately owned spy satellites taking images of competitors' facilities to determine activities through the number of cars in the corporate parking lot (Javers, 2010). Whether any of these activities are necessary in themselves is contentious to say the least, but what of counter-espionage? When a company suspects that it is subject to espionage, is it justified then in engaging in surveillance to limit the damage of lost company secrets? A possibly less contentious area is the surveillance of potential senior hires, looking at those moving into salaried positions worth millions. Such people will generally know that they are going to be subject to some level of surveillance to ensure that they are not quietly taking drugs or sleeping with prostitutes, or other activities which might bring the hiring company into disrepute. But when should such surveillance end? Can it extend to a school soccer fixture on a Saturday afternoon, or to family outings? Here there are clearly proportionality considerations to be borne in mind, but these will depend on the value placed on the wrongs visited on the innocent family members.

Not all private surveillance is as dubious as corporate espionage, but it may raise serious ethical questions, nonetheless. There are, for instance, commercial uses of surveillance such as targeting advertising in order that the return on investment of an advertising campaign can be maximised. This has been the financial model of many social networks in the second and third decades of the twenty-first century, but has also led to the targeting (and micro-targeting) of political advertising, which would not have been possible in the twentieth century (see various chapters in Macnish & Galliott, 2020). Even without the political angle, is such advertising a welcome democratisation of the personal service once restricted to the elite, or is it a weak facsimile, seducing someone to serve the interests of the corporate world? As with questions of state security mass surveillance and public health concerns, the relatively new development of 'big' data analytics has introduced new challenges to our understanding of how our information is collected and used by corporations.

Journalism may seem a more obviously justified form of surveillance than corporate or commercial surveillance. However, the ethics of journalism is itself a richly contested field of discourse, and much of this touches on the surveillance practices of journalists themselves. While political exposés such as that of Watergate seem clearly to be in the public interest, could this extend to journalists monitoring politicians 'just in case' they do something wrong, subjecting them to total surveillance (Lawlor & Macnish, 2019)? In such cases, who is it that gets to determine what is 'wrong'? This would seem to have been the behaviour of the *News of the World* and other newspapers in the UK in the wake of the hacking scandal in 2011. Related to the hacking scandal was also the question of fishing expeditions, a claim that was raised throughout the subsequent enquiry without ever being clearly defined. This chapter provides an analytic breakdown of the different uses of the term 'fishing expedition' to understand what it means and why each differing instance may be wrong.

Private investigators are subject to even less academic ethical reflection than corporate espionage, and yet, particularly in the USA, private investigation is a significant industry which supports the legal profession in investigating crimes, employers in identifying false claims of injury, and spouses suspicious of their partner's fidelity. To classify all these together would be a blunt response to a legitimate profession, albeit one that is under-regulated and therefore prone to unethical practices by some. Here questions arise regarding honesty, and the temptation for the private investigator to pretend to be someone they are not, so as to elicit information, and the practice of entrapment. This last involves the investigator flirting with the subject under suspicion to determine whether he (and it is more often a man) is faithful to his partner. Many are sceptical of this approach, but the chapter digs into why this is an unethical practice.

The last chapter on private surveillance is one that has touched many in the year of COVID-19: surveillance in the workplace by employers. With multiple lockdowns and the increase in working from home, this has extended from the office or factory to the home study, spare bedroom, or any place where a laptop can be balanced. There are companies that can offer employers software to log keystrokes and even take pictures of employees at regular intervals to ensure that they are at their desk and focussed on the monitor. This seems to be clearly excessive, but what of employers' duty of care for their staff? Employers may argue that they can only help with health and safety conditions 'at work' through surveillance techniques when the work is being carried out in the home. Even in the office, though, or on the road for drivers being monitored, it does not follow that employees should have no expectation of privacy. If they have a reasonable expectation of privacy in company toilets, then it does not follow that once off company property that expectation ceases. Instead, careful, and nuanced reflection is required to determine whether, where, and when such surveillance could be justified.

While the second, applied part of the book focusses on the public sector and the private sector, the last two chapters expand out to look at surveillance in public spaces and surveillance in family and other care situations. As to the former, it may be asserted by some that there is no reasonable expectation of privacy in public. However, this has not always been the view of the US Supreme Court, which has ruled that surveillance of public telephones and tracking devices placed on private vehicles driven on public roads are both breaches of the Fourth Amendment to the US Constitution, guaranteeing citizens' freedom from search and seizure (*Katz* v. *United States*, 1967; *United States* v. *Jones*, 2012). Even without appeal to judicial authority, we would feel it wrong if it transpired that someone had hidden a microphone in a park bench to record conversations. How much difference is there between that and the increasingly ubiquitous presence of CCTV and automated number plate recognition systems? What of cases in which communities (typically non-white) have been subject to so-called 'rings of steel' whereby no one can enter or leave the community on foot or by car without being registered by a camera? Facial recognition systems have been a further development on these technologies, resulting in similarly discriminatory practices (Hill, 2020).

The final chapter considers surveillance at the two ends of life, providing some further insight into why we may object so viscerally to surveillance in at least some contexts. As infants, we are subject to surveillance by our parents and communities and rightly so: to do otherwise would be negligent on their part. As we grow in independence, so we expect to be subject to diminishing surveillance from our parents as a sign of trust and adulthood. Hence, a return to childhood levels of surveillance may feel infantilising to the extent that we may start to act in a less responsible manner. This also makes it troubling when we age and enter end-of-life care, which may also employ surveillance practices, ostensibly for our care and benefit, but potentially also for the security of staff and of residents. More than this, though, to what degree do those of us not yet at this stage of life tend to assume that age implies a decline in cognitive abilities and autonomy, thus justifying the very surveillance that we would reject in our own lives? There is a risk that we use age as a proxy for incapacity in a way that is demeaning and leads to harm to the elderly in society.

CONCLUSION

In summary, this work is an attempt to introduce the key ethical questions and discussions surrounding many areas of surveillance practice and theory. While not comprehensive, its goal is to be both accessible and rigorous. As with much philosophical writing, it tends to ask more questions than it answers. At the same time, it does provide a solid and balanced overview of those issues which should prove helpful for those seeking guidance and this introduction helps steer the chapters in the following collection towards addressing substantively a selection of these key concerns.

REFERENCES

Ball, K., Lyon, D., Murakami Wood, D., Norris, C., & Raab, C. (2006). *A report on the surveillance society*. Produced for the Information Commissioner by the Surveillance Studies Network. Information Commissioner's Office, London.

Bellaby, R. W. (2014). *The ethics of intelligence: A new framework*. London: Routledge.

Doyle, T. (2009). Privacy and perfect voyeurism. *Ethics and Information Technology, 11*, 181–189.

Hill, K. (2020). Facial Recognition Tool Led to Black Man's Arrest. It Was Wrong. *The New York Times*, June 25, 2020, Section A, Page 1 (New York edition).

Javers, E. (2010). *Broker, trader, lawyer, spy: The secret world of corporate espionage* (1st ed.). New York, NY: Collins Business.

Katz v. *United States* (1967). U.S.

Klar, R., & Lanzerath, D. (2020). The ethics of COVID-19 tracking apps – Challenges and voluntariness. *Research Ethics, 16*, 1–9.

Lawlor, R., & Macnish, K. (2019). Protecting politicians' privacy for the sake of democracy. In C. Fox & J. Saunders (Eds.), *Media ethics, free speech, and the requirements of democracy*. New York, NY: Routledge.

Lyon, D. (2007). *Surveillance studies: An overview* (1st ed.). Cambridge: Polity Press.

Macnish, K. (2014). Just surveillance? Towards a normative theory of surveillance. *Surveillance and Society, 12*, 142–153.

Macnish, K. (2016). Persons, personhood and proportionality: building on a just war approach to intelligence ethics. In J. Galliott, W. Reed (Eds.), *Ethics and the future of spying: Technology, national security and intelligence collection* (pp. 111–122). New York, NY: Routledge.

Macnish, K. (2018). *The ethics of surveillance: An introduction* (1st ed.). London: Routledge.
Macnish, K., & Galliott, J. (Eds.). (2020). *Big data and democracy*. Edinburgh: Edinburgh University Press.
Nathan, C. (2017). Liability to deception and manipulation: The ethics of undercover policing. *Journal of Applied Philosophy, 34*, 370–388. https://doi.org/10.1111/japp.12243
Omand, D. (2012). *Securing the state*. London: Hurst.
Quinlan, M. (2007). Just intelligence: Prolegomena to an ethical theory. *Intelligence and National Security, 22*, 1–13.
United States v. *Jones* (2012).
Wertheimer, A. (2006). *Coercion*. Princeton, NJ: Princeton University Press.
Wertheimer, A. (1999). *Exploitation* (New ed.). Princeton, NJ: Princeton University Press.

CHAPTER 2

SCIENCE, ETHICS, AND RESPONSIBLE RESEARCH – THE CASE OF SURVEILLANCE

Alfonso Alfonsi and Maresa Berliri

ABSTRACT

This chapter, based on a sociological approach, addresses the ethical issues of surveillance research from the perspective of the profound transformations that science and innovation are undergoing, as part of a broader shift from modern to post-modern society, affecting also other major social institutions (such as government, religion, family, and public administration). The change occurring in the science and technology system is characterised by diminishing authority, uncertainty about internal mechanisms and standards, and a declining and increasingly difficult access to resources. Such changes, also related to globalisation and new digital technologies, have transformed the way research is conducted and disseminated. Research is now more open and its results more easily accessible to citizens.

Scientific research is also put under increased public scrutiny, while, at the same time, public distrust and disaffection towards science is rising. In such a context, it is more important than ever to make sure that research activities are not compromised by fraudulent and unethical practices. The legitimate expectations of citizens to enjoy their rights, including the ability to protect their private sphere, are growing. Scientific and technological development is deeply interrelated with the widespread awareness of these rights and the possibility of exercising them, but it produces also new risks, while a widespread sense

Ethical Issues in Covert, Security and Surveillance Research
Advances in Research Ethics and Integrity, Volume 8, 17–28
ISSN: 2398-6018/doi:10.1108/S2398-601820210000008003

of insecurity increases. The digital revolution, while improving people's qual-
ity of life, offers at the same time new opportunities for crime and terrorism,
which in turn has produced a demand to strengthen security systems through
increasingly advanced and intrusive surveillance technologies. Misconduct in
the field of surveillance may not only undermine the quality of research, but
also further impair society's trust in research and science as well as in the State
and its institutions.

Keywords: Surveillance; sousveillance; ethics; security; social sorting;
surveillance creep; privacy; trust

INTRODUCTION

Following a sociological perspective, which accounts for the overarching shift
from modern to post-modern society, this chapter focusses on the current
efforts to find a balance between two equally compelling social demands: that
of security and that of protection of personal rights, including privacy. In
particular, the social costs of surveillance are addressed, together with efforts
to minimise them. In this regard, the debate about contentious topics, such
as social sorting, surveillance creep, data slippage, dual use and the like are
examined to highlight the effects that inappropriate surveillance practices can
have in harming individuals and social groups. In a broader perspective, the
effect that such kinds of improprieties can have in diminishing social trust
are discussed with regard to the challenges to the authority of both the State
and scientific institutions. To this end, we will discuss the merit of broad
conceptualisations of surveillance, such as the notion of 'surveillance society'
advanced by the Surveillance Studies Network, or David Lyon's (2018) 'surveillance culture'. This broad view will be confronted with the more restricted
definitions of surveillance focussed on activities specifically targeted for law
enforcement and crime prevention, with the massive use of digital technologies (smart systems) and large amounts of data, both ad hoc and for other
purposes. On the other end of the spectrum, we will also examine the implications of the fact that new digital technologies allow more and more citizens
to perform a 'bottom up' surveillance activity with regard to the behaviour of
public officials, including law enforcement agents.

SURVEILLANCE IN THE CONTEXT OF
POST-MODERN SOCIETY

Addressing the ethical issues of surveillance from a sociological point of view
requires placing such reflection in the context of the profound transformation
that science and innovation are undergoing as part of the shift from modern to
post-modern society that is affecting all social institutions. In fact, at the core

of current surveillance activities is the massive use of different kinds of technologies, including ICTs,[1] in fields where research and innovation are moving and evolving at an extremely fast pace. This ongoing transformation has been described and conceptualised in different ways by scholars and researchers, like the shift from Mode1 to Mode2 scientific production (Gibbons et al., 1994), post-academic research (Ziman, 2000), or triple helix innovation model (Etzkowitz & Leydesdorff, 2000; Leydesdorff & Etzkowitz, 1998). Some of its features, however, tend to be highlighted in a similar way by many authors (d'Andrea, 2019; Nowotny, Scott, & Gibbons, 2001).

- Science and innovation are becoming a multiactor process, involving a wide range of different actors, from scientists and researchers to citizens and the public.
- The increasing tendency towards political steering of scientific research and to implement competitive mechanisms of access to public funds.
- The increasing pressure to obtain faster social and economic benefits out of scientific research by favouring investments in applied research rather than in fundamental research.
- The increasing tendency towards trans-disciplinary research, on one side, and to more specialisation within the different scientific disciplines, on the other.

Another important transformation is the decreasing authority of and people's increasing distrust of science and scientific institutions, which is leading to a growing demand for accountability and public scrutiny of research processes and products, also seen as a way of preventing risks and undesirable impacts.

Similar changes, in the context of the transition to what is termed 'late modernity' (or digital modernity, as David Lyon suggested), are occurring also in other social institutions, such as politics, economics, public administrations, with various forms of diminishing authority and lack of public trust. These include de-standardisation, fragmentation, and increasing social pressure on institutions to become more transparent, effective, productive, and sensitive to societal needs and expectations. Such processes of change are modifying the balance between social structures (including not only institutions, but also social norms, cultural views, behaviours, etc.) and the agency of individuals, that is, the capacity of individuals to more freely think and act as well as to 'build up' their own life, projects, and identity, even challenging the social structures. In late modernity, the agency or the subjectivity of people are weakening social institutions and are producing diversified configurations of social life which are facilitated thanks to other processes such as digitalisation, increasing mobility, and easier access to resources (Archer, 2007; Bauman, 2000; Beck, 1992; Giddens, 1991; Quaranta, 1986).

By and large there is an increasing pressure to close the gap between science and society promoting and deploying scientific and innovation ecosystems that are more open, transparent, and accessible. Science and research are challenged to be more open to citizens, allowing the possibility of public scrutiny of their activities and results (d'Andrea , Marta and only for Part Three Para 2.2. Kahma & Vase, 2017).

As mentioned in the Introduction, this process of change in the internal and external mechanisms of science might also facilitate malpractices or, for our discussion, the design of surveillance technologies, which are risky from a societal point of view, and can produce economic and social costs.

SOCIAL SUBJECTIVITY AND THE EMERGING DEMANDS FOR SECURITY AND AUTONOMY

Considering what we have noted so far, we can say that science and innovation are undergoing a long transitional phase which is characterised at the same time by a weakening of the main social institutions and by an increase in 'social subjectivity'.

With the term 'social subjectivity' we refer to the fact that contemporary societies – due to the processes discussed above – reflect a large-scale increase in the importance, complexity, and density of the cognitive, intellectual and emotional dimensions of individuals. The latter are also characterised by a high degree of uncertainty, since social structures are becoming weaker, more flexible, and more subject to change (Beck, 1992; Giddens, 1991; Quaranta, 1986). We can say that new forms of human agency are emerging, producing a 'surplus' of human energy, so that individuals are more and more 'capable' of generating new ideas, innovating and overcoming everyday life constraints, while their field of action is broader and less limited by territorial boundaries.

The digital ecosystem offers unprecedented opportunities to express such human agency, functioning as a multiplier of the social energy of groups and individuals, in cultural and social life as well as the economy. At the same time, it can jeopardise the identity and the personal security of individuals. Not least, the Internet offers increasing opportunities to criminal actors, both on-line and off-line (Mezzana & Krlic, 2013).

We can thus maintain that there is a connection between the scientific and technological developments and the increased assertiveness of individuals and groups, who can avail themselves of unprecedented opportunities for their expression and potency. The legitimate expectations of citizens to enjoy their rights, including the ability to protect their private sphere, are growing (Cannataci, 2015). Scientific and technological development is deeply interrelated with the widespread awareness of these rights and the possibility of exercising them, but it produces also new risks, while a widespread sense of insecurity increases. The digital revolution, in fact, while improving people's quality of life, offered at the same time, as said, new opportunities for various forms of crime and terrorism, which in turn produced the demand to strengthen security systems through increasingly advanced and intrusive surveillance technologies which themselves produce anxiety about intrusive State control or exploitation from over-the-top private companies.

In such a context, the problem becomes balancing two equally compelling social demands: that of security and that of protection of personal rights, including privacy (Alfonsi, Declich, & Berliri, 2019; Charitidis, Spyrakou, Markakis & Iphofen, 2019; Iphofen, 2014, chapter 5). The question of what is actually unethical is going beyond well-known issues such as fabrication, falsification, and plagiarism. Referring to surveillance, phenomena such as social profiling through the data science process, or the opacity in the use of advanced technologies for recording and analysing personal behaviour and inclinations challenge all concerned actors to take measures to avoid being involved in practices that could harm the rights of citizens. In fact, misconduct in the field of surveillance can harm not only individual citizens' rights, but can, in a broader perspective, further impair societal trust in science, and in the State and its institutions.

UNDERSTANDINGS OF SURVEILLANCE

To discuss the impact of issues related to surveillance on public trust and social interaction, we should consider how the application of this notion has broadened in recent times. At a first level, we have the more restricted and traditional definition, what can be termed 'State surveillance', that is, focussed on activities carried out by legal entities endowed with a special authority by State institutions and primarily targeted at law enforcement and crime prevention – including terrorism. Nowadays, such activities imply the massive use of digital technologies (smart systems) and the processing of large amounts of data, both collected ad hoc or collected for other purposes. In this view, surveillance activities can be considered as

> any monitoring or observing of persons, listening to their conversations or other activities, or any other collection of data referring to persons regardless whether this is content data or meta data, which is carried out by the State, or in its behalf or at its orders. (Cannataci, 2019)

In this regard, several authors (see for instance Mann & Ferebonk, 2013) point to the fact that the very word 'surveillance', of French origin, implies a 'gaze from above' (*sur veillance*), underscoring the hierarchical and asymmetric relationship between the 'watcher' and the 'watched'.

At the same time, this State activity is presently confronted by the use that organised crime and terrorists are making of new technologies and the Internet (including what is called Deep Internet and Dark Internet) for their criminal activities, off-line and on-line. Thus, law enforcement authorities are also faced with the need to increase their capacity to combat the criminal use and penetration of the new technological environment. Furthermore, in the present context old and new forms of surveillance co-exist, co-support, and feed off each other, thus producing 'mutual augmentation', which could possibly produce much greater and amplified surveillance (Colonnello, Alfonsi, Marta, & Mezzana, 2014; Trottier, 2011). Thus, a relevant area of discussion currently revolves around how to ensure an Internet where the citizens are safe from criminal activities as well as from undue surveillance from law enforcement agencies, while at the same time these same agencies are provided with sufficient capacity to effectively combat the actions of criminals and terrorists. This balance is considered by many to be difficult to strike.

It is important to observe that the deployment of new technologies to some extent challenges the State monopoly on surveillance and opens the way to a wider range of actors, not only to public authorities. This realisation has brought several authors, including those related to the Surveillance Study Network,[2] to broaden the definition of surveillance from an institutional function to a widespread social practice of which State surveillance is only a special case. Thus, the notion of surveillance society has been introduced, understood as a

> society which functions because of the extensive collection, recording, storage, analysis and application of information on individuals and groups as they go about their lives (big data). In this case private bodies, including big corporations, join the State actors as agents of surveillance for their own purposes, including business. (Surveillance Study Network[3])

This notion implies the need for more diffused and granular use of instruments to check the ways in which the data about personal behaviour are collected and perused. At the same time, the notion of surveillance society focusses on the idea that there are observers (above) and those observed (below) with basically the private sector interacting and competing with the State in *surveilling* the citizens in their private lives.

A further extension in the understanding of surveillance in the contemporary world is achieved by authors like David Lyon, who speaks of a 'Culture of surveillance'. This notion focusses on the agency of citizens/users who are not only passive subjects of surveillance, or merely 'devolve' their personal data, but actively participate in its operation by their daily actions, including surveillance of others (e.g. on social media, see Trottier, 2011), self-surveillance, and 'quantified self' practices (Lupton, 2020). What is to be noted is also the fact that the directionality of surveillance, albeit remaining asymmetrical in power relationships, no longer goes only in one direction, that is, top down, but moves also 'bottom up' (see the notion of 'Sousveillance', i.e. 'watching from below', of Mann, 2013). This means also that some individuals and groups have acquired the capability of recording and monitoring the behaviour of public officials and law enforcement agents, and to some extent of big companies. This multiactor and multilateral surveillance gives rise to various power configurations, both cooperative (e.g. community policing[4]) and confrontational, which challenge the monopoly (now 'oligopoly') of the State and of large corporations on data collection and evaluation. One current example is the case of the death of the American citizen George Floyd, whose last minutes were recorded not only by the police bodycams, and nearby CCTVs, but also by several bystanders, so that the social meaning of the event was from the start framed in a way that highlighted the misbehaviour of the police officials involved. It must be noted that this plurality of visual sources played a significant role also in the legal trial that brought to the conviction of officer Derek Chauvin.

SOCIAL COSTS OF SURVEILLANCE AND SOCIETAL TRUST

As we have discussed, at present surveillance technologies are multiple, ubiquitous, pervasive, heavily relying on ICTs, and are changing fast and becoming more and more sophisticated so that there is a heated debate about their possible problems, harms, and costs for individuals, groups, and society as a whole. This is by no means a recent development: since the last half of the twentieth century, the ever-increasing use of technology for the discovery and collection of personal information for surveillance and security purposes has raised concerns about risks (e.g. with regard to privacy protection), harms and costs to individuals and groups by social scientists, jurists, ethicists, researchers, and by advocacy and citizens' organisations. Surveillance studies provided interesting categories to analyse the application of such technologies in order to identify the main issues to be taken into account (Lyon, 2007; Marx, 2002; Macnish, 2018). Based on a review of the relevant literature, we provide here a quick overview of the social costs that can derive from the use of contentious, inappropriate, or non-proportionate practices. As a preliminary observation, we can note that privacy protection is always at the centre of concern, in the reflection about surveillance activities. Also in this case there are different definitions of privacy and personal data protection (from the right to be let alone, to privacy as a fundamental right of identity protection and self-determination and freedom of expression). For our purposes, we define privacy as a dynamic social form of defence of the self and of its subjectivity, at various levels: from the ethological level, linked to the defence of one's own personal territory, to the psychological level, and gradually up to the legal level (Mezzana & Krlic, 2013). On the basis of the relevant literature, it is possible to identify three areas of concern about the social costs of surveillance. For identifying these areas, we used the findings of the EU Project RESPECT (Rules, Expectations & Security through Privacy-Enhanced Convenient Technologies) contained in the 'Final report on social costs of surveillance' (Colonnello et al., 2014).

A first area of concern is related to the use and management of data (Big data and personal data) and data processing technologies (including smart and automated ones). This area includes:

- Social sorting, that is, social classification and selection for valuative purposes of individuals and groups often based on not accessible/transparent criteria (often biased by stereotypes – categorical suspicion related to gender, ethnic, racial, religious, or political aspects) incorporated in algorithms and in automated technologies (e.g. in the case of CCTV it can contribute to the construction and reinforcement of a condemnatory gaze on the powerless).
- Surveillance/function creep, that is, the interchangeability of digital technologies, or in other words the gradual widening of the use of a technology or system beyond the purpose for which it was originally developed to other uses and ends; or data collected for one purpose being used for another.
- Data slippage, that is, moving of data from one context to another.
- False positives, exposing people to the harm that can arise from errors or misidentification or misinterpretation of data or behaviours recorded.
- Leaky containers, namely the practices by which, with the development of new technologies and greater national and global interconnections, there is a

'loss' (intentional or accidental) of personal information from one system to another, which may damage the reputation of another person, causing harm to their private, social, and economic life, undermining their credibility within a social group or community.

This area includes also the important ethical issue of dual use, defined as the fact that a product or a technology can be used with both good and bad intentions/aims (bad intentions that have to be considered among the case of malpractices, like e.g. deliberate or accidental releases of private information – data breach). In the case of surveillance technologies, dual use is a very relevant topic, which involves using crime prevention technologies like phone interception, face recognition in social media, or cryptography, for political uses against dissidents or minority groups, with a violation of human rights. Part of the current debate veers on the necessity and possibility to incorporate remedies for such concerns in the very design and deployment of surveillance technologies.

A second area of concern focusses on the social costs related to the deployment and use of inappropriate or non-proportionate surveillance technologies and activities on individuals and groups. As we said before, privacy is important for protecting the identity and the subjectivity of individuals. Inappropriate or non-proportionate surveillance activities might produce effects and harms on personal identity (defined as the capacity of individuals to control the reality in which they operate), on autonomy (defined as decision making power and freedom of movement and action) and on the reputation (defined as the protection of the good names of people). In this context, the possible common harms identified include exclusion and discrimination; stigmatisation of groups and lifestyles; constraints to mobility; stalking and harassment; limitation and self-censorship; change in social behaviour (e.g. in public space for the presence of CCTV, or public shaming in social media); loss of opportunities in one's private, social and professional life; loss of personal/group social capital and relations. In this context, particular attention has to be devoted to gender-based discrimination and to the stigmatisation of persons with disabilities, indigenous people, or migrants (Cannataci, 2018, 2019).

A third area concerns, in a broader perspective, the effects that inappropriate and non-proportionate surveillance practices, even if enacted in the name of security, produce in further diminishing social and public trust and confidence in government, public institutions, and private organisations, including the de-legitimisation of the police in their role and on how this role is performed. Furthermore, such surveillance activities, in some cases, might affect also the quality of democracy and the full participation in the social, political, and economic life of individuals and groups, with phenomena such as abuse of power in the name of national security and protection from terrorism, suppression, or inhibition of political dissidence, reduction of fundamental civil liberties and fundamental rights, or forms of mass espionage/surveillance. Furthermore, some bad practices of surveillance like categorical suspicion, judicial errors, manipulation of evidence, or miscarriage of justice (tied with the use of biometric surveillance) might also affect the virtuous operation of the administration of justice.

Finally, beyond the deployment of *sousveillance* activities by citizens that we discussed earlier, the surveillance technologies can produce, as a reaction, also phenomena of resistances and non-compliance performed by individuals and groups using different forms and tools.

At this point of our reflection, the question is how to design and deploy responsible, appropriate, and proportionate surveillance technologies and activities able to cope with both the demand for security and autonomy, and to the new challenges posed by the new frontiers of surveillance technologies.

TOWARDS RESPONSIBLE SURVEILLANCE

From what we have discussed so far, it does appear that surveillance and its culture are a fundamental feature of contemporary societies. In fact, surveillance activities in the different definitions that we have presented are becoming more and more pervasive and granular, by means of increasingly diversified and advanced technologies. At the same time, however, their deployment has become multilateral not only because State actors are interacting/competing with private actors but also because citizens individually and as organised groups can play an active role and, at certain conditions, reverse the 'gaze' from the bottom up. This gives rise to several overall power configurations that, albeit asymmetrical in terms of potency, are by no means exclusively top down. These new configurations can include also horizontal relationships such as peer-to-peer surveillance or self-surveillance.

Thus, the context of surveillance can be seen as closely connected to those forms of enhanced social subjectivity that we have discussed above and represents also a major challenge, in that the many layered issues that it poses, including the risks and social costs discussed in the previous paragraph, are not yet fully socialised, or, we might say, are 'under-socialised'. By this we mean that security and surveillance technologies, strategies, and arrangements are being developed at a very fast pace so that their embeddedness in society is still weak, developed with scant interaction with the different stakeholders and with insufficient public control and assessment of their impacts, including considerable heterogeneity in the evaluation instruments. This lack of socialisation is at the origin of economic and social costs to individuals, groups, and societies, also due to the implementation of questionable practices of surveillance. Furthermore, this occurs in a context in which societies and citizens are much more reactive and attentive with respect of malpractice and this might reinforce distrust in science and research, and in institutions. On the contrary, what we mean by socialisation is the capacity to adapt technologies to the needs, expectations, and problems of society and the capacity to control social dynamics incorporated in science and technology. This socialisation of science, technology, and research is not to be regarded as a unitary and linear process, but a composite and multidirectional one, requiring the involvement of actors and groups (Bijker & d'Andrea, 2009; d'Andrea, Quaranta, & Quinti, 2005; Mezzana Ed., 2011).

To sum up, what seems to be lacking is a shared awareness of what is at stake and of viable ways to exercise social responsibility in view of inclusive and multilateral forms of governance, in line with what authors like David Lyon have called 'digital citizenship'.

A possible path towards a full socialisation of surveillance could perhaps be traced by looking at the perspective of Responsible Research and Innovation (RRI) launched by the European Commission to manage science–society relations in the European Research Area (Burget, Bardone, & Pedaste, 2017; European Commission, 2012; Owen et al., 2013; van den Hoven, 2014; Von Schomberg, 2011, 2019). To be sure, currently there is a widespread debate on the merits of the RRI approach, that is, questioning its very definition and purpose. In our understanding, RRI can be viewed as a policy reaction to the changes already occurring in science and innovation or, better, an attempt to drive these changes towards desirable or at least manageable outputs.

In this regard, RRI can be considered as an umbrella concept, that is supposed to advocate an action to better embed science, research, and innovation in the fabric of society, by pointing to certain key elements of concern such as: gender equality in science, open access to research data and publications, research ethics and integrity, citizen engagement, science education, and governance. These key elements are often integrated by four dimensions: inclusiveness, anticipation, responsiveness, and reflexivity, which might be relevant in the context of surveillance (Compass, 2018; Floridi, 2012; Klimburg-Witjes & Huettenrauch, 2021; Kormeling, 2018; Menevidis, Mohd Nor, Briege and Mitrou, 2014; Stahl, 2013; SIENNA, 2020; Van de Poel et al., 2020).

Inclusiveness seems in fact to respond to the multilateral feature of present-day surveillance. This requires that all actors and stakeholders involved (State agencies, technologists, scientists, companies, policymakers, citizens, civil society organisations, etc.) are able to interact with each other. To fully satisfy the condition of inclusiveness, appropriate means need to be devised to allow citizens to voice their perspectives and concerns about the deployment of surveillance technologies in everyday life situations. At the same time, the anticipatory dimension is of paramount importance in a field where a fast-paced technological development constantly produces new technical possibilities that in turn call for ethical decisions, social acceptance, and normative frameworks. Furthermore, the pace at which technological developments tend to happen requires the capacity for timely responses to the challenges of a constantly changing landscape. Finally, as we pointed out already, what is also required is the attitude of all concerned actors to be able to reflect on the implications of such developments in order to build a shared vision of what is at stake in order to cope with an environment in which surveillance with its contribution to public security and with its risks and drawbacks is so much intertwined in the fabric of contemporary social life.

In conclusion, it is necessary to understand the conditions by which emerging social subjectivity can be informed by what has been termed an 'ethics of care' in order to assure fundamental instances of fairness, data justice, visibility, and recognition in the design, deployment, and use of surveillance technologies.

NOTES

1. These include CCTV, RFID, SMART technologies, geo-localisation technologies, biometric technologies, voice identification, face recognition, Data science and Big Data, Artificial intelligence, ICTs, Internet of things, wearable technologies, encryption and anonymisation technologies, use of malicious malware and spyware, social media scan, etc.

2. *Surveillance Studies Network* (https://www.surveillance-studies.net/) is a charitable company registered in UK, but international in its membership, dedicated to the study of surveillance in all its forms. They publish the peer reviewed journal *Surveillance and Society* (http://surveillance-and-society.org/) and acts as a clearing house for social science and policy research and consultancy about surveillance.

3. This is the definition provided by the Surveillance Study Network, in its blog post 'An introduction to the surveillance society', available at https://www.surveillance-studies.net/?page_id=119.

4. See Mifsud Bonnici and Cannataci (2018).

REFERENCES

Alfonsi, A., Declich, G., & Berliri, M. (2019). Surveillance, privacy and covert research: Current challenges to the research ethics and integrity. In *PRO-RES workshop on covert research, privacy and surveillance* (PRO-RES PROmoting integrity in the use of RESearch results), Rome, April 11, 2019.

Archer, M. S. (2007). *Making our way through the world: Human reflexivity and social mobility*. Cambridge: Cambridge University Press.

Bauman, Z. (2000). *Liquid society*. Cambridge: Polity Press.

Beck, U. (1992). *Risk society: Towards a new modernity* (Vol. 17). London: Sage.

Bijker, W., & d'Andrea, L. (Eds.). (2009). *Handbook on the socialisation of scientific and technological research (Social Sciences and European Research Capacities (SS-ERC) Project)*. Rome: European Commission.

Burget, M., Bardone, E., & Pedaste, M. (2017). Definitions and conceptual dimensions of responsible research and innovation: A literature review. *Science and Engineering Ethics, 23*(1), 1–19.

Cannataci, J. (Ed.). (2015). *The individual and privacy. The library of essays on law and privacy* (Vol. 1). New York, NY: Routledge.

Cannataci, J. (2018). *Right to privacy. Report of the special rapporteur on the right to privacy*. General Assembly, Human Rights Council, Fortieth Session, 26 February–23 March 2018.

Cannataci, J. (2019). *Right to privacy. Report of the special rapporteur on the right to privacy*. General Assembly, Human Right Council, Fortieth Session, 25 February–22 March 2019.

Charitidis, C., Spyrakou, E., Markakis, V., with the contribution of Iphofen, R. (2019). Thematic priorities report D2.1. PRO-RES D2.2. PRO-RES PROmoting ethics and integrity in non medical RESearch.

Compass. (2018) Responsible innovation roadmap cyber security. Retrieved from https://innovation-compass.eu/roadmaps/roadmaps/ri-labs-cyber-security/

Colonnello, C., Alfonsi, A., Marta, F. L., & Mezzana, D. (2014). Final report on social costs of surveillance. RESPECT (Rules, Expectations & Security through Privacy-Enhanced Convenient Technologies) Deliverable D13.4.

d'Andrea, L., Quaranta, G., & Quinti, G. (2005). *Manuale sui processi di socializzazione della ricerca scientifica e tecnologica*. Rome: CERFE.

d'Andrea L., Marta, F. L., and only for Part Three Para 2.2. (2017). *FIT4RRI D1.1 – Report on the literature review*. doi:10.5281/zenodo.1434349

d'Andrea, L. (2019). *State-of-the-art review of documented experiences – Document 6 – Approaches to RRI*. GRACE – Grounding RRI Actions to Achieve Institutional Change in European Research Funding and Performing Organisations. Knowledge & Innovation Srls.

European Commission. (2012). *Responsible research and innovation. Europe's ability to respond to societal challenges*. Luxembourg: Publication Offices of the European Union.

Etzkowitz, H., & Leydesdorff, L. (2000). The dynamics of innovation: From national systems and "mode 2" to a triple helix of university–industry–government relations. *Research Policy, 29*(2), 109–123.

Floridi, L. (Ed.), (2012). *The Cambridge handbook of information and computer ethics*. Cambridge: Cambridge University Press.

Gibbons, M., Limoges, C., Nowotny, H., Schwartzman, S., Scott, P., & Trow, M. (1994). *The new production of knowledge: The dynamics of science and research in contemporary societies*. London: Sage.

Giddens, A. (1991). *Modernity and self-identity: Self and society in the late modern age*. Palo Alto, CA: Stanford University Press.

Iphofen, R. (2014). Ethical issues in surveillance and privacy. In A. W. Stedmon and G. Lawson (Eds.), *Hostile intent and counter-terrorism: Human factors theory and application*. 59–72. Aldershot: Ashgate.

Klimburg-Witjes, N., & Huettenrauch, F. C. (2021). Contextualizing security innovation: Responsible research at the smart border?. *Science and Engineering Ethics*. doi.org/10.1007/s11948-021-00292-y

Kormeling, G. (2018). *Responsible innovation, ethics, safety and technology. How to deal with risks and ethical questions raised by the development of new technologies* (2nd ed.). Delft: TU Delft Open.

Leydesdorff, L., & Etzkowitz, H. (1998). The triple helix as a model for innovation studies. *Science and Public Policy*, *25*(3), 195–203.

Lyon, D. (2007). *Surveillance studies: An overview*. Cambridge: Polity Press.

Lyon, D. (2018). *The culture of surveillance. Watching as a way of life*. Cambridge: Polity Press.

Lupton, D. (2020). *Data selves. More-than-human perspectives*. Cambridge: Polity Press.

Macnish, K. (2018). *The ethics of surveillance. An introduction*. New York, NY: Routledge.

Mann, S. (2013). The inevitability of the transition from surveillance-society to a veillance-society: Moral and economic grounding for sousveillance. In *2013 IEEE international symposium on technology and society (ISTAS)*. 18–34. 27–29 June 2013, University of Toronto, Toronto, Canada.

Mann, S., & Ferebonk, J. (2013). New media and the power of politics of sousveillance in a surveillance-dominated world. *Surveillance and Society*, *11*(1/2), 18–34.

Marx, G. T. (2002). What's new about the "new surveillance"? Classifying for change and continuity. *Surveillance & Society*, *1*(1), 9–29.

Mezzana, D. (Ed.). (2011). *Technological responsibility. Guidelines for a shared governance of the processes of socialization of scientific research and innovation, within an interconnected world, SET-DEV, 7th Framework Programme for Technological Research and Development of the European Commission*. Rome: Consiglio Nazionale delle Ricerche.

Mezzana, D., & Krlic, M. (2013). The current context of surveillance: An overview of some emerging phenomena and policies. *European Journal of Law and Technology*, *4*(2). https://ejlt.org/index.php/ejlt/article/view/187/380

Mifsud Bonnici, J. P., & Cannataci, J. (Eds.). (2018). *Changing communities, changing policing*. Graz: NWV.

Menevidis, Z., Mohd Nor, R., Briege, C. & Mitrou, L. (2014). Responsibility. *D6.2. Policy brief: RRI for security*. doi.10.13140/2.1.2996.3846

Nowotny, H., Scott, P., & Gibbons, M. (2001). *Rethinking science: Knowledge and the public in the age of uncertainty*. Cambridge: Polity Press.

Owen, R., Stilgoe, J., Macnaghten, P., Gorman, M., Fisher, E., & Guston, D. H. (2013). Framework for responsible innovation. In R. Owen, M. Heintz, & J. Bessant (Eds.), *Responsible innovation*. 27–50. Chichester: Wiley.

Quaranta, G. (1986). *L'era dello sviluppo*. Milano: Franco Angeli.

SIENNA. (2020). *Project policy brief #1. Enhancing EU legal frameworks for AI & robotics*. Zenodo. http://doi.org/10.5281/zenodo.4332661

Stahl, B. C. (2013) Responsible research and innovation: The role of privacy in an emerging framework. *Science and Public Policy*, *40*(6), 708–716.

Trottier, D. (2011) *Mutual augmentation of surveillance practices on social media*. Kingston: Queen's University.

Van de Poel, I., Asveld, L., Flipse, S., Klaassen, P., Kwee, Z., Maia, M., ... Yaghmaei, E. (2020). Learning to do responsible innovation in industry: Six lessons. *Journal of Responsible Innovation*, *7*(3), 697–707.

van den Hoven, J. (2014). *Responsible innovation in brief*. Delft: The Delft University of Technology.

Von Schomberg, R. (Ed.). (2011). *Towards responsible research and innovation in the information and communication technologies and security technologies fields. A report from the European Commission Services*. doi.10.2777/58723

Von Schomberg, R. (2019). Why responsible innovation. In R. Von Schomberg & J. Hankins (Eds.), *The international handbook on responsible innovation. A global resource*. 12–32. Cheltenham and Northampton: Edward Elgar Publishing doi:10.4337/9781784718862

Ziman, J. (2000). *Real science. What it is, and what it means*. Cambridge: Cambridge University Press.

CHAPTER 3

RESEARCH IS NOT A PRIVATE MATTER

Paul Spicker

ABSTRACT

The received wisdom underlying many guides to ethical research is that information is private, and research is consequently seen as a trespass on the private sphere. Privacy demands control; control requires consent; consent protects privacy. This is not wrong in every case, but it is over-generalised. The distorted perspective leads to some striking misinterpretations of the rights of research participants, and the duties of researchers. Privacy is not the same thing as data protection; consent is not adequate as a defence of privacy; seeking consent is not always required or appropriate. Beyond that, the misinterpretation can lead to conduct which is unethical, limiting the scope of research activity, obstructing the flow of information in a free society, and failing to recognise what researchers' real duties are.

Keywords: Privacy; information privacy; consent; public sphere; ethical review; rights and duties

Many of the ethical rules relating to research begin with a presumption that the information that is being obtained is, in some sense, private. The Australian National Health and Medical Research Council's guidance explains:

Individuals have a sphere of life from which they should be able to exclude any intrusion .... A major application of the concept of privacy is information privacy: the interest of a person in controlling access to and use of any information personal to that person. (ANHMRC, 1999, p. 52)

Ethical Issues in Covert, Security and Surveillance Research
Advances in Research Ethics and Integrity, Volume 8, 29–40

ISSN: 2398-6018/doi:10.1108/S2398-601820210000008004

In later advice, they describe privacy as 'a domain within which individuals and groups are entitled to be free from the scrutiny of others' and states that 'An ethically defensible plan for research ... should ... include measures to protect the privacy desired by participants' (ANHMRC, 2018, pp. 102 and 50). The central test is that people decide for themselves what they are prepared to reveal. If the information is under the control of the research participants, it can only be used by a researcher if the research participant gives consent. From this we go to the idea that all research concerning human beings must be subject to the free, fully informed consent of the people concerned.

There are lots of things wrong with this account. It leads to some striking misinterpretations of the rights of research participants, and the duties of researchers; but beyond that, it can lead to conduct which is frankly unethical.

PRIVACY

John Stuart Mill wrote of privacy as a 'reserved territory'.

> There is a part of the life of every person who has come to years of discretion, within which the individuality of that person ought to reign uncontrolled either by any other individual or by the public collectively.' (Mill, 1848, chapter 11)

Some ideas of privacy seem to work on the principle that people's affairs are nobody else's business until the person in question says otherwise – a position which holds, not that no one else should interfere, but that the person must be in control of the process (Rössler, 2005, p. 72). Within that model, people can give up their privacy; they choose what to reveal; they can sell their information. That seems, however, to conceive of privacy as a sort of ownership. Judges Warren and Brandeis (1890), who are commonly credited with the introduction of the principle of privacy into US law, took a very different view:

> The principle which protects personal writings and all other personal productions ... is in reality not the principle of private property, but of an inviolate personality .... The intensity and complexity of life, attendant upon advancing civilization, have rendered necessary some retreat from the world, and man, under the refining influence of culture, has become more sensitive to publicity so that solitude and privacy have become more essential to the individual .... (p. 205)

No one, the Universal Declaration of Human Rights states, 'shall be subjected to arbitrary interference with his privacy, family, home or correspondence' (United Nations, 1948). This is about respect for persons. It is not framed in terms of having a say; it is not about control or choice, though it could well enhance both. The suggestion that this principle can be breached with consent is an excuse, used to legitimate the intrusion into personal space that the principle of privacy is supposed to prevent. If one accepts that information is truly private and personal, research – or any other activity that violates the reserved territory – ought to minimise intrusion and accept that some things cannot be examined.

There are exceptions and limits to this understanding of privacy, but I will come to those later. The invasion of privacy is objectionable both in its own right, and because it is liable directly to affect how people live – what they can do, where they can go, and how they should act. That is the case for maintaining confidentiality, and anonymity in circumstances where it helps protect the subject of research from identification. Arguments about privacy have tended to get lost somewhere in arguments about data protection and control, but the test of privacy is quite different. It is about the preservation of an 'inviolate personality', and the sanctity of personal data has little directly to do with that.

INFORMATION PRIVACY: CONSENT AND CONTROL

The second stage of the argument is about information privacy, 'the claim of individuals, groups or institutions to determine for themselves when, how and to what extent information about them is communicated to others'. (Westin, cited in Kimmel, 1988). Information privacy is usually matched with the principle of informed consent: that people have to agree to the use of information, and that they have to be sufficiently informed to know what they are agreeing to.

> As far as possible participation in sociological research should be based on the freely given informed consent of those studied. This implies a responsibility on the sociologist to explain in appropriate detail, and in terms meaningful to participants, what the research is about, who is undertaking and financing it, why it is being undertaken, and how it is to be distributed and used. (British Sociological Association (BSA), 2017, p. 5)

There are two subtly different principles outlined here. The first, information privacy, puts in charge the person to whom the information relates. (The principle of data protection is derived from this general approach. The terms are used almost interchangeably in the literature – arguably information privacy is a little wider – but for practical purposes, I will treat information privacy and data protection as being roughly equivalent.) In the context of research, information privacy and data protection imply that consent has to be negotiated. People who are being researched are entitled to be informed; they have to consent to the project; consent is a continuous process; they have the right to withdraw at any time.

The other set of principles relates to the conduct of the researcher. Guides to research ethics are typically directed to the researcher, not to the research participant. The duties of the researcher are to explain, to avoid coercion, and to make sure that they are not stepping over the line. Some people might want to argue that rights are correlative with duties, so that these two principles boil down to the same thing; if researchers have a duty, it is does not seem to be saying anything different from the idea that people participating in research have rights. However, even if the distinction between information privacy and informed consent is not immediately evident, they are not the same. The key difference is this: it is quite possible that they refer to different people. One important example is included in Westin's definition of information privacy: the subjects who have the right to decide about privacy might be groups or institutions. Organisational research is often done for or about an organisation; it is the organisation that gives consent, not the participants. The people who take part in that research are contacted on the basis of their organisational role or position, and placed under an obligation to cooperate with the research.

An even more important distinction lies between research participants and research subjects. Information privacy is supposed to protect the subjects – the people to whom the information relates. Research participants are not necessarily people who are engaged with the research, and the information in question may not be about them. A participant in research on domestic violence vouches information about an abusive partner. A professional recounts experience working with children with mental disorder. A person claiming social security complains about the treatment given to her by an officer. In every case, that information does not belong to the person who is reporting it. The consent of the participant is not enough. The data relate to third parties, and the principle of information privacy has been breached.

The distinction between subjects and participants is rather too often elided in the literature. The UK's Economic and Social Research Council, for example, defines research 'participants' in these terms:

> Human participants are defined as including living human beings, human beings who have recently died (cadavers, human remains and body parts), embryos and foetuses, human tissue and bodily fluids, and human data and records (such as, but not restricted to medical, genetic, financial, personnel, criminal or administrative records and test results including scholastic achievements). (ESRC, 2015, p. 42)

The idea that cadavers and human tissue samples 'participate' in research is slightly surreal. (I am not sure what qualifies as a 'recent' death, but I cannot see that the strength of feeling people may have about, e.g., the organs of their dead child, grow dimmer with the passing of years. What matters is surely the relationship, not the length of time.) What the ESRC intends to say is that these subsidiary sources of information are also protected by the principle of information privacy. Where information privacy applies, the control of the research subject extends to every scrap of private data – including bodily fluids and historic records – and that someone who has the right to hold that data must be consulted.

This seems to be connected only very loosely with the idea of 'privacy' I have been discussing. Data protection and consent are not properly speaking ethical principles in their own right; they are methods intended to protect privacy, and it is as methods that they need to be judged. On one hand, consent is not enough to defend privacy. Privacy is a human right, and people cannot consent to give up their human rights; and while some requests are less intrusive than others, there is no way of asking for explicit consent that is not in itself an intrusion. On the other hand, data protection can be violated with no intrusion, and no immediate implications for personal privacy. The secondary analysis of data, based on information that was gathered for a different purpose for the original research, is illustrative. Research and data archives exist precisely to make this sort of analysis possible. It is difficult to see what implications for privacy there might be in working with tissue. Of course, one has to take care that the use of derived information should not be constructed in such a way as to compromise the position of individuals illegitimately. We usually use anonymity and confidentiality to cover that eventuality.

It could be argued that privacy is simply the wrong principle to refer to. Faden and Beauchamp argue that consent has much more to do with self-determination and personal autonomy than it does to privacy. Consent is about the exercise of personal choice (Faden, Beauchamp, 1986). There are limits, however, to how far the person giving up the information is in control, or should be, in so far as there is a potential for conflict; what matters are the duties of the researcher, rather than the rights of the participant. I think that most researchers will accept that they have some obligations to the people who participate in their research, but there is a large gap between that and 'information privacy'. There will be circumstances where the two approaches combine, where there is no practical difference between respecting the participant and giving the participant a degree of control; but there are also circumstances where control over information becomes a way to protect the powerful, exploit the vulnerable, such as when it is a means to hide corruption or abuse. The principle of information privacy (or data protection) is a poor guide to ethical conduct. If we are hoping for researchers to act ethically, it is not clear that ceding control to participants is the way to go about it.

THE LIMITS OF PRIVACY

Even at the level of the individual, it is debatable whether we can ever treat ourselves as wholly private. We are social animals. We communicate with each other in common terms. Our understanding of ourselves, Gilbert Ryle argued, is based substantially on our knowledge of other people; we cannot have a sense of self until we know about others (Ryle, 1963). When we extend the principle to two people, difficulties arise. Each person has rights, and their rights are conditioned and mediated in terms of the society they live in. The contexts can be complex: the Dutch idea of 'sphere sovereignty', initially stated by Kuyper (1899) and later by Dooyeweerd (1979), is based on the idea that that there are several spheres of life where different rules apply – spheres such as the home, religion, business, and politics. We have come to reject – I think rightly – the claim that domestic violence is a private matter between husband and wife, or that parental chastisement in one's own home has nothing to do with the world outside (Schneider, 1994).

The limitations of this kind of privacy are marked by the idea of the private sphere – Mill's 'reserved territory'. The private sphere stands in contradistinction to the public sphere – the areas of life where society or the state have the right to pass information to others. All criminal acts are, by definition, public; the public authorities have declared that certain acts must be treated legally as public matters. (That makes it rather questionable that so many researchers think they should protect their participants from the consequences of actions revealed by the research. Public actions are not protected by principles of privacy, and it is troubling when they are made the subject of data protection.) Where general rights are at stake – such as human rights – the privacy or confidentiality of the research process does not override them.

Many of the codes of guidance issued by professional associations get this wrong. The Social Policy Association offers as a general principle the idea that

'Information provided to a researcher in the context of a research study should be treated as confidential' (SPA, 2009). That implies that the information is presumed to be private. But social policy is concerned with public issues and public information; much of the point of the field is to subject public action to open scrutiny. If information is found in the course of research, there has to be a very good reason not to reveal it. The British Society of Criminology states that 'Researchers should not breach the 'duty of confidentiality' and not pass on identifiable data to third parties without participants' consent'. It goes on to advise that 'In general in the UK people who witness crimes or hear about them before or afterwards are not legally obliged to report them to the police' (BSC, 2006). (There are three main legal exceptions – terrorism, child protection and money laundering.) Criminal law defines a range of actions as public, not private. It is not always clear whether an action is criminal – but privacy is too often used as a defence against legitimate public scrutiny.

Similarly, the Social Research Association cites US guidance:

> The US Office for Protection from Research Risks allows observational research to be exempt from consent unless:
>   a) 'information obtained is recorded in such a manner that human subjects can be identified, directly or through identifiers linked to the subjects; and
>   b) any disclosure of the human subjects' responses outside the research could reasonably place the subjects at risk of criminal or civil liability or be damaging to the subjects' financial standing, employability, or reputation'. (SRA, 2003, p 33)

If there is a risk of criminal or civil liability, it is because the subjects have harmed other people. That is exactly the point at which the duties a researcher has to a subject are likely to be outweighed by the need to avoid harm to others.

Defining what is private, and what is public, can be difficult. Different rules apply in different circumstances. Private actions can take place in public settings, and public actions can happen in private ones. There are circumstances where people do things in private that are public in their nature – people who are abusing public authority often try to do it behind closed doors. While justice should in principle be open and transparent, there are special cases where justice is better served in private – for example, in decisions about the care of children.

As a general proposition actions are public if:

- They occur in the public domain, and are open to be witnessed by members of the public. There are exceptions to this: circumstances where people legitimately do things in public places that are not meant to be witnessed or public – adjusting clothing, falling over, or sleeping. There is a judgement to make; social media fizzle with examples of people doing silly things that they may regret. But there is no obvious moral duty to ignore public behaviour; if there is a default position, it is that behaviour in public occurs in the public domain unless there are good reasons to the contrary.
- They have been defined as public by a lawfully constituted authority. All criminal acts are public, because the law declares them to be – that is what a 'crime' is. The same applies to some things that may otherwise seem personal – rules about marriage, sexuality, motoring, taxable income, workers'

rights, public companies (which have to report their financial activity publicly) and much else besides.
- They concern public affairs, such as government, legislation, and the system of justice. Part of the argument for considering these things as public is the shared, social nature of the activity, but that is not the whole story. The legitimacy and authority of democratic governments rests not just on a process of voting, but on a degree of openness, transparency, and the opportunity to engage in public fora. Treating governance as public is not just a description; it is a moral positioning its own right.

Researchers who are working primarily in the public sphere are often fired by ethical concerns, but those concerns look rather different from the traditional focus of guides to research ethics. Policy analysts aim to 'tell truth to power'. The American Society for Public Administration aims to 'serve the public interest' and 'uphold the law', including 'constitutional principles of equality, fairness, representativeness, responsiveness and due process'. (ASPA, 2012) My own discipline, social policy, has a critical role in holding governments to account. [One of my last research projects was based on speaking to officials administering social security, and it was done without asking the government department which controls access to those officials, because the department would have refused. However, more than 200 officials participated (PCS, 2017).]
- They concern issues that are already accepted as being in the public domain – typically, because they have been published. That is the standard defence of secondary analysis, meta-analysis, and critical reappraisal of evidence. Secondary analysis and research archives use data in ways that neither the participant nor the researcher can reasonably anticipate, and if the data belongs to the participant, that appears to be unethical. So, in principle, would be repetition of comments or information provided by one person for a different purpose. In my own work, I have used previously published accounts to discuss some of the intensely personal issues around dementia, incontinence, and learning disability. I did not of course ask the people concerned – I do not know who they are – but I would not have asked them if I did. I was citing other people's research.

I claimed at the start of this chapter that some of the misinterpretations about the scope and process of research could be unethical, and this is an example. Treating public information as if it must be private is at best ethically questionable, at worst repugnant. Restricting truthful accounts of the things that people do in public, and subsequent discussion of them, is a restraint on free speech and a free press; that kind of restraint infringes the right of everyone else, as members of the public, to know. Obstruction of the examination of public norms, rules, and laws is a prescription for tyranny. Discussion and examination of published material is fundamental to science, learning, education, and a free society. And examination of government and policy is essential to democracy, which has been defined as 'government by discussion' (Cohen, 1997). The defence of the public sphere is in all our interests.

RESEARCH WITHOUT CONSENT

Much of the literature on informed consent starts from the assumption that there is something intrinsically wrong with research where no consent is given. The development of that doctrine began with a legitimate concern, about the use of pointless, invasive 'experiments' by Nazi doctors, and the Nuremberg Code became the model for bio-medical research everywhere. The doctrines that I have been examining reflect those concerns, but they have gone some way beyond them. The doctrine of information privacy can only legitimately apply in circumstances where the person who gives the consent is the person who legitimately controls the release of that information to the researcher. There are many circumstances where that is not the case. They include, most obviously, information that is public in its nature. Even in the private sphere, however, there is information over which the research participant does not hold the rights. This includes information that relates to organisations, to third parties (and other people), and to other participants – and most research based on evidence from participants calls for some 'triangulation', cross-validation, or corroboration to be useful, at which point it ceases to be under the control of individual respondents. It might still be good practice (and good manners) for a researcher to behave as if their research participant was a valued source – I have tried to do that – but I have also, without compunction, used freedom of information legislation, which requires public officials to respond to queries. We should not suppose that the researcher's primary duty is to the respondents.

Much of the literature concerned with involuntary participation in research is concerned with 'covert research', a term which generally refers to circumstances where the researcher does not tell research subjects or participants that research is taking place. [That is often muddled with the different, and relatively unusual, situation where researchers do not tell people that research is going on and actively deceive participants about what they are doing. Most cases of deception take place within the framework of a research project that seems to be about something else (Kimmel, 1996, p. 73).] It is more helpful to think of covert research as being undisclosed, or having 'limited disclosure' (ANHMRC, 2007). Legitimate examples of research where no disclosure was necessary or appropriate might be taken to include monitoring the use of mobile phones while driving (Walker, Williams, & Jamrozik, 2006), considering health and safety issues in the management of major sporting events (Lekka, Webster, & Corbett, 2010), or surveillance of internet use to produce economic indicators (McLaren & Shanbhogue, 2011). All three of those pieces of research have taken place in the public sphere, and they were all clearly done for the public benefit; it would be shocking if they were not permitted.

Undisclosed research could be considered a breach of privacy if it led to the publication of material that was private – but the same would be true of research with full disclosure. The doctrine of privacy does imply a default – a set of barriers and protections that researchers can only cross subject to permission, co-operation, and safeguards, and sometimes, particularly when there is a risk of harm, not even then. Consent may contribute to the protection of research subjects, but it is not a guarantee of it. I was part of a research team developing an instrument to assist with planning social care provision for people with dementia (Spicker & Gordon, 1997). The main objective of the instrument was to use data to inform planners about the needs of the population, and so to minimise intrusion in individual circumstances. Wherever possible, information was obtained from people who were already in possession of the data, and the information was anonymised and dealt with collectively. The study was designed to obtain the information in a manner which would minimise disturbance or cost to the subjects of the research, and to process and use the information in a manner which would not impose costs or otherwise harm them.

There were no problems raised during formal ethical review, because as far as the review committee was concerned this was not an invasive process. Ethical concerns were, however, raised as we proceeded. There was no effective way of obtaining consent from people with dementia; explaining the purpose of the research to people with dementia and their carers, even in outline, would itself carry risks (many people with dementia have not been told); even minimal intervention could be intrusive – questions about memory loss, behaviour, insecurities, or personal care are inevitably difficult to ask. We sought to protect and safeguard the interests of the respondents – our interviewers were professionally qualified and experienced social workers. Ultimately, however, this all depends on a series of moral judgments, and a question of whether the benefits of the research (a less invasive procedure than current assessments) could justify the process. There cannot be blanket rules.

ETHICAL RESEARCH: THE DUTIES OF RESEARCHERS

I began this chapter with a widely accepted model of ethical behaviour in research: privacy demands control, control requires consent, and consent protects privacy. This is not wrong in every case, but there are more than enough counter-examples to show that it cannot be taken as a default position.

Researchers do have duties to protect people, but those duties are badly described in conventional codes of guidance. First, there are duties to everyone and anyone – human rights, the rights of citizens, the rights of vulnerable people, and so on. Researchers have a duty at least to avoid, and where the information is clear to report, crimes against humanity, the abuse of power, and the abuse of persons. These rights should have the highest priority in research – certainly, they trump any issue about the research itself, and any undertakings the researcher might make to specific persons. The supposition that researchers have a duty to conceal the wrongs that some people do to others, that powerful people have the right to control information, and that nothing can be done without their consent, is plainly unethical.

Second, there are duties arising from the research that is being done – its potential use, its application, and its effects on research subjects. Research should be beneficent (aiming to do something good), or at least non-maleficent (doing no harm). Privacy can be an important constraint on research, but there are acts of observation, recording, and reporting that have no evident implications for privacy. Google and Twitter commonly monitor people's use of terms or the subject of searches; many researchers are involved in similar activities. When people complain about the mass use of internet-based data, they are assuming that in some way that this has trespassed on their rights. How? Are Icelanders somehow violated because their government manages (and sells) genetic information about the population? Merz and his colleagues are highly critical of the Icelandic example. In their view, an action that would be legitimate if it was solely for governmental purposes ceases to be legitimate if it is used commercially (Merz, McGee, & Sankar, 2004). There is a distinct argument to make here about the research relationship – how the research might be affected by obligations incurred as a result of funding or sponsorship – but the simple fact of whether this relates to government or the private sector does not seem to me to have anything to do with the process of research. Neither the aims of the action, nor the process, nor the outcomes have any evident implications that affect any individual person. The objections to such measures are being represented, questionably, as a point of absolute principle, without considering whether there is actually a violation of privacy or of rights. If research is beneficent, does no harm and does not intrude on personal space, there should be no obstacle to it.

Third, there are duties to participants – which I take to mean the people with whom researchers interact directly (a much more limited category than appeared earlier in this argument). The rights of participants are 'particular', not 'general'; they define the duties which are negotiated with the researcher. The defence of particular rights is a matter of integrity. Researchers should avoid, for example, making promises they cannot legitimately keep – such as promises of confidentiality made to people engaged in criminal activity. It is important, however, to recognise that duties to participants are contingent, and must have a lower priority than general duties such as human rights, human dignity, or the rights of citizenship. That is a still more important example of the ways in which treating research as private may be unethical.

Much of the process of research is concerned with making information public, in the broad sense of that term. The process of research generally involves taking data, of whatever sort, and processing it in a form that will be presented to other people. Whenever research is done with the intention of producing a report, or making the findings known to people other than the researcher and the participants, it can be said to be a 'publication'. The very word 'publication' might reasonably be taken to suggest that the material is made available to the public, but that is not requisite; in law, a 'publication' might refer simply to communication to a third party. Sometimes the presentation itself is confidential – for example, when an organisation has commissioned research about its operations – but even then, information is likely to be taken from one place and moved to another. [In an American case, confidential communications within a company have been held to be 'publications' (*Bals* v. *Verduzco*, 1992).] The transmission of material across boundaries is fundamental to research work.

There are topics which cannot be broached without some degree of intrusion into people's private space, and wherever that is done, it needs to be approached with a sense of ethical integrity and a degree of sensitivity. Where information is private, there may be a case for confidentiality and anonymity. That is not true in every situation, and where the activity falls clearly into the public sphere, there is no duty to consult with participants, to negotiate the terms of the research, or even to disclose that research is taking place. In most circumstances, research is not a private matter, and the assumption that it must be private is itself a violation of another ethical principle – one of the foundational principles of modern civilisation. We have to be able to examine the world we live in.

REFERENCES

American Society for Public Administration (ASPA). (2012). Retrieved from http://www.aspanet.org/public/ASPADocs/Principles%2012-09-10.pdf

Australian National Health and Medical Research Council (ANHMRC). (1999). National statement on ethical conduct in research involving humans: Commonwealth of Australia.

Australian National Health and Medical Research Council (ANHMRC). (2007). National statement of ethical conduct in human research. Retrieved from http://www.nhmrc.gov.au/publications/ethics/2007_humans/contents.htm

Australian National Health and Medical Research Council (ANHMRC). (2018). National statement on ethical conduct in human research: Commonwealth of Australia.

Bals v. *Verduzco*, 600 N.E.2d 1353 (Ind. 1992).

British Sociological Association (BSA). (2017). Statement of ethical practice (p. 5). Retrieved from https://www.britsoc.co.uk/media/24310/bsa_statement_of_ethical_practice.pdf

British Society of Criminology (BSC). (2006). Code of ethics for researchers in the field of criminology. Retrieved from http://www.britsoccrim.org/ethical.htm

Cohen, J. (1997). Deliberation and democratic legitimacy. In R. Goodin & P. Pettit (Eds.), *Contemporary political philosophy*. Oxford: Blackwell.

Dooyeweerd, H. (1979). *Roots of western culture*. Toronto: Wedge.

UK Economic and Social Research Council (ESRC). (2015). ESRC framework for research ethics. Retrieved from https://esrc.ukri.org/files/funding/guidance-for-applicants/esrc-framework-for-research-ethics-2015/

Faden, R., & Beauchamp, T. (1986). *A history and theory of informed consent*. Oxford: Oxford University Press.

Kimmel, A. (1988). *Ethics and values in social research*. London: Sage.

Kimmel, A. (1996). *Ethical issues in behavioural research*. Oxford: Blackwell.

Kuyper, A. (1899). *Calvinism: Six stone lectures*. Amsterdam: Hoeveker and Wormser.

Lekka, C., Webster, J., & Corbett, E. (2010). *A literature review of the health and safety risks associated with major sporting events*. Merseyside: Health and Safety Executive.

McLaren, N., & Shanbhogue, R. (2011). Using internet data as economic indicators. *Bank of England Quarterly Bulletin Q2, 51*, 134–140.

Merz, J., McGee, G., & Sankar, P. (2004). "Iceland Inc."?: On the ethics of commercial population genomics. *Social Science & Medicine, 58*, 1201–1209.

Mill, J. S. (1848). The principles of political economy. Retrieved from http://ebooks.adelaide.edu.au/m/mill/john_stuart/m645p/book5.11.html

PCS. (2017). *The future of social security in Scotland: Views from within the system*. Glasgow: Public and Commercial Services Union.

Rössler, B. (2005). *The value of privacy*. Cambridge: Polity.

Ryle, G. (1963). *The concept of mind*. Harmondsworth: Penguin.

Schneider, E. (1994). The violence of privacy. In M. Fineman & R. Mykitiuk (Eds.), *The public nature of private violence*. New York, NY: Routledge.

Social Policy Association (SPA). (2009). Social policy association guidelines on research ethics. Retrieved from http://www.social-policy.com/documents/SPA_code_ethics_jan09.pdf

Spicker, P., & Gordon, D. (1997). *Planning for the needs of people with dementia*. Aldershot: Avebury.

Social Research Association (SRA). (2003). Ethical guidelines.

United Nations. (1948). Universal declaration of human rights, art 12.

Walker, L., Williams, J., & Jamrozik, L. (2006). Unsafe driving behaviour and four wheel drive vehicles. *British Medical Journal, 331*, 71.

Warren, S., & Brandeis, L. (1890). The right to privacy. *Harvard Law Review, 4*(5), 193–220.

CHAPTER 4

COVERT RESEARCH ETHICS

Marco Marzano

ABSTRACT

Covert research has a mixed reputation within the scientific community. Some are unsure of its moral worth, others would proscribe it entirely. This reputation stems largely from a lack of knowledge about the reasons for choosing the covert method. In this chapter, these reasons will be reconstructed in detail and all the elements that will allow one to judge the level of ethicality of covert research will be laid out for the reader. In particular, the chapter will answer the following questions: What harms can result from covert research to the subjects participating in the research? Is covert research necessarily deceptive? In which cases is it ethically permissible for a researcher to deceive? What is the scientific added value of the covert research, that is, what does covert research discover that overt research does not? What are the risks to researchers acting undercover? Finally, some suggestions will be offered to research ethics reviewers to help in their appraisal of covert research.

Keywords: Covert research; deception; research ethics committees; social research ethics; qualitative research; investigative social research

Covert research is clearly not to everyone's analytic taste but the commitment is to explore different and creative ways of constructing ethnographic narratives. The covert ethnographic role can be a deeply artful one that offers a way to form intimate insider accounts about a wide range of topics. It should become a more standard part of the ethnographic

Ethical Issues in Covert, Security and Surveillance Research
Advances in Research Ethics and Integrity, Volume 8, 41–53
ISSN: 2398-6018/doi:10.1108/S2398-601820210000008005

craft (Atkinson, 2015) rather than be outcast as a methodological pariah. In certain forms of autoethnography, online lurking within cyber ethnography and bystander observations of public behaviours, there seems to be a growing appetite for covert research, although it is certainly not becoming mainstream. There remains a classic fear and fascination about covert research. (Calvey, 2019, p. 259)

INTRODUCTION

Covert research – research which is done without informing those involved (i.e. the 'subjects' of research) – has been labouring under a negative reputation in the academic community for some decades (Barnes, 1963; Calvey, 2017; Erikson, 1966; Herrera, 1999; Homan, 1980; Shils, 1982; Warwick, 1982). The origin of the disgrace into which covert research has fallen, after a long period of grace,[1] is to be sought in the fact that it is seen as extremely ethically and morally dubious. This suspicion of the perceived dangers of covert research is shared by both the members of many research ethics review committees (RECs) or institutional review boards (IRBs) which promote a rigorous code of ethics, believing that it violates many of the rights of those being studied in an unacceptable way, and many scholars, especially sociologists and anthropologists, who have done various forms of collaborative research over recent years. These latter believe that covert research does incalculable damage to the pact between researchers and those they study that they have taken such care to construct (Christians, 2000; Denzin, 1997; Guba & Lincoln, 1989; Noddings, 2003). These attitudes as a whole have led to the complete marginalisation of covert research, with many RECs and IRBs beginning to ban it in all circumstances and many researchers having stopped doing it altogether. Today covert research is a method used, with some difficulty, by a markedly limited number of researchers (Calvey, 2017).

I would argue that this is a highly negative development in academic terms and that the stigmatising of covert research on ethical grounds is excessive and unjust. In this chapter, I will argue that there are many reasons why covert research can be considered ethically acceptable. I will abstain from listing the accusations traditionally levelled at covert research[2] as these are extremely well known and I focus instead on the motives which have, both implicitly and explicitly, been marshalled in support of this research method.

In general, I believe that it is possible to distinguish between two overall approaches to the defence of covert research, one moderate and one radical. These two perspectives reflect different visions of research ethics, the duties of researchers and the rights of those involved particularly in social science research. I will illustrate both perspectives, starting from the moderate approach. But first I should clarify that my thinking will refer primarily to qualitative research (Hammersley, 2020) and not other forms of research (such as experiments), and focus on work in sociology and social psychology and, to a lesser extent, anthropology.

THE MODERATE DEFENCE OF THE GROUNDS FOR COVERT RESEARCH

The moderate approach to covert research has certainly been the most widespread of the two approaches within the social science community (Calvey, 2008; Lugosi, 2006; Perez, 2019; Roulet, Gill, Stenger, & Gill, 2017; Spicker, 2011).

The exponents of this approach do not invoke total researcher freedom calling for an end to all forms of ethics regulation. Quite the contrary, they assert that, if done in a certain way, covert research can and must be considered compatible with the ethics standards currently prevalent in the academic community. This approach might even be called 'reformist', as its objective is to bring certain types of covert research into the legitimate and recognised methods fold and demonstrate its compatibility with overt methods.

To this end, the moderates or reformers have put forward the following arguments:

Lying Must Be an Exception

In the first place the 'reformers' argue that lying is not to be considered a 'normal', natural part of social sciences research and that, where possible, researchers must behave honestly and make participants aware of the real reason for their presence in the field. This is especially the case where research is on vulnerable or fragile people. And in any case social scientists should be called on to justify their ethical behaviour and field work choices before ethics committees or, in the absence of these, in the sections of their articles dealing with methodology and ethics (Lugosi, 2006).

Overt and Covert Research Are Not Clearly Distinguishable

Reiterating this point, that is, that intentional and blatant lying cannot be tolerated as a normal research method (Spicker, 2011), the moderate defenders of covert research argue that a situation in which the subjects of research are truly fully informed and aware of a researcher's purposes and intentions is closer to myth than to real life (Fine, 1993; Fine & Shulman, 2009). From this perspective, it is argued, covert and overt research cannot be seen as easily identifiable and distinguishable entities (Calvey, 2017; McKenzie 2009)) and even in the best overt research there are inevitably many opaque elements, ambiguities and a lack of transparency and clarity. In this respect, the informed consent practices now widespread do not avert doubt and confusion (Marzano, 2012; Traianou & Hammersley, 2020) and would frequently seem, beyond significantly limiting research freedom, to serve more to defend the interests and reputation of academic institutions than to protect the people studied (Hedgecoe, 2016; Murphy & Dingwall, 2007; Van den Hoonard, 2011).

Informing Subjects Is Sometimes Really Impossible

Sometimes it is a research location which determines whether or not research work can be performed in a fully open way (Lugosi, 2006; Spicker, 2011). This is the case of ethnographic work done in public places such as town squares, open air markets, football stadiums and so on. In such situations, it is obviously impossible for ethnographers to inform everyone they meet of the fact that research is underway (Traianou & Hammersley, 2020). In any case, those going to public places know that they are exposing themselves to the public gaze and thus any social analysts that could be present.[3] This is also true of those lacking private spaces and living permanently in public places (such as the homeless people studied by Perez, 2019).

Informed Consent Can Never Cover Everything That Happens in the Field

A further element rendering much research at least partially covert is the fact that isolating research from other contexts can be an extremely complex matter and much of researchers' most significant information is acquired in the field in informal, random conversations in corridors, exchanges of opinion and friendly chats on the margins of formal interviews. What could researchers do about this? Shed all information acquired in this context? Should such valuable information regarding an understanding of, say, an organisational culture really be thrown away solely because it has been sourced from ordinary human conversations outside a research protocol formally approved by an ethics committee? Not to speak of all those behaviours which researchers put into practice in their contacts with those they study designed to manage impressions or rather improve their reputations in the eyes of those they are studying for the purposes of obtaining specific benefits and better access to the information of interest to them.

Sometimes the Most Important Things Are Learned through Unintentional Covert Research

More generally, we should not imagine that the places in which ethnographic work takes place resemble the Trobriand islands in Malinowski's work, where strangers are rarely to be seen. In contemporary advanced industrial (and post-industrial) societies, the lion's share of places and spaces are packed with people coming and going freely, appearing on the scene briefly or barging in without researchers being given the chance to warn them of their presence. I can illustrate with a personal experience of mine relating to research into people dying of cancer which I did some years ago in a large Italian hospital. The research began in a semi-covert way (Marzano, 2007) in the sense that the hospital staff knew about the project and that the head of the hospital ward had approved it. The last part of this ethnographic project was overt, with everyone (staff, patients and their relatives) being informed of its nature and purposes. It was, however, precisely in this last phase of my field work that something totally unforeseen occurred: one day I was in the staff room of the palliative care ward intent on writing up some of my field notes when a doctor (dietician) suddenly came in together with the wife and daughter of a patient. The three of them acted as if I was not there (perhaps the doctor assumed I was a colleague although I was not wearing a white coat), sat down at the other end of the table and the doctor proceeded to explain the best diet and food to be given to the patient (last stage terminally ill) to the two women. I witnessed the whole conversation in silence and it was an extremely chilling conversation in which a patient entirely unaware of his real condition was treated like a pet to be induced to eat certain foods with little tricks. I wrote out the dialogue in my diary and then added it to my research in rigorously anonymous form (Marzano, 2004). Many years later, I still believe I was right to do so because those few minutes of dialogue were a stark representation of the dehumanisation of the patient and brought across very clearly the way the terminally ill were treated in Italy to my readers. Unintentional covert research can also sometimes be very fruitful.

Informed Consent Inevitably Concerns Only the Initial Research Design

It should also be borne in mind that, as is well known, the qualitative research framework is extremely flexible (Hammersley & Atkinson, 1995, p. 265; Wiles et al., 2007), subject to ongoing restructuring and redefining and changing frequently during the course of a researcher's field work (Calvey, 2008; Lugosi, 2006). For this reason, it can indeed happen that the information supplied at the outset of research, and for which informed consent may have been obtained from participants, will no longer be complete or up-to-date at a later point in the research. Researchers are very rarely able (or willing) to inform participants of such changes and these latter are, in any case, not sociologists and anthropologists and unlikely to be interested in finding out more about the details of what social scientists do, their curiosities and research interests. Very frequently, what participants are most interested in is something researchers are also keen to ensure, namely being able to get on with what they are doing, without too many interruptions and excessive disturbances, working, interacting and going about their normal lives without being disturbed by ethnographers' presence or words. Keeping them constantly informed as to changing research strategies would be a nuisance, a source of irritation, to them. The result, however, is that in this case, too, researchers' objectives and intentions are partially covert.

A Covert Method May Be the Most Suitable Way of Getting Into the Field

The moderate defenders of research also argue that acting covertly can sometimes be ethically admissible on the grounds that its time frame is limited as is its purpose, serving solely to facilitate the researcher's access to the field. In certain contexts, in fact, researchers revealing their true identity may be prejudicial to the very potential for the research, in the last analysis. For example, at the time of his research into gay bars, Lugosi (2006) believed that it would have been dangerously counterproductive for him to have revealed, right from the start, the real reasons for his presence and that it was far better to build up solid friendships during his hours of work as a barman, and the many free time hours he chose to spend there, before doing so. In all cases such as this, acting covertly is an exceptional and momentary state in which researchers commit to making their true identity known as soon as possible to the largest possible number of people. Acting covertly is simply a necessary expedient with which to initiate research in a social environment to which it would otherwise have been very difficult to gain access. It is possible that most if not all field research can begin in this state of 'naturally covert observation' which gives rise to a topic of research enquiry in the first place.

It Is Not Always the Researcher Who Chooses to Hide His/Her Identity

In certain situations working undercover is not an independent or free choice and it is researchers' gatekeepers who require this as a precondition for allowing them access to the field (Traianou & Hammersley, 2020). This has happened to me twice (Marzano, 2018): the first time when I was studying people dying of cancer and the head of the hospital's oncology ward whom I had contacted through a common friend told the doctors and nurses on the ward who I was and then that if I wanted to observe what went on there all I needed to do was to put on a white coat and tell patients and their relatives that I was a trainee. The second time was when the heads of a Catholic group I was studying proposed that I take part in an educational week of theirs but only on condition that I did not tell the other participants that I was a sociologist and not a member of the community like all the others: 'The risk would that they would feel like laboratory guinea pigs', I was told, 'and would get annoyed.' In both cases the only alternative would have been breaking off the research. The fact is that, in the groups and organisations we study there are significant power imbalances and these can be visible not only in the decisions of the organisation's heads to impose the researcher's presence (disregarding the consent of the others) but also, in some cases, not revealing the presence of the researcher to those involved. In such cases, challenging this norm, making one's identity explicit, would mean challenging the hierarchy, casting doubt on the right of the heads to decide (Traianou & Hammersley, 2020).

Sometimes Asking for Subjects' Consent Is Impractical or Inappropriate

In other research, the obstacles to overt research consist in the fact that (a) the subjects are not, for various reasons, capable of understanding the nature of the researcher's work or that (b) asking them to sign an informed consent form would be an ethically inopportune action (Marzano, 2012). The first situation is very frequent (how many of those who sign informed consent forms are truly aware of its consequences?) and in some cases glaring. An example is Lawton's research into hospices and the terminally ill (Lawton, 2001; see also Paterniti, 2000). This British researcher tried to keep patients coming to the hospice informed about the nature of her work but she could only rarely be sure that they had fully understood, given the late stage of their illness and their frequent dementia. The second situation is a matter of those social contexts in which signing a consent form (even simply informed consent) is bound up with painful memories and has exploitation and domination associations. This is the case of the waste pickers studied by Perez (2019, see also Gubrium et al., 2014, p. 1609). Perez herself has spoken of preferring, at many stages in her career, to use covert methods including to avoid offending the people she was observing. For example, despite fearing that they would forget, she did not remind the waste pickers she spent the day with what she had told them at the outset, that is, that she was recording them. Doing so would, she believed, have been ethically 'required' but it might have meant implying that their mental faculties were in some way lacking and so ethically compromised. This could be a very serious accusation for people subjected to stigmatisation and social disparagement on a daily basis which they refuted by reminding others, including the ethnographer, of their qualifications.

Autoethnography and Online Research: Two Research Methodologies That Are Difficult to Reconcile with Overt Research

There are also new forms of research which have become very popular over recent years and are difficult to reconcile with informed consent and conventional codes of ethics. These are autoethnography (Ellis, 2004; Jones, Adams, & Ellis, 2016) and online research (Calvey, 2017; Hennell, Limmer, & Piacentini, 2020). In autoethnography, scholars recount events from their own lives in detail and then critically analyse them. Clearly the narrator is never the only character in such texts, as is generally true of autobiographies, with other people being mentioned and their actions described. It is equally clear that this takes place without the prior consent of these latter. The facts described have already happened and frequently the people spoken of are no longer there or no longer in contact with the ethnographer. The cyberethnography situation is similar, namely ethnographic study of online material. Whilst it is theoretically possible to envisage researchers informing subjects of their presence in many situations, there is no doubt that online work exponentially increases the potential for 'lurking', namely doing very easy covert research into what happens on a certain site or social media page without intervening (and thus revealing one's true purpose) (Calvey, 2017). This is particularly true in the case of studies of social media (Woodfield, 2017) in which many of the ethical issues examined in relation to 'research in public places' arise (Iphofen, 2011).

The Risk of Causing Harm with Qualitative Research Is Very Limited

If we reread the history of ethnographic research objectively, we are obliged to accept that the harm done to the subjects of covert ethnographic research, including the most controversial, has been negligible to non-existent. Take the most controversial of all covert ethnography, the one universally cited as a negative example by all the critics of this method, Laud Humphrey's *Tearoom Trade*, a covert study of casual homosexual sex in public toilets in the second half of the 1960s. Even this much criticised research has been seen to have caused no harm to those Humphrey (1975) observed and then interviewed. Quite the contrary, it contributed to increasing tolerance of gay people in America and to bringing an end to repressive policies (Yanow & Schwartz-Shea, 2018). The most significant risks were those its author himself, who later became a well-known activist in the defence of the civil rights of homosexuals, took in order to carry it out (Galliher, Brekhus, & Keys, 2004). And in some ways a similar argument, though on a smaller scale, can be made as regards Wacquant's (2004) book on boxers in an African-American ghetto in Chicago.

Covert Research Must Always Be Considered as a Kind of Last Resort

From a moderate perspective, scholars never opt for covert research without giving it serious thought. Quite the opposite, they make recourse to it only when strictly necessary, sometimes uneasily and with feelings of guilt and in any case always preferring to come out into the open and reveal their identities as soon as possible. For example, Virtová, Stöckelová, and Krásná (2018) have recounted that the member of the group who undertook the field work got herself hired at the electronic goods factory chosen for the study and kept her identity concealed in order to be able to carry out her research work freely without interference by the firm's management. As time went on, however, the moral urge to drop her mask and tell her worker colleagues the truth intensified and, after revealing her identity to some of her department colleagues, she went as far as to allow one of them, who had in the meantime become a close friend, to have a say on research strategy, decide who could be told the truth and which parts of the research needed to be terminated or rewritten. A similar decision was taken by Perez (2019) and myself, years ago and in similar terms, described the moral quandary which led to me seeking out and finding a way to do overt research (Marzano, 2007).

The Superiority of Situated Ethics

In summary, the exponents of what I have called a moderate form of covert research espouse a situated ethics (Calvey, 2008) in which they conceal their research identities only in certain situations and with specific limits and constraints ensuring full moral responsibility for their actions. In the view of its exponents, situated ethics and a sense of 'positionality' supply those involved in its research with much wider, more authentic and incisive protection than that given by mere informed consent, that is, a process which is frequently solely formal and defensive in purpose (regarding the reputation of the researcher or the academic institution he or she belongs to).

THE RADICAL APPROACH

The approach to covert research I have termed moderate or reformist has certainly been the most popular approach over the last two decades and it has, to some extent, rehabilitated this approach. That said, I cannot avoid citing here, however summarily, what I see as a more radical approach to covert research. It starts from the assumption that knowledge of the truth is a complicated business which requires getting over the defensive barriers put up by subjects to stop the truth coming out (Mitchell, 1993). In this context, covert research is seen as an absolute necessity and the sharing of information and research projects between scholars and subjects dangerously utopian. This perspective sees the research world as marked by conflict and the juxtaposition of interests with those observed on one side and researchers on the other.

This decidedly minority view is rare today and its great prophet is Jack Douglas, a very original theoretician and passionate researcher (Johnson, 2015). The book in which he set out his 'research philosophy' most clearly (Douglas, 1976) begins with this striking phrase: 'The goal of all social research is to discover, understand and communicate truth about human beings in society'. Douglas is certainly well aware that this affirmation is replete with problems, heuristic complications and huge epistemological and methodological difficulties, believing that it must be considered the starting point for all knowledge acquisition all the same. Naturally the truth Douglas spoke of is not the absolute truth of the positivists but the everyday life truth we all seek out in our lives. For Douglas, in seeking out the truth, sociologists have no option but to prioritise one source in particular in their everyday lives and academic work equally, namely direct experience, first person participation, getting into the shoes, at least for a whilst, of a member of the social group or organisation to be studied. What can be gleaned from interviews comes second, as the direct experience of other people, with what can be deduced from mere logic or common sense coming last. The reason behind this research methods 'hierarchy' is to be sought in the fact that nothing is more reliable than direct experience. In interviews, there is always the chance that interviewees are lying or, at least, concealing part of the truth and the likelihood of this increases on certain themes (primarily sex, money and power) and above all in a society as divided and conflicted as contemporary America.

Douglas does not deny that there are research situations and contexts in which scholars can proceed by means of relationships of trust with the people they study and base their studies on the willingness of the latter to co-operate with them. There are, however, according to Douglas, others, and they are certainly not few in number, in which finding out the truth requires adopting a different research strategy, namely lying, acting under false pretences and infiltrating. I have already referred to the basic reasons behind this: the people sociologists often study are likely to lie and deceive often, they resist with all their power, and frequently in an organised way, any attempt by researchers to penetrate their worlds to get to know and describe them. And this is not only the case of criminals but also of the most normal of people, of us all, when things we prefer to keep hidden are involved. The perimeter of lies, deceit and half-truths is, for Douglas, so wide in social life that giving up covert methods would mean giving up casting light on the lion's share of human activities and thwart the knowledge gathering mission of the social sciences, relegating these to innocuous and moralistic disciplines.

It would, however, be mistaken to deduce an overall indifference to research ethics from the orientation of Douglas's research. In my view, and Douglas might perhaps agree, it would be closer to the truth to argue that the ethical principles his work is inspired by are not those of the currently prevalent code of ethics approach but rather inspired by the need to prioritise 'parrhesia' wherever possible, namely telling the truth, above all to the powerful, who don't want to hear it (Alvesalo-Kuusi & Whyte, 2018, Galliher, 1979). Parrhesia, as Michel Foucault (1983, 2011, 2012) reminded us in a reworking of ancient philosophy, is in some cases a courageous gesture (exposing the researcher to the anger and revenge of the powerful) and, in others, a gesture of friendship and brotherhood. In other words, telling the truth may serve to condemn an abuse but also to help a friend to take stock of reality. This is what Douglas (1976, p. 115) is implicitly reminding us when he argues that investigative research also means stating, or rather putting into writing, a truth which might wound some of those in the field who have become friends, people we sympathise with but who we have done research on and who, when the results are written up, we must treat like all the others, no concessions. For Douglas (1976 p. 115), truth tellers are duty bound to report

> illegal, shady or deviant activities (from the standpoint of the middle-class public) which the member would prefer were not reported, which could be used against the members by political enemies, and which the authors might prefer did not exist.

Truth tellers stop before nothing in their desire to tell the truth. In his book, Douglas describes frankly and in detail the academic world's many hypocrisies and lies and also sets out in full the many lies he himself has told in his private life. For Douglas ethics is not a bureaucratic issue which can be relegated to a board or protocol, but a profound moral duty bound up with telling the truth, whatever the cost and always. For him, the institutionalisation of the professional behavioural codes from which sanctions could be applied are a threat to freedom and constitute a tool by which to impose grey, depressing conformity and thus avert the emergence of new ideas which might jeopardise consolidated power balances (Douglas, 1979). The laws of liberal democratic states are more than sufficient to safeguard research ethics without the need for sanctions from specific ethics boards.

Douglas's very unusual approach has prompted bitter criticism by some, but also admiration and applause from others who have, however, only rarely emulated his approach to investigative research. Of these latter, many of his students can certainly be cited (Adler, 1993; Adler & Adler, 1987; Johnson, 1975, 2015; Melnikov & Kotarba, 2017, 2020), as well as certain contemporary authors whose approach is very close to the 'critical sociology' approach (Brannan, 2015, 2017; Lloyd, 2020; Sugden & Tomlinson, 1999), a formidable highly *sui generis* anthropologist like Nancy Scheper-Hughes (2004) and, above all, some of the greatest researchers in the history of ethnography from Dalton of *Men Who Manage*, (cited more than once by Douglas himself as a sublime example of investigative research), Rosenhan of *Being Sane in Insane Places*, Festinger of *When Prophecy Fails* and Goffman of *Asylums* (see also Mitchell, 1993).

CONCLUSIONS

Covert research was, for decades, a method made use of by social scientists without especial difficulty, feelings of guilt or inadequacy or negative implications for those studied. The change in cultural climate which took place in the 1980s and its newly introduced ethics standards has made covert research increasingly difficult, and frequently impossible when monitoring by ethics committees is required. However, covert research has not died out and many of the researchers adopting it (those I have called moderate or reformist) have done so in an attempt to demonstrate its compatibility with the generally accepted principles of ethics regulation. Outside this perimeter, a covert research tradition (which I have called radical) which is incompatible with codes of ethics but not with the ethical principles involved in social research has struggled, all the same, to survive on the strength of those uncomfortable truths which many do not want to hear.

NOTES

1. Much of the epic social sciences research of the past was covert, with a few examples being Dalton (1959), Festinger, Riecken, and Schachter (1956), Goffman (1961) and Rosenhan (1973). For a complete list see Calvey (2017).
2. This has been analysed fully in the works cited at the beginning of this chapter.
3. Incidentally things are not simple even here, given the fact that, as Spicker, (2011) has noted, it is not solely public action which takes place in public places but also private actions which should be observed and reported with greater caution by social scientists.

REFERENCES

Adler, P. A. (1993). *Wheeling and dealing: An ethnography of an upper-level drug dealing and smuggling community*. New York, NY: Columbia University Press.

Adler, P. A., & Adler, P. (1987). *Membership roles in field research* (Vol. 6). Thousand Oaks, CA: Sage.

Alvesalo-Kuusi, A., & Whyte, D. (2018). Researching the powerful: A call for the reconstruction of research ethics. *Sociological Research Online, 23*(1), 136–152.

Atkinson, P. (2015). For Ethnography. London: Sage.

Barnes, J. A. (1963). Some ethical problems in modern fieldwork. *The British Journal of Sociology, 14*(2), 118–134.

Brannan, M. J. (2015). 'You're not going anywhere': Employee retention, symbolic violence and the structuring of subordination in a UK-based call centre. *The Sociological Review, 63*(4), 801–819.

Brannan, M. J. (2017). Power, corruption and lies: Mis-selling and the production of culture in financial services. *Human Relations, 70*(6), 641–667.

Calvey, D. (2008). The art and politics of covert research: doing situated ethics' in the field. *Sociology, 42*(5), 905–918.

Calvey, D. (2017). *Covert research: The art, politics and ethics of undercover fieldwork*. Los Angeles, CA: Sage.

Calvey, D. (2019). The everyday world of bouncers: A rehabilitated role for covert ethnography. *Qualitative Research, 19*(3), 247–262.

Christians, C. G. (2000). Ethics and politics in qualitative research. In N. K. Denzin & Y. S. Lincoln (Eds.), *Handbook of qualitative research* (2nd ed., pp. 133–155). Thousand Oaks, CA: Sage.

Dalton, M. (1959). *Men who manage. Fusions of feeling and theory in administration [With a chart]*. New York, NY: John Wiley & Sons.

Denzin, N. K. (1997). *Interpretative ethnography: Ethnographic practices for the 21st century*. Thousand Oaks, CA: Sage.

Douglas, J. D. (1976). *Investigative social research: Individual and team field research*. Beverly Hills, CA: Sage.

Douglas, J. D. (1979). Living morality versus bureaucratic fiat. In C. B. Klockars & F. W. O'Connor (Eds.), *Deviance and decency: The Ethics of Research with Human Subjects* (pp. 13–33).

Ellis, C. (2004). *The ethnographic I: A methodological novel about autoethnography*. Walnut Creek, CA: Rowman Altamira.

Erikson, K. T. (1966). A comment on disguised observation in sociology. *Social Problems, 14*, 366–373.

Festinger, L., Riecken, H., & Schachter, S. (1956). *When prophecy fails: A social and psychological study of a modern group that predicted the destruction of the world*. Minneapolis, MN: University of Minnesota Press.

Fine, G. A. (1993). Ten lies of ethnography: Moral dilemmas of field research. *Journal of Contemporary Ethnography, 22*(3), 267–294.

Fine, G. A., & Shulman, D. (2009). Lies from the field: Ethical issues in organizational ethnography. In S. Ybema, D. Yanow, H. Wels, & F. H. Kamsteeg, (Eds.), *Organizational ethnography: Studying the complexities of everyday life* (pp. 177–195). London: Sage.

Foucault, M. (1983). *Discourse and truth: The problematization of Parrhesia.* Berkeley, CA: University of California Press.

Foucault, M. (2011). *The government of self and others: Lectures at the Collège de France, 1982–1983.* Houndmills: Palgrave Macmillan.

Foucault, M. (2012). In F. Gros (Ed.), *The courage of truth (The government of self and others II): Lectures at the Collège de France, 1983–1984.* New York, NY: Macmillan-Picador. C.

Galliher, J. F. (1979). Social Scientists' Ethical Responsibilties to Superordinates: Looking Upward Meekly. *Social Problems., 27*(3), 298–308

Galliher, J. F., Brekhus, W., & Keys, D. P. (2004). *Laud Humphreys: Prophet of homosexuality and sociology.* Madison, WI: University of Wisconsin Press.

Goffman, E. (1961). *Asylums: Essays on the social situation of mental patients and other inmates.* Garden City, NY: Doubleday.

Guba, E. G., & Lincoln, Y. S. (1989). *Fourth generation evaluation.* Newbury Park, CA: Sage.

Gubrium, A. C., Hill, A. L., & Flicker, S. (2014). A situated practice of ethics for participatory visual and digital methods in public health research and practice: A focus on digital storytelling. *American Journal of Public Health, 104*(9), 1606–1614.

Hammersley, M. (2020). Ethics of ethnography. In R. Iphofen (Ed.), *Handbook of research ethics and scientific integrity* (pp. 445–457). Cham: Springer.

Hammersley, M., & Atkinson, P. (1995). *Ethnography: Practices and principles.* East Sussex: Psychology Press.

Hedgecoe, A. (2016). Reputational risk, academic freedom and research ethics review. *Sociology, 50*(3), 486–501.

Hennell, K., Limmer, M., & Piacentini, M. (2020). Ethical dilemmas using social media in qualitative social research: A case study of online participant observation. *Sociological Research Online, 25*(3), 473–489.

Herrera, C. D. (1999). Two arguments for 'covert methods' in social research. *The British Journal of Sociology, 50*(2), 331–343.

Homan, R. (1980). The ethics of covert methods. *The British Journal of Sociology, 33*(1), 46–59.

Humphreys, L. (1975). *Tearoom trade, enlarged edition: Impersonal sex in public places.* Piscataway, NJ: Transaction Publishers.

Iphofen, R. (2011). *Ethical decision making in social research: A practical guide.* New York, NY: Palgrave.

Johnson, J. M. (1975). *Doing field research.* New York, NY: Free Press.

Johnson, J. M. (2015). Freedom works! The vision and broken heart of Jack D. Douglas. *Symbolic Interaction, 38*(2), 285–297.

Jones, S. H., Adams, T. E., & Ellis, C. (Eds.). (2016). *Handbook of autoethnography.* London: Routledge.

Lawton, J. (2001). Gaining and maintaining consent: ethical concerns raised in a study of dying patients. *Qualitative Health Research, 11*(5), 693–705.

Lloyd, A. (2020). Efficiency, productivity and targets: The gap between ideology and reality in the call centre. *Critical Sociology, 46*(1), 83–96.

Lugosi, P. (2006). Between overt and covert research: Concealment and disclosure in an ethnographic study of commercial hospitality. *Qualitative Inquiry, 12*(3), 541–561.

Marzano, M. (2004). Scene finali. In *Morire di cancro in Italia.* Bologna: Il Mulino.

Marzano, M. (2007). Informed consent, deception, and research freedom in qualitative research. *Qualitative Inquiry, 13*(3), 417–436.

Marzano, M. (2012). Informed consent. In J. F. Gubrium, J. A. Holstein, A. B. Marvasti & K. D. McKinney (Eds.), *The SAGE handbook of interview research: The complexity of the craft.* (pp. 443–445). Beverly Hills, CA: SAGE Publications.

Marzano, M. (2018). The ethics of covert ethnographic research. In C. I. Macleod, J. Marx, P. Mnyaka & G. J. Treharne (Eds.), *The Palgrave handbook of ethics in critical research* (pp. 399–413). Cham: Palgrave Macmillan.

McKenzie, J. S. (2009). 'You don't know how lucky you are to be here!': Reflections on covert practices in an overt participant observation study. *Sociological Research Online, 14*(2), 60–69.

Melnikov, A., & Kotarba, J. A. (2017). Jack D. Douglas. In M. H. Jacobsen (Ed.). *The interactionist imagination* (pp. 291–314). London: Palgrave Macmillan.

Melnikov, A., & Kotarba, J. A. (2020). *Douglas, Jack D.* Beverly Hills, CA: SAGE Publications Limited.

Mitchell, R. G. (1993). *Secrecy and fieldwork* (Vol. 29). Newbury Park, CA: Sage.

Murphy, E., & Dingwall, R. (2007). Informed consent, anticipatory regulation and ethnographic practice. *Social science & medicine, 65*(11), 2223–2234.

Noddings, N. (2003). *Caring: A feminine approach to ethics and moral education* (2nd ed.). Berkeley, CA: University of California Press.

Paterniti, D. A. (2000). The micropolitics of identity in adverse circumstance: A study of identity making in a total institution. *Journal of Contemporary Ethnography, 29*(1), 93–119.

Perez, T. S. (2019). In support of situated ethics: Ways of building trust with stigmatised 'waste pickers' in Cape Town. *Qualitative Research, 19*(2), 148–163.

Rosenhan, D. L. (1973). On being sane in insane places. *Science, 179*(4070), 250–258.

Roulet, T. J., Gill, M. J., Stenger, S., & Gill, D. J. (2017). Reconsidering the value of covert research: The role of ambiguous consent in participant observation. *Organizational Research Methods, 20*(3), 487–517.

Scheper-Hughes, N. (2004). Parts unknown: Undercover ethnography of the organs-trafficking underworld. *Ethnography, 5*(1), 29–73.

Shils, E. (1982). Social inquiry and the autonomy of the individual. In M. Bulmer (Ed.), *Social research ethics: An examination of the merits of covert participant observation* (pp. 125–141). London: Macmillan.

Spicker, P. (2011). Ethical covert research. *Sociology, 45*(1), 118–133.

Sugden, J., & Tomlinson, A. (1999). Digging the dirt and staying clean: Retrieving the investigative tradition for a critical sociology of sport. *International Review for the Sociology of Sport, 34*(4), 385–397.

Traianou, A., & Hammersley, M. (2020). Is there a right not to be researched? Is there a right to do research? Some questions about informed consent and the principle of autonomy. *International Journal of Social Research Methodology, 24*(4), 443–452.

Van den Hoonard, W. (2011). *The seduction of ethics: Transforming the social sciences*. Toronto: University of Toronto Press.

Virtová, T., Stöckelová, T., & Krásná, H. (2018). On the track of c/overt research: Lessons from taking ethnographic ethics to the extreme. *Qualitative Inquiry, 24*(7) 453–463.

Wacquant, L. J. (2004). *Body & soul*. Oxford: Oxford University Press.

Warwick, D. P. (1982). Tearoom trade: Means and end in social research. In M. Bulmer (Ed.), *Social research ethics: An examination of the merits of covert participant observation* (pp. 38–58). London: Macmillan

Wiles, R., Crow, G., Charles, V., & Heath, S. (2007). Informed consent and the research process: following rules or striking balances?. *Sociological Research Online, 12*(2), 99–110.

Woodfield, K. (2017). *The ethics of online research (Advances in Research Ethics and Integrity, Vol. 2)*. Bingley: Emerald Publishing Limited.

Yanow, D., & Schwartz-Shea, P. (2018). Framing "deception" and "covertness" in research: Do Milgram, Humphreys, and Zimbardo justify regulating social science research ethics?. In *Forum Qualitative Sozialforschung/Forum: Qualitative Social Research, 19*(3). Retrieved from https://www.qualitative-research.net/index.php/fqs/article/view/3102/4274

CHAPTER 5

TAKING SHORTCUTS: CORRELATION, NOT CAUSATION, AND THE MORAL PROBLEMS IT BRINGS

Kevin Macnish

ABSTRACT

Large-scale data analytics have raised a number of ethical concerns. Many of these were introduced in a seminal paper by boyd and Crawford and have been developed since by others (boyd & Crawford, 2012; Lagoze, 2014; Martin, 2015; Mittelstadt, Allo, Taddeo, Wachter, & Floridi, 2016). One such concern which is frequently recognised but under-analysed is the focus on correlation of data rather than on the causative relationship between data and results. Advocates of this approach dismiss the need for an understanding of causation, holding instead that the correlation of data is sufficient to meet our needs. In crude terms, this position holds that we no longer need to know why $X+Y=Z$. Merely acknowledging that the pattern exists is enough.

In this chapter, the author explores the ethical implications and challenges surrounding a focus on correlation over causation. In particular, the author focusses on questions of legitimacy of data collection, the embedding of persistent bias, and the implications of future predictions. Such concerns are vital for understanding the ethical implications of, for example, the collection and use of 'big data' or the covert access to 'secondary' information ostensibly 'publicly

Ethical Issues in Covert, Security and Surveillance Research
Advances in Research Ethics and Integrity, Volume 8, 55–70

ISSN: 2398-6018/doi:10.1108/S2398-601820210000008006

available'. The author's conclusion is that by failing to consider causation, the short-term benefits of speed and cost may be countered by ethically problematic scenarios in both the short and long term.

Keywords: Correlation; causation; ethics; big data analytics; legitimacy; bias

INTRODUCTION

This is a world where massive amounts of data and applied mathematics replace every other tool that might be brought to bear. Out with every theory of human behaviour, from linguistics to sociology. Forget taxonomy, ontology, and psychology. Who knows why people do what they do? The point is they do it, and we can track and measure it with unprecedented fidelity. With enough data, the numbers speak for themselves. (Chris Anderson, then Editor-in-Chief of *Wired*, writing in 2008. Cited in boyd & Crawford, 2012; see also Ananny, 2016; Hildebrandt, 2011).[1]

Large-scale data analytics have raised a number of concerns in recent years. Many of these were helpfully introduced by boyd and Crawford and have been developed since by others (boyd & Crawford, 2012; Lagoze, 2014; Martin, 2015; Mittelstadt et al., 2016). One such concern which has led to only limited discussion is that of a focus on correlation of data to results in preference to a focus on the causative relationship between the data and the results (boyd & Crawford, 2012; Mittelstadt et al., 2016). Adherents to this approach, captured eloquently in the above quote by Anderson, dismiss the need for an understanding of causation. Instead the correlation of data is assumed sufficient to meet our needs.

An example of the focus on correlation rather than causation can be found in a TED talk by Jennifer Golbeck (2013). Research linked the enjoyment of curly fries to a higher level of intelligence than 'normal'. This is almost certainly not because eating curly fries *makes* a person more intelligent, nor because being intelligent *causes* a person to like curly fries. Rather, it may simply be because one person with a higher-than-average intelligence liked curly fries on Facebook as a joke, and her friends continued that joke. As people who have a higher-than-average intelligence tend to be friends on social media with others with higher-than-average intelligence, this leads to the strange correlation between intelligence and liking curly fries. The consequences, however, are that companies wishing to market products to people of higher-than-average intelligence may choose to target people who like curly fries, knowing that there is an established correlation and irrespective of the reason for that correlation. Worse, recruiters may start to look for apparently random but established correlations in seeking candidates for jobs. While being the subject of a marketing campaign is not typically intrusive (although it can be: see Ebeling, 2016, pp. 49–66), being turned down for a job in preference for another person simply because *they* like curly fries is definitely objectionable.

At the same time, large-scale data analytics can provide a wealth of benefits to individuals and society. This extends well beyond personalised coupons or targeted advertising to significant advances in public health and welfare. If research can establish clear connections on a national scale with existing data regarding links between, for example, red meat consumption and bowel cancer, or between obesity and particular foods, then governments may have an obligation to carry out this research. The purpose of this chapter is not to dismiss data analytics as unethical *en masse*, nor to provide an overview of ethical concerns. It is rather to draw attention to the ethical issues arising from one particular aspect of data analytics, namely the attention paid to correlation in preference to (or instead of) causation.

The curly fries example is relatively easy for non-statisticians to understand. In that case, a correlation occurs between people with a higher-than-average IQ and people who 'like' curly fries. However, data analytics is typically far more opaque than in this example. A more complex case is the famous case of retail chain Target discovering that a teenage girl was pregnant before she told her father (Duhigg, 2012). In his article, Charles Duhigg suggests a number of items in the teenager's shopping basket would, when taken together, indicate to the data analytics team at Target that she is pregnant. These include buying more moisturiser, switching to unscented moisturiser, and buying a large bag that could double as diaper bags when the baby arrives. Independently none of these would bear much significance. It is when taken together that they take on a relevance not seen in the individual parts.

The items Duhigg lists bear an obvious relation to the pregnancy of the teen, but this need not be the case. The data analytics team at Target were not deciding which items were relevant based on their intuitions and then tracking these. Rather they were reverse engineering the known shopping baskets of customers who were also known to be pregnant to see what goods they had bought, and then searching for these prospectively with customers whose state of pregnancy was not known.

In Duhigg's example, then, there is an understandable causative role played by the items in the shopping basket: we can quickly see why at least some of these items, when taking together, might give an indication that the customer is pregnant. Likewise, in the curly fries example, there is a confounding variable (one not measured but which has an influence on seemingly unconnected results), namely the fact that the correlation is noted on a social media platform where like-minded people commonly cluster together.

However, it is not implausible that there could well be other items in a shopping basket which, again taken together, could indicate that a customer is pregnant. Imagine that these include 2lbs of carrots, 1lb of celery, scented candles, pillow cases, four AA batteries, and a CD. These could compare with a normal shopping basket of 3lbs of carrots, no celery, scented candles, eight AA batteries and two CDs. The first basket, through a long series of correlations, could provide an indication that the customer is pregnant, while the latter does not provide such an indication. That is, in this example, I want to stipulate a lack of *any* causative connection between the items bought and the results of the data analysis, and a lack of *any* confounding variables. Nonetheless, the correlation holds in 70% of cases and so it appears to be a reasonable assumption to make that this shopper is pregnant.[2]

In this chapter, I look at the ethical issues that arise from this focus on the correlative rather than the causative. I argue that this focus may be effective in the short term but it is ethically problematic. In particular, I hold that there are three reasons why we should be cautious of this approach. Firstly, this approach leads us away from considering the legitimacy of the data collected. Secondly, the approach lends itself to the embedding of persistent outliers and bias. Thirdly, the approach may miss the fact that, as any investor in financial services will say, past performance is no guarantee of future success. As noted above, there may be confounding variables that could be found to underpin a number of discoveries in big data. However, to stress the point that I am making about an unhealthy focus on correlation of data to the detriment of understanding causation, I will assume cases where there are no confounding variables.

LEGITIMACY

Central to the approach currently taken to big data analysis is that the data scientist frequently does not know which data will be relevant and which data will not. The response is to collect all of the data available in order to see which prove to be relevant. Does this matter? Clearly there are ethical questions that need to be raised about how the data are obtained, particularly whether the person providing the data has given valid and fully informed consent for that data to be collected and used in this way. Assuming this is the case, though, does it matter that all available data are collected and processed?

I want to argue that there is a significant difference here between what data are effectively legitimate, what are legally legitimate, and what are morally legitimate to collect. The current paradigm confesses its ignorance of what are effectively legitimate, and so seeks to collect all the data available, in order to discover which are effective in producing the results that interest the data scientist. This is tempered by legal restrictions as to what data are permissible to collect and what are not. Depending on the particular site or nation state, it may be illegal to collect data on a person's voting or health records. Also important of course is who is doing the collecting: it may be legal for a government to collect some data which it is not legal for a business to collect, or vice versa. One consideration that can be overlooked in this decision, though, is what data are *morally* legitimate to collect.

Whether it is morally legitimate to collect the data may never occur to the data scientist. It is not that they are necessarily malicious: their intentions are good and they want the best results for all concerned. However, intentions only go so far and consequences (intended and unintended) need to be considered as well. They may also choose not to see the collection of the data as their problem. Their job is to analyse the data provided. How that data are gathered is an issue for someone else.

Imagine a case in which data are collected by a university on the educational achievement of its students and the skin colour of its students. Then imagine that a clear correlation is drawn between the academic achievement of a student and the colour of their skin, so that it transpires that black students perform worse than white. There could of course be any number of reasons for this, from the university running scholarship programmes for black students from deprived backgrounds who have further to go in order to catch up with white colleagues who tend to come from more privileged backgrounds, to racism among the university staff who grade papers.[3] The discovery of this correlation, though, could lead to a number of outcomes. Among these are that the university may choose to do nothing, or it could carry out an audit of staff and students to uncover any hitherto undiscovered racist assumptions, or it could choose to focus on recruiting white students in order to raise its results in national league tables.

While these consequences differ in their ethical acceptability, they also raise the question as to whether the data should have been collected in the first place. In this instance, the good that can be achieved by discovering staff with racist assumptions might be sufficiently advantageous to justify the collection of these data. However, this response implies that the *cause* of the correlation is of interest to the university. This seems to be morally unproblematic and not my focus here. By contrast, my starting assumption has been that the cause is not of interest but rather the results themselves (in Anderson's words, 'the numbers speak for themselves'). If that is the case, then the university would ask not '*why* is this data the way it is' but 'what could we *do* with these results?' The consequences of the collection are therefore focussed on action, which is itself governed by a series of values, rather than on research or discovery.

Even if the data were used for beneficent ends, it does not follow that all data that could be collected *would* be used for beneficent ends. Could a university morally collect the voting records of its students, or a list of their sexual partners? These seem to be more problematic. Certainly there might be a beneficent desire to uncover causes and help the students in some way, but the potential for abuse may increase with ever more intrusive data collection. Ultimately, the point may be reached at which the potential for abuse outweighs the potential for benefit to the students. At this point it would seem that the university would not be justified in collecting the data. The scale of intrusiveness of the data collected is clearly also a problem.

Thirdly, it is worth noting that different data may be collected for different reasons. The ethnicity of students may be collected for the morally legitimate end of ensuring that the university's recruitment process is not biasing against students on the grounds of their ethnicity, or to pass to government records aimed at monitoring social trends. Likewise, the university would be legitimate in collecting data about student performance. Indeed, it would be failing in its role as an educational institution if it neglected to pay attention to the academic performance of its students. However, the scenario becomes more problematic when these independent data sets are combined and subsequently used for a hitherto unforeseen or unanticipated end.

Ultimately, the collection of data on people is a form of surveillance, which raises a number of ethical issues (Lyon, 2002). In order to be ethical, surveillance should be subject to a number of limits regarding who is carrying it out and whether they are accountable, why they are doing so, whether it is proportionate, whether there are less intrusive ways of arriving at the same end, whether the collection is likely to be successful in achieving the justifying cause, and whether the surveillance is discriminating between those who are liable and those who are not (Macnish, 2014). It does not seem unreasonable that the collection of data for analysis should be subject to the same ethical considerations as other forms of surveillance.

One response to the surveillance objection may relate not to the collection of new data, but the use of historic data already collected. This is not, it may be argued, an act of surveillance. The surveillance occurred at the point of collection. This is data arising from past surveillance which is now available for data scientists to use. Furthermore, given that the data exist, there may even be an obligation for it to be subject to analysis in the interests of, for example, public health.

The immediate counter to this response is to point out that surveillance does not involve merely the collection of data, but the collection *and processing* of that data. Surveillance may exist without the processing of data (i.e. it is not a necessary condition), but in this case, taking a broad understanding of what is meant by processing, there would be little purpose in the surveillance. As such it would not be justified on the grounds of the aforementioned need for a just cause. Furthermore, if my government collected my emails five years ago but did not read them at the time of collection but chose to read them today, I would argue that I have been under surveillance both at the time of collection and at the time of processing (i.e. reading) of my emails. This distinction gets to the heart of the revelations made by Edward Snowden in 2013 that the USA, UK and other governments were collecting large quantities of internet data relating to domestic citizens. While the intelligence communities at the time protested there was no violation of privacy as the internet data had not been accessed, it was nonetheless an act of surveillance (Macnish, 2016).

A further problem to arise from the processing of historic data is the possible lack of informed consent given by the owners of that data for its processing (see, e.g., Foster & Young, 2011). This has been one problem with the UK government's recent attempts to capture citizens' health data in a centralised database known as 'care.data'. This concerns health data which were initially given by patients to their GPs (general practitioners – their primary care physicians). Their reasons for doing so were probably legion, although one reason was almost certainly not the pooling of that data for future analysis. Certainly some may not have found the pooling of their data for analysis objectionable, just as many do not find this objectionable today. However, the fact remains that in giving the data to the GP, the patient did not give informed consent for this particular use of that data. As such, it is right that the patient be sought out in order to gain informed consent for this secondary use of the data.

There are understandable concerns with this focus on informed consent such that public health could suffer as a result of paying too much attention to finding and addressing the concerns of every citizen before accessing their data, a price that is too high to pay when the costs are minimal (Ganesh, 2014). However, this is to underplay the procedural importance of informed consent and the potential harms involved in the pooling of medical data.

Procedurally, the gaining of informed consent is central to the ethics surrounding the collection of data relating to individuals. This was emphasised in the Nuremburg Code and again in the Helsinki Declaration. There is a concern that a precedent will be established in ignoring the need for informed consent, with long-term ramifications. If liberal democracies cannot abide by their own standards in medical ethics, then they sacrifice any moral high ground in responding to others that do the same in more objectionable instances. To act on information over which people should have control without their consent is an abuse of their autonomy and can have a severe impact on their lives.

Secondly, there are a number of potential harms arising from the pooling of medical records, not least the discovering of health records of individuals, be they public figures, employees, or insurance applicants. It may be objected that this is not the intention of data scientists, and that there are security measures in place to prevent the leaking of information. However, it should be remembered that Edward Snowden managed to walk out of what is one of the most secure buildings in the world with millions of documents of top secret information on a memory stick. Given that Snowden had been subject to some of the most intense scrutiny before being allowed into those buildings, including polygraphs and background checks, it is naïve to suggest that health records will not be discovered and removed for the purpose of personal gain from large-scale pooled databases.

A final concern with the focus on legality rather than the moral legitimacy of the collection of data is that technology moves apace of legislation. Problems usually have to arise for a number of years before they lead to the introduction of legislation, and then a few more years before the response is passed into law. This enables unethical practices to continue unaffected for a considerable period before they are ultimately ended by legislation. It also overlooks the fact that while legislators generally try to ensure that laws are ethical, this is not always the case. Competing interests are often brought to bear on the legislative process and laws passed today have to be consistent with laws passed yesterday. As such, it may be that the law, when it is passed, does not go far enough to protect those it was designed to protect.

In speaking of collecting legitimate data we may therefore be using the term in one of at least three ways: effective, legal, or moral. What is legal and effective to collect may not be moral. Or, it may be moral to collect data for one purpose but then unethical to use it for a different purpose. This latter concern is especially pertinent to historic data. A standard approach to alleviate the concerns regarding inappropriate collection or use of a person's data is to seek their informed consent. While this may be cumbersome and slow the process of analysis with a clear public benefit, there are sound ethical, procedural, and practical concerns that mean we should not sidestep this. Finally, there are dangers in an over-reliance on legislation to guide morally legitimate collection owing to the pace of change in the former, which can easily be outstripped by developments in technology.

EMBEDDING OF PERSISTENT OUTLIERS AND BIAS

A second problem for large-scale data analytics is the introduction of bias and discrimination. Bias can be obvious, such as the aforementioned case leading to the increased recruitment of white students over black students, or through similar forms of social sorting such as upmarket stores sending coupons to regular customers but not occasional customers. The end result of this process is that the wealthier regular customers pay less to use the store than poorer occasional customers (Lyon, 2002). When this is seen to be the case, that bias can be guarded and, to some extent, legislated against.

More problematic is hidden bias which is by its nature less easy to discover. As an example of hidden bias, imagine a public transport system which is successfully designed to serve the needs of 90% of the public. This sounds laudable: no system is perfect and 100% use is unrealistic without coercion. What, though, if the 10% who are not served by the transport system all fall into this category because they are unable to use it, owing to some form of disability? Certainly one cannot please all of the people all of the time, but to discriminate against someone *purely* for that person's disability, even if the discrimination is unwitting, is clearly unethical.

In the case of everyday statistics, such hidden bias is a possibility. Given the scale and focus on likelihood of correlation of big data analytics, though, it is not only probable that hidden bias would be present, but probable also that such bias would remain hidden for longer. That a system has a 90% success rate may be indicative of a highly effective and desirable system. Yet, if the 10% of occasions when the system fails always involves the same people, or group of people, then there is a problem.

Returning to the scenario of university recruitment, imagine that a university is seeking to improve its place in the national league tables. To this end, it carries out data analysis on the students currently achieving the highest grades and looks at their behaviour in the last two years of school before attending university. This avoids the obvious bias encountered before of correlating grades with skin colour. The results, when they are collected, then indicate that the best-performing students all played polo, golf, and sailed in this crucial two-year period. This leads to the university increasing its recruitment efforts among school students who sail and play golf and polo. There is a reasonable likelihood at this point that the university would effectively be focussing its recruitment efforts on fee-paying schools rather than state schools, in the process recruiting more white than black students, as well as more wealthy than under-privileged students.

It is logically possible that most students who attended fee-paying and predominantly white schools are more successful at university than those who attended state schools. This could be because they are more intelligent or because they are advantaged in some way by the fee-paying education system, or a number of other reasons. It is demonstrably false that people have higher intelligence purely because their parents had sufficient money to send them to a fee-paying school. It might, though, be possible that students at fee-paying schools are trained better in critical thinking or independent work than those at state schools, and so are better prepared for university when they arrive. The result is that they 'hit the ground running' while those from state schools feel as if they are constantly trying to catch up. Alternatively, they may simply be better prepared by the school for the requirements to get into university and are as such better at 'playing the game' than those who attended state schools.

In this case, the university faces a choice as to whether to improve its place in the national rankings by recruiting from fee-paying schools, or by providing an opportunity for those less privileged to develop their skills in critical thinking and independent working. If the former is true, then the university's actions could be justified by (and may even genuinely be determined by) the results of the data analysis. They are not seeking to be elitist or racist, although these are likely to be the results of their actions.

The above scenario imagined one university engaged in this practice. However, if one imagines every university taking a similar approach then an obvious problem emerges. In the first instance, recruitment becomes focussed on and heavily competitive for students from fee-paying schools. With time, though, further accumulated data will predominantly come from students who have attended fee-paying schools, thus focussing recruitment still further on a few key fee-paying schools and not even considering state schools at all. It is also entirely feasible that some schools become aware of which extra-curricular activities are favoured by the best universities (some schools are capable of conducting their own data analytic processes on historic cases) and start to offer and endorse those activities to pupils. Once more, the better-resourced schools will be more successful than those with more stretched budgets. In both cases, though, rather than being liberated by education, those less privileged find that university education at least, and the opportunities that go with it, have returned to being a preserve of the wealthy.[4]

While this is a hypothetical example, one does not have to look far to uncover cases in which hidden bias persists in algorithmic approaches to social problem-solving. Perhaps the best known of these is the city of Boston's adoption of a smart phone app to automatically locate potholes in public roads (the city fixes 20,000 potholes every year). This meant that rather than wait for people to complain about the state of the roads, the city could respond more quickly. The app may even have been perceived as having a social levelling effect, given that underprivileged groups in society may be less likely to complain about the state of their roads than other groups. If this was the case, though, the app was unsuccessful. As Kate Crawford (2013) notes,

> People in lower income groups in the US are less likely to have smartphones, and this is particularly true of older residents, where smartphone penetration can be as low as 16%. For cities like Boston, this means that smartphone data sets are missing inputs from significant parts of the population – often those who have the fewest resources.

As Crawford notes, Boston's Office of New Urban Mechanics was aware of this problem and worked hard to adjust for it, but it does not take a leap of the imagination to consider the impact of this thinking had the Office been less careful.

One such instance has been noted in relation to motor insurance policies, which are increasingly being tied to the installation of a 'black box' in the owner's vehicle and which monitors driving habits. These can then be correlated with the habits of other drivers so that profiles are developed regarding 'safe' drivers and 'unsafe drivers' based on their driving. The immediate effect is to penalise unsafe drivers for their more risky behaviour and, one hopes, in the long term promote safer driving for all.

One such example of an indicator of unsafe driving is the time of day or night at which a person is on the roads and the frequency with which they drive. According to Robinson and colleagues, one system operated by insurer Progressive favours drivers who do not go out at night and who drive infrequently. However, they go on to point out, drawing on research by Maria E. Enchautegui (2013), the unintended effects of this may serve to punish particular communities, and especially those on low incomes, who 'are more likely to work the night shift, putting them on the road late at night, and to live further from work' (Robinson, Yu, & Rieke, 2014, p. 6).

In essence, the Progressive system puts late night workers into a similar category as late night party-goers,

> forcing them to carry more of the cost of intoxicated and other irresponsible driving that happens disproportionately at night. Statistically speaking, this added cost does not simply reflect the risk that the late night commuter may be hit by a drunk driver. It also reflects the possibility that, as far as the insurer can tell, the late responsible night worker may be a drunk driver. (Robinson et al., 2014, p. 6)

Rather than spreading risk among the insured population, then, the system focusses that risk on particular groups who are already marginalised in society.

A final case which deserves mention is that of Latanya Sweeney's discovery that online searches for names typically associated with black people had a significantly greater chance of returning advertisements which related to arrests than names associated with white people. Names associated with black people

> generated ads suggestive of an arrest in 81 to 86 percent of name searches on one website and 92 to 95 percent on the other, while those assigned at birth primarily to whites, such as Geoffrey, Jill and Emma, generated more neutral copy: the word 'arrest' appeared in 23 to 29 percent of name searches on one site and 0 to 60 percent on the other. On the more ad trafficked website, a black-identifying name was 25% more likely to get an ad suggestive of an arrest record. (Sweeney, 2013, p. 1)

Sweeney notes that this occurs not because of an explicit bias in the software, but because that software

> learns over time which ad text gets the most clicks from viewers of the ad. It does this by assigning weights (or probabilities) based on the click history of each ad copy. At first all possible ad copies are weighted the same, they are all equally likely to produce a click. Over time, as people tend to click one version of ad text over others, the weights change, so the ad text getting the most clicks eventually displays more frequently. (Sweeney, 2013, p. 34)

In essence, then, the software learns over time to reflect the biases which exist in society (Robinson et al., 2014, p. 16).

In this section, we have seen a number of cases, hypothetical and real, in which a focus on correlation and not causation of results is ethically problematic in that this can mask discrimination and bias. There is hence a concern that through focussing on correlations and failing to uncover the story behind those correlations, hidden biases might remain hidden for longer. Worse still, those biases could be exacerbated through decisions made on the basis of correlative data which has not been subject to adequate scrutiny regarding the causes of those correlations.

PREDICTING THE FUTURE ON THE STRENGTH OF THE PAST

It is an oft-repeated phrase in financial services that past performance is no guarantee of future success. Just because an investor has done well in the past there is no way of being sure that she will continue to do well in the future. Past results may have come about through luck or through a confluence of events that have since ceased to pertain.

The same is true in data analytics when causation is ignored for correlation. On an entertaining website, and now book, Tyler Vigen (2015a, 2015b) has provided graphs of a number of examples which fit the concerns raised in this chapter of seeking correlation without concern for causation. These include the following from among a list of 30,000:

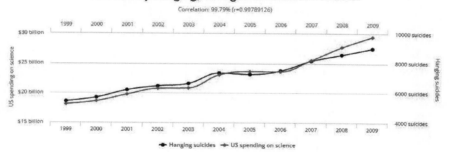

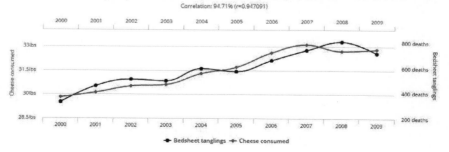

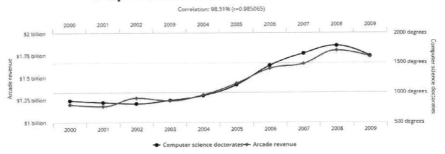

Total revenue generated by arcades
correlates with
Computer science doctorates awarded in the US

In using these charts I am clearly oversimplifying, and drawing on oversimplifications, for ease of illustration. No one would attempt to predict the number of science doctorates to be awarded in the USA by basing the prediction purely on the total revenue generated by arcades. However, the focus on the correlation effect in big data analytics at the expense of causation could have similarly absurd, but less obvious, effects.

Imagine a case in which an analysis of all terrorists of any stripe, up to the present, have all walked at precisely 57 metres/minute (leaving to one side the thorny question of how we define a terrorist). Further analysis might also demonstrate that anyone who is not a terrorist has always walked faster or slower than 57 metres/minute. Does this mean that it would be reasonable to develop an automated security system that recognises and disables only those who walk at 57 metres/minute? To some degree this might be sensible: the statistics as stipulated appear to be overwhelming. However, there are a number of problems with this approach.

Firstly, returning to the opening quote of this section, the past is not always a reliable indicator of the future. Aside from standard challenges to inductive logic regarding geese at Christmas, whereby the goose is always welcomed into the farmhouse kitchen with food until Christmas morning when she is welcomed with a cleaver, when there is no confounding variable (such as the knowledge of Christmas traditions) or known reason for the correlation, there is no reason to presume that correlation will continue. Hence, just because all and only terrorists have until now walked at 57 metres/minute, there is no guarantee that all and only terrorists in the future will walk at 57 metres/minute. Indeed, should it become known that all and only terrorists walk at 57 metres/minute (and that this is being used as a means of identification of terrorists) then future terrorists are likely to consciously adopt a different walking speed.

Secondly, it is important to understand where the data are drawn from in these cases. It is, after all, impossible to measure the walking pace of every person on the planet and even if we were to do this it would only be relevant to the time at which the measurement occurred. Walking speeds change with age and circumstance, as well as with culture. Currently, data sets regarding walking behaviour tend to be developed in the West and so have a predominantly western bias (Macnish, 2012). Hence, the aforementioned problem of hidden bias can enter the system through the choice of data set and have a significant impact on the system's applicability and ability to accurately predict the future. The implications of this are that the use of a seemingly strong correlation to identify terrorists could be flawed either over geography or over time, with the result that innocent people are harassed and stigmatised (Macnish, 2012).

The terrorist example is one with serious consequences. It is no light matter to be mistaken for a terrorist. However, if the outcomes of the analysis are comparatively trivial then this is less of a problem. One might be tempted to say that the pregnant teenager in Duhigg's story was a fairly trivial case of data analytics. The father did not presume that his daughter was pregnant but rather that Target was acting irresponsibly in sending her coupons for items that a pregnant woman might want. If he had thought that she was pregnant on the basis of the coupons alone, and if he had a particularly low view of pregnant teenagers, then the consequences for the daughter could have been far more severe. Taking this not to be the case in this instance, though, the worst that would happen in a scenario in which Target had a 60% success rate in identifying pregnant women, would be that 40% of those identified received coupons that they would never use. Furthermore, in signing up to a loyalty card programme, customers accept that they will get coupons through the post (indeed, many do it for this reason), often assuming that these will be fairly arbitrary and that some will therefore be of little interest to them. Indeed, Duhigg (2012) notes in his article the creepiness for a customer of realising that Target knows she is pregnant on receipt of such tailored coupons. The response, he claims, has been to include coupons for random items that it is known no pregnant woman is likely to want, such as lawn mowers or garden furniture. This is not to say that pregnant women would not want these items, merely that they do not relate to pregnancy in the way that other coupons might.

Serious cases are not restricted to security, though. They might also emerge in the health and public welfare sectors. For example, the discovery of a correlation between those who use a certain prescription drug and those who die when under general anaesthesia should rightly lead to hospitals warning patients not to use this drug when they are about to undergo an operation requiring a general anaesthetic. If, though, both the drug and the operation are significant to the patient's life, then the patient will be forced to choose between the two.

As things stand, this is a regrettable but not unconscionable scenario. Such things happen. However, it may be that the manufacturer of the drug used a particular compound in the composition of the drug which was inert in the delivery of the drug but which reacted negatively with a certain level of anaesthetic. If the supplier stopped using this compound, purely by chance, then the forced decision would cease to be an issue. Owing to the use of historic data in deriving the correlation, though, no one would know this without further tests being carried out.

It is not implausible that the manufacturer of the drug stopped using the compound after the data were collected but before the results were published, and so the ensuing warnings would be unnecessarily harmful.

Each of these cases is to a greater or lesser extent plausible. Furthermore, it is not unreasonable to draw conclusions and base future predictions on past data. Once more, though, the concern in this chapter is not the basing of future predictions on past data but the basing of such on past data alone without seeking the reasons for any correlations. For example, the correlation between the drug and death while under anaesthesia is plausible, and it is a valuable activity to notice this correlation and warn others in the light of the perceived pattern. However, without working to understand why there is a correlation, subsequent changes to the drug might go unperceived.

The practical challenge to this warning in particular is likely to be that such practices (seeking correlation as grounds for prediction without uncovering causative factors) are more likely to proliferate in business than in security or medicine. In such cases, the harms are more akin to receiving irrelevant coupons than people dying or terrorists evading capture. Yes, the response would come, the system is not perfect but then we do not seek perfection, and where is the harm?

To this my response would be that people's behaviour is governed in part by the expectations that are placed on them. If these expectations are derived from an arbitrary group then the expectations themselves risk being arbitrary. If the data set used is of current customers, who are overwhelmingly male, then the predictions may be significantly more pertinent to men than women. If this governs not only coupons but also marketing and design of stores, this may make it harder for women to use those stores (if maybe only for social reasons such as a predominance of certain styles and colours in the store windows and no female assistants such that the average woman needs to sum up greater courage in entering the store and prepare herself for a degree of mansplaining). This in turn has a societal impact of at best embedding and condoning existing social divisions, and at worst implicitly endorsing and furthering those divisions, which should be avoided. Hence, even apparently harmless or low risk uses of correlative data for predictions can have significant outcomes.

CONCLUSION

I have warned here against an *exclusive* focus on correlations in big data analytics. Failing to consider causation may be effective in the short term but it will prove to be ethically problematic in both the short and long term. Paying attention to causes could overcome the three problems explored here: the legitimacy of the data collected, the emergence of bias and persistent outliers, and the difficulty of predicting future events on the basis of current data.

The challenge is that in considering causes, the data scientist will lose the advantages of speed and complexity that accompany big data. Being forced to examine why a particular correlation occurs might slow the publishing or using of that data, with potentially significant social effects. If, for instance, a strong correlation is found between eating a certain food and colon cancer, then it may well be prudent to advise people to refrain from eating that food prior to discovering the reason for that relationship, which could take years to uncover. At the same time, as I hope to have demonstrated, there are also potentially significant social effects that arise from ignoring causes as well. It is hence short-sighted to promote the quick returns that can be gained by ignoring causes as being justified by social benefit. The fuller picture shows social benefit *and harm* that can arise from this approach and so it is not one to be taken lightly.

NOTES

1. I believe that Anderson has since retracted this statement, although cannot find reference to this retraction.
2. Clearly, the dark arts of big data (Target's chief data analyst was prevented from communicating with Duhigg when Target discovered that he had discussed his work with a reporter) are vastly more complex than I have suggested here (Duhigg, 2012). However, to attempt to capture this complexity would detract from the central argument. I shall therefore continue to use simplified cases to press home the concerns with this approach of favouring correlation over causation.
3. Although intended as a hypothetical example, this is sadly the case in UK universities at least. See Alexander and Arday (2015). I am grateful to Rosemary Hill for drawing my attention to this report as well as for comments on an earlier draft.
4. A similar situation in the workplace is imagined by boyd, Levy, & Marwick (2014).

REFERENCES

Alexander, C., & Arday, J. (2015). *Aiming higher: Race, inequality and diversity in the academy.* Runnymede Perspectives. London: Runnymede.

Ananny, M. (2016). Toward an ethics of algorithms convening, observation, probability, and timeliness. *Science, Technology & Human Values, 41*(1), 93–117. doi:10.1177/0162243915606523

boyd, d., & Crawford, K. (2012). Critical questions for big data. *Information, Communication & Society, 15*(5), 662–679. doi:10.1080/1369118X.2012.678878

boyd, d., Levy, K., & Marwick, A. (2014). The networked nature of algorithmic discrimination. In S. P. Gangadharan, V. Eubanks, & S. Barocas (Eds.), *Data and discrimination: Collected essays* (pp. 53–57). Washington, DC: Open Technology Institute.

Crawford, K. (2013). The hidden biases in big data. *Harvard Business Review.* April 1. Retrieved from https://hbr.org/2013/04/the-hidden-biases-in-big-data

Duhigg, C. (2012). How companies learn your secrets. *The New York Times,* February 16. Retrieved from http://www.nytimes.com/2012/02/19/magazine/shopping-habits.html

Ebeling, M. (2016). *Healthcare and big data: Digital specters and phantom objects.* New York, NY: Springer.

Enchautegui, M. E. (2013). *Nonstandard work schedules and the well-being of low-income families.* Paper 26, Urban Institute, Washington DC. Retrieved from http://www.urban.org/research/publication/nonstandard-work-schedules-and-well-being-low-income-families

Foster, V., & Young, A. (2011). The use of routinely collected patient data for research: A critical review. *Health: An Interdisciplinary Journal for the Social Study of Health, Illness and Medicine, 16*(4), 448–463. doi:10.1177/1363459311425513

Ganesh, J. (2014). Big data may be invasive but it will keep us in rude health. *Financial Times,* February 21. Retrieved from http://www.ft.com/cms/s/62a5aaaa-9a55-11e3-8232-00144feab7de,Authorised=false.html?siteedition=uk&_i_location=http%3A%2F%2Fwww.ft.com%2Fcms%2Fs%2F0%2F62a5aaaa-9a55-11e3-8232-00144feab7de.html%3Fsiteedition%3Duk&_i_referer=&classification=conditional_standard&iab=barrier-app#axzz4JeevuGEk

Golbeck, J. (2013). The curly fry conundrum: Why social media 'likes' say more than you might think. *TED*. Retrieved from http://www.ted.com/talks/jennifer_golbeck_the_curly_fry_conundrum_why_social_media_likes_say_more_than_you_might_think

Hildebrandt, M. (2011). Who needs stories if you can get the data? ISPs in the era of big number crunching. *Philosophy and Technology*, *24*(4), 371–390. doi:10.1007/s13347-011-0041-8

Lagoze, C. (2014). Big data, data integrity, and the fracturing of the control zone. *Big Data and Society*, *1*(2), 1–11. doi:10.1177/2053951714558281

Lyon, D. (2002). *Surveillance as social sorting: Privacy, risk and automated discrimination*. New York, NY: Routledge.

Macnish, K. (2012). Unblinking eyes: The ethics of automating surveillance. *Ethics and Information Technology*, *14*(2), 151–167. doi:10.1007/s10676-012-9291-0

Macnish, K. (2014). Just surveillance? Towards a normative theory of surveillance. *Surveillance and Society*, *12*(1), 142–153.

Macnish, K. (2016). Government surveillance and why defining privacy matters in a post-Snowden world. *Journal of Applied Philosophy*, *35*(2), 417–432. doi:10.1111/japp.12219

Martin, K. E. (2015). Ethical issues in the big data industry. *MIS Quarterly Executive*, *14*(2), 67–85.

Mittelstadt, B. D., Allo, P., Taddeo, M., Wachter, S., & Floridi, L. (2016). The ethics of algorithms: Mapping the debate. *Big Data & Society*, *3*(2), 1–21. doi:10.1177/2053951716679679

Robinson, D., Yu, H., & Rieke, A. (2014). *Civil rights, big data, and our algorithmic future*. Washington, DC: Upturn.

Sweeney, L. (2013). *Discrimination in online ad delivery*. SSRN Scholarly Paper ID 2208240. Rochester, NY: Social Science Research Network. Retrieved from http://papers.ssrn.com/abstract=2208240

Vigen, T. (2015a). 15 insane things that correlate with each other. Retrieved from http://tylervigen.com/spurious-correlations

Vigen, T. (2015b). *Spurious correlations*. New York, NY: Hachette Books.

CHAPTER 6

THE BIG DATA WORLD: BENEFITS, THREATS AND ETHICAL CHALLENGES

Marina Da Bormida

ABSTRACT

Advances in Big Data, artificial Intelligence and data-driven innovation bring enormous benefits for the overall society and for different sectors. By contrast, their misuse can lead to data workflows bypassing the intent of privacy and data protection law, as well as of ethical mandates. It may be referred to as the 'creep factor' of Big Data, and needs to be tackled right away, especially considering that we are moving towards the 'datafication' of society, where devices to capture, collect, store and process data are becoming ever-cheaper and faster, whilst the computational power is continuously increasing. If using Big Data in truly anonymisable ways, within an ethically sound and societally focussed framework, is capable of acting as an enabler of sustainable development, using Big Data outside such a framework poses a number of threats, potential hurdles and multiple ethical challenges. Some examples are the impact on privacy caused by new surveillance tools and data gathering techniques, including also group privacy, high-tech profiling, automated decision making and discriminatory practices. In our society, everything can be given a score and critical life changing opportunities are increasingly determined by such scoring systems, often obtained through secret predictive algorithms applied to data to determine who has value. It is therefore essential to guarantee the fairness and accurateness of such scoring systems and that the decisions

Ethical Issues in Covert, Security and Surveillance Research
Advances in Research Ethics and Integrity, Volume 8, 71–91
ISSN: 2398-6018/doi:10.1108/S2398-601820210000008007

relying upon them are realised in a legal and ethical manner, avoiding the risk of stigmatisation capable of affecting individuals' opportunities. Likewise, it is necessary to prevent the so-called 'social cooling'. This represents the long-term negative side effects of the data-driven innovation, in particular of such scoring systems and of the reputation economy. It is reflected in terms, for instance, of self-censorship, risk-aversion and lack of exercise of free speech generated by increasingly intrusive Big Data practices lacking an ethical foundation. Another key ethics dimension pertains to human-data interaction in Internet of Things (IoT) environments, which is increasing the volume of data collected, the speed of the process and the variety of data sources. It is urgent to further investigate aspects like the 'ownership' of data and other hurdles, especially considering that the regulatory landscape is developing at a much slower pace than IoT and the evolution of Big Data technologies. These are only some examples of the issues and consequences that Big Data raise, which require adequate measures in response to the 'data trust deficit', moving not towards the prohibition of the collection of data but rather towards the identification and prohibition of their misuse and unfair behaviours and treatments, once government and companies have such data. At the same time, the debate should further investigate 'data altruism', deepening how the increasing amounts of data in our society can be concretely used for public good and the best implementation modalities.

Keywords: Big Data; artificial intelligence; data analytics; ethics challenges; individuals' control over personal data; dataveillance

THE ERA OF BIG DATA AND THE 'DATAFICATION' OF SOCIETY

We live in the era of Big Data, where governments, organisations and marketers know, or can deduce, an increasing number of data items about aspects of our lives that in previous eras we could assume were reasonably private (e.g. our race, ethnicity, religion, politics, sexuality, interests, hobbies, health information, income, credit rating and history, travel history and plans, spending habits, decision-making capabilities and biases and much else). Devices to capture, collect, store and process data are becoming ever-cheaper and faster, whilst the computational power to handle these data is continuously increasing. Digital technologies have made possible the 'datafication' of society, affecting all sectors and everyone's daily life. The growing importance of data for the economy and society is unquestionable and more is to come.[1]

But what does 'Big Data' mean? Though frequently used, the term has no agreed definition. It is usually associated with complex and large datasets on which special tools and methods are used to perform operations to derive meaningful information and support better decision making. However, the Big Data concept is not just about the quantity of data available, but also encompasses new ways of analysing existing data and generating new knowledge. In public discourse, the term tends to refer to the increasing ubiquity of data, the size of datasets, the growth of digital data and other new or alternative data sources. From a more specifically technical perspective, Big Data has five essential features:

- *Volume*: the size of the data, notably the quantity generated and stored. The volume of data determines its value and potential insight. In order to have Big Data, the volume has to be massive (Terabytes and Petabytes or more).[2]
- *Variety*: the type and nature of the data, as well as the way of structuring it. Big Data may draw from text, images, audio, video (and data fusion can complete missing pieces) and can be structured, semi-structured or unstructured. Data can be obtained from many different sources, whose importance varies depending on the nature of the analysis: from social networks, to in-house devices, to smartphone GPS technology. Big Data can also have many layers and be in different formats.
- *Velocity*: the time needed to generate and process information. Data have to flow quickly and in as close to real-time as possible because, certainly in a business context, high speed can deliver a competitive advantage.
- *Veracity*: data quality and reliability; it is essential to have ways of detecting and correcting any false, incorrect or incomplete data.
- *Value*: the analysis of reliable data adds value within and across disciplines and domains. Value arises from the development of actionable information.

BIG DATA AS AN ENABLER OF GROWTH BUT HARBINGER OF ETHICAL CHALLENGES

Big Data is increasingly recognised as an enabling factor that promises to transform contemporary societies and industry. Far-reaching social changes enabled by datasets are increasingly becoming part of our daily life with benefits ranging from finance to medicine, meteorology to genomics, and biological or environmental research to statistics and business.

> Data will reshape the way we produce, consume and live. Benefits will be felt in every single aspect of our lives, ranging from more conscious energy consumption and product, material and food traceability, to healthier lives and better health-care .... Data is the lifeblood of economic development: it is the basis for many new products and services, driving productivity and resource efficiency gains across all sectors of the economy, allowing for more personalised products and services and enabling better policy making and upgrading government services .... The availability of data is essential for training artificial intelligence systems, with products and services rapidly moving from pattern recognition and insight generation to more sophisticated forecasting techniques and, thus, better decision making .... Moreover, making more data available and improving the way in which data is used is essential for tackling societal, climate and environment-related challenges, contributing to healthier, more prosperous and more sustainable societies. It will for example lead to better policies to achieve the objectives of the European Green Deal. (COM, 2020b)

The exploitation of Big Data can unlock significant value in areas such as decision making, customer experience, market demand predictions, product and market development and operational efficiency. McKinsey & Company (Bailly & Manyika, 2013) report that the manufacturing industry stores more data than any other sector, with Big Data (soon to be made available through Cyber-physical Systems) expected to have an important role in the fourth industrial revolution, the so-called 'Industry 4.0' (Kagermann & Wahlster, 2013). This revolution has the potential to enhance productivity by improving supply chain management (Reichert, 2014) and creating more efficient risk management systems based on better-informed decisions. Industry 4.0 is also aimed at developing intelligent products (smart products) capable of capturing and transmitting huge amounts of data on their production and use. These data have to be gathered and analysed in real-time so as to pinpoint customers' preferences and shape future products. Data are also expected to fuel the massive uptake of transformative practices such as the use of digital twins in manufacturing.

As mentioned, Big Data also creates value in many other domains including health care, government administration and education. The application of transparency and open government policies is expected to have a positive impact on many aspects of citizens' lives. This will hopefully lead to the development of more democratic and participative societies by improved administrative efficiency, alongside perhaps more obvious uses such as better disease prevention in the health sector or self-monitoring in the education sector.

However, these positive effects must be offset against complex and multidimensional challenges. In the health care sector, an area that could benefit enormously from Big Data solutions, concerns relate, for instance, to the difficulty of respecting ethical boundaries relating to sensitive data where the volume of data may be preventing the chance to acquire the informed and specific consent required before each processing instance takes place. Another example, in the education sector, is the risk that students feel under surveillance at all times due to the constant collection and processing of their data, thus potentially leading to a reduction of their creativity and/or in higher levels of stress.

When considering Big Data, the debate needs to highlight the several potential ethical and social dimensions that arise, and explore the legal, societal and ethical issues. Here, there is a need to elaborate a societal and ethical framework for safeguarding human rights, mitigating risks and ensuring a consistent alignment between ethical values and behaviours. Such a framework should be able to enhance the confidence of citizens and businesses towards Big Data and the data economy. As acknowledged by the European Data Protection Supervisor (EDPS), 'big data comes with big responsibility and therefore appropriate data protection safeguards must be in place'.[3]

Recent ethical debate has focussed on concerns about privacy, anonymisation, encryption, surveillance and, above all, trust. The debate is increasingly moving towards artificial intelligence (AI) and autonomous technology, in line with technological advances. It is likely that as technology changes even further upcoming new types of harms may also be identified and debated.

THE CONTINUITY (OR NOT) OF DATA SCIENCE RESEARCH ETHICS WITH SOCIAL AND BEHAVIOURAL SCIENCE RESEARCH ETHICS

Given data-intensive advances, a pertinent question is whether ethical principles developed in the social and behavioural sciences using core concepts such as informed consent, risk, harm, ownership, etc. can be applied directly to data science, or whether they require augmentation with other principles specifically conceived for 'human-subjects' protection in data-intensive research activities. Traditionally, human-subjects' protection applies when data can be readily associated with the individual who bears a risk of harm in his or her everyday life. However, with Big Data there may be a substantial distance between everyday life and the uses of personal data. If technical protections are inadequate, and do not prevent the re-identification of sensitive data across distinct databases, it is challenging to predict the types of possible harms to human subjects due to the multiple, complex reasons for sharing, re-using and circulating research data.

If these difficulties are insurmountable within existing paradigms of research ethics, we will need to re-think the traditional paradigms. Here, a new framework of research ethics specific to data science could perhaps be built that could better move the 'person' to the centre of the debate. The expanding literature on privacy and other civil rights confirms that the ethical dimension of Big Data is becoming more and more central in European Union (EU) debate, and that the common goal is to seek concrete solutions that balance making the most of the value of Big Data without sacrificing fundamental human rights. Here, the Resolution on the fundamental rights implications of Big Data (2016/2225), adopted by the European Parliament, underlines that though Big Data has valuable potential for citizens, academia, the scientific community and the public and private sectors, it also entails significant risks namely with regard to the protection of fundamental rights, the right to privacy, data protection, non-discrimination and data security. The European Parliament has therefore stressed the need for regulatory compliance together with strong scientific and ethical standards, and awareness-raising initiatives, whilst recognising the importance of greater accountability, transparency, due process and legal certainty with regard to data processing by the private and public sectors.

Likewise, the European Commission (EC) recognises the importance of safeguarding European fundamental rights and values in the data strategy and its implementation (COM, 2020b), whilst in the COM (2020a), built upon the European strategy for AI, it is underlined that in order to address the opportunities and challenges raised by AI systems and to achieve the objective of trustworthy, ethical and human-centric AI, it is necessary to rely on European values and to ensure 'that new technologies are at the service of all Europeans – improving their lives while respecting their rights' (COM, 2020a). In the same direction, a coordinated European approach on the human and ethical implications of AI, as well as a reflection on the better use of Big Data for innovation, was announced in her political guidelines by the Commission President Ursula von der Leyen (2019).

BIG DATA AND ITS IMPACT ON PRIVACY

Human Dignity at Risk Due to the 'Creep Factor' of Big Data

The use of Big Data, new surveillance tools and data gathering techniques represent a fundamental step for the European economy. Nevertheless, it also poses significant legal problems from a data protection perspective, despite the renewed legal framework (General Regulation on the Protection of Personal Data, GDPR). In the Big Data paradigm, traditional methods and notions of privacy protections might be inadequate in some instances (e.g. informed consent approaches), whilst the data are often used and re-used in ways that were inconceivable when the data were collected.

As acknowledged by the EDPS, the respect for human dignity is strictly inter-related with the respect for the right to privacy and the right to the protection of personal data. That human dignity is an inviolable right of human beings is recognised in the European Charter of Fundamental Rights. This essential right might be infringed by violations like objectification, which occurs when an individual is treated as an object serving someone else's purposes (European Data Protection Supervisor, Opinion 4/2015).

The impact of Big Data technologies on privacy (and thereby human dignity) ranges from group privacy and high-tech profiling, to data discrimination and automated decision making. It is even more significant if people disseminate personal data in the digital world at different levels of awareness throughout their main life phases. Here, people can often make themselves almost completely transparent for data miners who use freely accessible data from social networks and other data associated with an IP address for profiling purposes.

This 'creep factor' of Big Data, due to unethical and deliberate practices, bypasses the intent of privacy law. Such practices are allowed by advances in analysing and using Big Data for revealing previously private individual data (or statistically close proxies for it) and often have the final aim of targeting and profiling customers.

Another concern in relation to Big Data is the possibility of the re-identification of the data subject after the process of anonymisation. This might occur using technologies of de-anonymisation made available by the increased computational power of modern day personal computers, enabling a trace back to the original personal data. Indeed, traditional anonymisation techniques, making each data entry non-identifiable by removing (or substituting) uniquely identifiable information, has limits: despite the substitution of users' personal information in a dataset, de-anonymisation can be overcome in a relatively short period of time through simple links between such anonymous datasets, other datasets (e.g. web search history) and personal data. Re-identification of the data subject might also derive from the powerful insights produced when multiple and specific datasets from different sources are joined. This might allow interested parties to uniquely identify specific physical persons or small groups of persons, with varying degrees of certainty.

The re-identification of data poses serious privacy concerns: once anonymised (or pseudo-anonymised), data may be freely processed without any prior consent by the data subject, before the subject is then re-identified. The situation is exacerbated by the lack of adequate transparency regarding the use of Big Data: this affects the ability of a data subject to allow disclosure of his/her information and to control access to these data by third parties, also impacting civil rights.

It is advisable that organisations willing to use Big Data adopt transparent procedures and ensure that these procedures are easily accessible and knowable by the public. In this way, an ethical perspective would truly drive innovation and boundary setting, properly taking into account the individual's need for privacy and self-determination.

New Types of Stigmatisation and Manipulation of Civil Rights in the 'Group Privacy' Landscape

The right to privacy is undergoing an evolution. Originally arising as the right to be let alone and to exclude others from personal facts, over the years it has shifted to the right to being able to control personal data, and is now moving further in the direction of improved control. The current direction is towards the right to manage identity and the analytical profile created by third parties which select the relevant patterns to be considered in metadata. This third phase dwells not only on data that enable the identification of specific physical persons, but more on data suitable for finding out specific patterns of behaviour such as health data, shopping preferences, health status, sleep cycles, mobility patterns, online consumption, friendships, etc., of groups rather than of individuals. Despite the data being anonymous (in the sense of being de-individualised), groups are increasingly becoming more transparent: indeed, stripping data from all elements pertaining to any sort of group belongingness would result in stripping the collection itself from its content and therefore its usefulness.

This information gathered from Big Data can be used in a targeted way to encourage people to behave or consume in a certain way. Targeted marketing is an example, but other initiatives (for instance, in the political landscape), based on the ability of Big Data to discover hidden correlations and on the inferred preferences and conditions of a specific group, could be adopted to encourage or discourage a certain behaviour, with incentives whose purposes are less transparent (including not only market intelligence, but other forms of manipulations in several sectors – such as in voting behaviour).

New types of stigmatisation might also arise, for instance, in relation to the commercial choices and other personal information of groups. Forms of discrimination are likely, especially when the groups get smaller (identified by geographical, age, sex, etc. settings). In this sense, Big Data techniques might eclipse longstanding civil rights protections.

What increases ethics concern is the related collection and aggregation of mass Big Data, and the resulting structured information and quantitative analysis for this purpose that are not subject to the application of current data protection regulations. Therefore, innovative ways of re-thinking citizens' protection are needed, capable of offering adequate and full protection.

The 'Sharing the Wealth' Model and the 'Personal Data Store' Approach for Balancing Big Data Exploitation and Data Protection

As pointed out by the EU Agency for Network and Information Security (ENISA), it is necessary to overcome the conceptual conflict between privacy and Big Data and between privacy and innovation. The need is to shift '... the discussion from "big data versus privacy" to "big data with privacy"', and to recognise the privacy and data protection principles as 'an essential value of big data, not only for the benefit of the individuals, but also for the very prosperity of big data analytics' (ENISA, 2015, p. 5). There is no dichotomy between ethics and innovation if feasible balancing solutions are figured out and implemented. The respect for citizens' privacy and dignity and the exploitation of Big Data's potential can fruitfully coexist and prosper together, balancing the fundamental human values (privacy, confidentiality, transparency, identity, free choice and others) with the compelling uses of Big Data for economic gains. This is aligned with EDPS's recent opinion (European Data Protection Supervisor, Opinion 3/2020 on the European strategy for data) underlining that data strategy's objectives could encompass 'to prove the viability and sustainability of an alternative data economy model – open, fair and democratic' where, in contrast with the current predominant business model,

> characterised by unprecedented concentration of data in a handful of powerful players, as well as pervasive tracking, the European data space should serve as an example of transparency, effective accountability and proper balance between the interests of the individual data subjects and the shared interest of the society as a whole.

The key question is how to ensure this coexistence and the underlying balance is achieved. The answer is not simple and relies on multiple dimensions. From a technological perspective, Privacy by Design and Privacy Enhancing Technologies (PETs) come into play.[4]

As stated by the EU Regulation 2016/679, the data protection principles should be taken into consideration at a very early stage, as well as privacy measures and PETs should be identified in conjunction with the determination of the means for processing and deployed at the time of the processing itself. ENISA proposed an array of privacy by design strategies, ranging from data minimisation and separate processing of personal data, to hiding personal data and their interrelation, opting for the highest level of aggregation. The PETs to implement these strategies are already applied in the Big Data industry: they rely on anonymisation, encryption, transparency and access, security and accountability control, consent ownership and control mechanisms. Even so, an adequate investment in this sector is required, as confirmed by the small number of patents for PETs compared to those granted for data analytics technologies. Efforts need to be directed towards strengthening data subject control thereby bringing transparency and trust in the online environment. In fact, trust has emerged as a complex topic within the contemporary Big Data landscape. At the same time, it has become a key factor for economic development and for the adoption of new services, such as public e-government services, as well as for users' acceptance to provide personal data. In some instances, such as in the medical field, the choice not to provide a full disclosure of the requested information might impact the individual's wellbeing or health (besides indirectly hindering progress in research), given that these are personal data and the trust relationship with the data collector (e.g. the staff of a hospital) is functional to the individual's wellbeing and/health.

The 'sharing the wealth' strategy proposed by Tene and Polonetsky (2013) for addressing Big Data challenges is based on the idea of providing individuals access to their data in a usable format and, above all, allowing them to take advantage of solutions capable of analysing their own data and drawing useful conclusions from it. The underlying vision is to share the wealth individuals' data helps to create with individuals themselves, letting them make use of and benefit from their own personal data. This approach is also aligned with the vision of the Big Data Value Association (BDVA Position Paper, 2019), which outlines opportunities of data economy arising over the next decade for the industry (business), the private users (citizens as customers), the research and academic community (science) and local, national and European government and public bodies (government).

Other authors (Rubinstein, 2013) underline the potentialities of a new business model based on the personal data store or personal data space (PDS). Such a business model shifts data acquisition and control to a user-centric paradigm, based on better control of data and joint benefits from its use. This solution (and the necessary implementing technology), if developed, might enable users' empowerment and full control over their personal data. In fact, it would permit users to gather, store, update, correct, analyse and/or share personal data, as well as having the ability to grant and withdraw consent to third parties for access to data. In this way, it would also work towards more accountable companies, where the commitment in personal data protection might become an economic asset for digital players.

PDS are also aligned with the importance of data portability, strongly advocated by the EDPS in view of guaranteeing people the right to access, control and correct their personal data, whilst enhancing their awareness. Data portability also nurtures the suggested approach of allowing people to share the benefits of data and can foster the development of a more competitive market environment, where the data protection policy is transformed into a *strategical economic asset*, thus triggering a virtuous circle. Companies would be encouraged to invest to find and implement the best ways to guarantee the privacy of their customers: indeed, data portability allows customers to switch providers more easily, also by taking into account the provider more committed to respecting personal data and to investing in privacy-friendly technical measures and internal procedures.

The 'sharing the wealth' paradigm and the potentialities of a new ethically driven business model relying on personal data are at the basis of the European Project DataVaults – 'Persistent Personal DataVaults Empowering a Secure and Privacy Preserving Data Storage, Analysis, Sharing and Monetisation Platform' (Grant Agreement no. 871755), funded under the H2020 Programme.[5] This project, currently under development, is aimed at setting, sustaining and mobilising an ever-growing ecosystem for personal data and insights sharing, capable of enhancing the collaboration between stakeholders (data owners and data seekers). Its value-driven tools and methods for addressing concerns about privacy, data protection, security and Intellectual Property Rights (IPR) ownership will enable the ethically sound sharing both of personal data and proprietary/commercial/industrial data, following strict and fair mechanism for defining how to generate, capture, release and cash out value for the benefit of all the stakeholders involved, as well as securing value flow based on smart contract, moving towards a win–win data sharing ecosystem.

The European Privacy Association even proposes to see data protection for digital companies not as mere legal compliance obligations, but as part of a broader corporate social responsibility) and socially responsible investments in the Big Data industry. It is recommended to valorise them as assets within renewed business models, able to help companies responsibly achieve their economic targets.

From a wider perspective, as also underlined by BDVA (2020) in particular in relation to the Smart Manufacturing environment, the soft law in the form of codes of conduct could bring a set of advantages at ecosystem level in each domain. In fact, such sources are expected to offer guidance and to address in meaningful, flexible and practical ways the immediate issues and ethical challenges of Big Data and AI innovations in each sector, going beyond current gaps in the legal system: they can operate as a rulebook, providing more granular ethical guidance as regards problems and concerns, resulting in an increase of confidence and legal certainty of individuals which also encompass trust building and consolidation.

In parallel, this calls for promoting the acquisition of skills on privacy as a value and right, on ethical issues of behaviour profiling, ownership of personal contents, virtual identity-related risks and digital reputation control, as well as on other topics related to Big Data advancements. On this purpose, Bachelor's and Master's degree programmes in Data Science, Informatics, Computer Science, Artificial Intelligence and related subjects could be adequately integrated in order to cover these themes. In this way, human resources in Big Data businesses could include ad hoc professional figures.

At the same time, in order to promote the commitment of the business world, it is advisable that the efforts of those companies which invest in ethical relationships with customers are recognised by governments and properly communicated by the companies themselves to their customer base. The certification approach should also be explored, as inspired by the Ethics Certification Program for Autonomous and Intelligent Systems launched by the Institute of Electrical and Electronics Engineers for AIS[6] products, services and systems.

This would let them further benefit in terms of improved reputation and let them increase the trust of customers towards their products and services. At the same time, information on business ethics violations occurring through the improper use of Big Data analytics should be transparent and not kept opaque to consumers.

A Critical Perspective on the 'Notice and Consent' Model and on the Role of Transparency in the Evolving World of Big Data Analytics

Emerging commentators argue that the data protection principles, as embodied in national and EU law, are no longer adequate to deal with the Big Data world: in particular, they criticise the role of transparency in the evolving world of Big Data analytics, assuming that it no longer makes sense considering the complex and opaque nature of algorithms. They also debate the actual suitability of the so-called 'notice and consent' model, on the grounds of consumers' lack of time, willingness or ability to read long privacy notices.

Others prefer to emphasise accountability, as opposed to transparency for answering Big Data ethics challenges, being focussed on mechanisms more aligned with the nature of Big Data (such as assessing the technical design of algorithms and auditability). GDPR itself highlights, besides the role of transparency, the growing importance of accountability.

Instead of denying the role of transparency in the Big Data context, others suggest that it is not possible to offer a wholesale replacement for transparency and propose a more 'layered' approach to it (for instance, as regards privacy notices to individuals and also the information detail), in conjunction with a greater level of detail and access being given to auditors and accredited certification bodies.

On the contrary, transparency itself might be considered as a requirement needed for accountability and seems unavoidable in the context of respect for human dignity. Traditional notice and consent models might be rather insufficient and obsolete in view of the effective exercise of control and in order to avoid a situation where individuals feel powerless in relation to their data. Nevertheless, to overcome this weakness, an alternative, more challenging path is to make consent more granular and capable of covering all the different processing (and related) purposes and the re-use of personal data. This effort should be combined with increased citizens' awareness and a higher participation level, as well as with effective solutions to guarantee the so-called right to be forgotten.

In the same user-centric approach, based on control and joint benefits and promoted by EC and European-wide initiatives,[7] a number of views foster new approaches premised on consumer empowerment in the data-driven business world. These approaches strongly aligned with the transparency and accountability requirements, ask for proper internal policies and control systems, focussed on pragmatic, smart and dynamic solutions and able to prevent the risk of companies becoming stuck in bureaucracy.

DISCRIMINATION, SOCIAL COOLING, BIG DATA DIVIDE AND SOCIAL SORTING

A possible side effect of datafication is the potential risk of discrimination of data mining technologies in several aspects of daily life, such as employment and credit scoring (Favaretto, De Clercq, & Elger, 2019). It ranges from discriminatory practices based on profiling and related privacy concerns (e.g. racial profiling enabled by Big Data platforms in subtle ways by targeting characteristics like home address and misleading vulnerable less-educated groups with scams of harmful offers),[8] to the impact of Big Data in the context of the daily operation of organisations and public administrations (e.g. within human resources offices). In the latter context, crucial decisions, like those about employment, might rely on the use of Big Data practices which might bring the risk of unfair treatment through discrimination based on gender, race, disability, national origin, sexual orientation and so on.

Social Cooling as a Side Effect of Big Data

We live in a society where everything can be given a score and critical life chang-ing opportunities are increasingly determined by such scoring systems, often obtained through secret predictive algorithms applied to data to determine which individuals or which social group has value. It is therefore essential to consider human values as oversight in the design and implementation of these systems and, at the same time, to guarantee that the policies and practices using data and scoring machines to make decisions are realised in a legal and ethical man-ner (including avoiding automated decision-making practices not compliant with regulatory boundaries set forth by art. 22 GDPR). Fair and accurate scoring sys-tems have to be ensured, whilst also avoiding the risk that data might be biased to arbitrarily assign individuals to a stigmatising group. Such an assignment might potentially allow that decisions relevant for them are not fair and, in the end, might negatively affect their concrete opportunities.

Any Big Data system has to ensure that, if existing, automated decision mak-ing, especially in areas such as employment, health care, education and financial lending, operates fairly for all communities, and safeguards the interests of those who are disadvantaged. The use of Big Data, in other words, should not result in infringements of the fundamental rights of individuals, neither in differential treatment or indirect discrimination against groups of people, for instance, as regards the fairness and equality of opportunities for access to services.

As indicated by the European Parliament, all measures possible need to be taken to minimise algorithmic discrimination and bias and to develop a com-mon ethical framework for the transparent processing of personal data and auto-mated decision making. This common framework should guide data usage and the ongoing enforcement of EU law. From this perspective, it is necessary that the use of algorithms to provide services – useful for identifying patterns in data – rely on a comprehensive understanding of the context in which they are expected to function and are capable of picking up what matters. It is also essential to establish oversight activities and human intervention in automated systems as well, besides considering that Big Data needs to be coupled with room for politics and with mechanisms to hold power to account. In this way, unintended negative societal consequences of possible errors introduced by algorithms, especially in terms of the risk of systematic discrimination across society in the provision of services, might be prevented or at least minimised.

This will also limit the widening of one of the chilling effects of Big Data related to discrimination, the so-called social cooling. Social cooling could limit people's desire to take risks or exercise free speech, which, over the long term, could 'cool down' society.[9] The term describes the long-term negative side effects in terms, for instance, of self-censorship, risk-aversion and exercise of free speech, of living in a reputation economy where Big Data practices that lack an ethical dimension are increasingly apparent and intrusive.

Social cooling is due to people's emerging perception that their data, including the data reflecting their weaknesses, is turned into thousands of different scores and that their resulting 'digital reputation' could limit their opportunities. As a consequence, they feel pressure to conform to a bureaucratic average, start to apply self-censorship and tend to change their behaviour to achieve better scores. This might result, especially if public awareness remains very low, in increased social rigidity, limiting people's ability and willingness to protest injustice and, in the end, in a subtle form of socio-political control. The related societal question is whether this trend will have an impact on the human ability to evolve as a society, where minority views are still able to flourish.

The social cooling effect emphasises another dimension of a mature and nuanced perception of data and privacy: its ability to protect the right to be imperfect, in other words the right to be human.

Big Data Divide

The expression Big Data Divide has a two-fold meaning. First, it refers to the difficulty in accessing services delivered through the use of the Internet and other new technologies and to the complexity in understanding how these technologies and related services work. This kind of digital divide might have consequences, for instance, with regard to online job hunting: senior citizens, who are unfamiliar with this new way of job hunting, can be harmed in terms of lost job opportunities. The same may happen with regard to other tools such as online dating services for finding a new partner or for social interactions. The consequences might be frustration and social withdrawal. Similarly, inclusion concerns are related to the possible definition of new policies based on a data-driven approach (e.g. data collected via sensors, social media, etc.); there is the concrete possibility that some individuals or portions of a society might not be considered. The risk is that the new policy will only take into account the needs of people having access to the given technological means. Secondly, the notion of a 'Big Data divide' refers to the asymmetric relationship between those 'who collect, store, and mine large quantities of data, and those whom data collection targets' (Andrejevic, 2014). The Big Data divide is perceived as potentially able to exacerbate power imbalances in the digital era and increase the individual's sense of powerlessness in relation to emerging forms of data collection and data mining.

Furthermore, it has been argued that Big Data and data mining emphasise correlation and prediction and call to mind the emergent Big Data-driven forms of social sorting (and related risk of discrimination). This remark refers to the ability – enabled by Big Data and data mining – of discerning unexpected, unanticipated correlations and of generating patterns of actionable information. Such ability provides powerful insights for decision making and prediction purposes, unavailable to those without access to such data, processing power and findings: those with access are advantageously positioned compared to those without it.

Predictive analytics for data-driven decision making and social sorting can also lead to 'predictive policing' (Meijer & Wessels, 2019), where extra surveillance is set for certain individuals, groups or streets if it is more likely that a crime can be committed. Though systematic empirical research, capable of generating an evidence base on the benefits and drawbacks of this practice, seems to be still missing, the predictive policy encompasses a political challenge: if it is difficult to ignore these kinds of findings and doing nothing to prevent the occurrence of the crime, at the same time the risk of stigmatisation of such individuals or groups has to be tackled. A balance could be sought considering, for instance, the intervention threshold and correlating the type of intervention with the likelihood of crime anticipated by the algorithms, being careful to exclude incidental co-occurrences.

Big Data from the Public Sector Perspective

Big Data for Public Use

Another area to investigate is how Big Data might be used for public good and with public support.

Both in the 'European Strategy for Data' (COM, 2020b) and in the recent Proposal for a Regulation on European Data Governance ('Data Governance Act') which is the first of a set of measures announced in the strategy, data altruism is facilitated, meaning 'data voluntarily made available by individuals or companies for the common good' (COM, 2020c). The increasing amounts of data in society might change the type of evidence that is available for policy makers and, at the same time, policy makers can linger over computer models and predictive analytics as a basis for their decisions. The chance to draw meaningful insights (relevant for policy elaboration purposes) from data would require a comprehensive data infrastructure, where data sources are well organised and can be accessed by authorised people for the appropriate use. The discussion mainly explores the opportunities in local services in view of accompanying local decisions by evidence for securing investment from central budget holders. The surveys ranged from identifying what approaches work better for the public at a lower cost to efficaciously demonstrate and show where resources are lacking and investment needed. However, the possible use of data analysis in many local authorities is being confronted by more traditional approaches, as well as with civil servants' diffidence in exploiting the potentialities of cutting-edge technologies. Thereby an organisational and cultural change needs to be supported, through awareness campaigns and other initiatives.

An interesting example of how Big Data can be exploited for the common good and public interest in conjunction with private business' priorities is the solution developed in the project AEGIS – 'Advanced Big Data Value Chain for Public Safety and Personal Security' (Grant Agreement no. 732189), funded by the European Commission in the H2020 Programme. The project brought

> together the data, the network and the technologies to create a curated, semantically enhanced, interlinked and multilingual repository for public and personal safety-related Big Data. It delivers a data-driven innovation that expands over multiple business sectors and takes into consideration structured, unstructured and multilingual datasets, rejuvenates existing models and facilitates organisations in the Public Safety and Personal Security linked sectors to provide better & personalised services to their users.[10]

The services enabled by this technology aim to generate value from Big Data and renovate the Public Safety and Personal Security sector, positively influencing the welfare and protection of the general public. Project achievements aim to have positive impacts in terms of economic growth and enhanced public security, as well as for individuals, by improving safety and wellbeing through prevention and protection from dangers affecting safety (such as accidents or disasters).

Dataveillance, Big Data Governance and Legislation

Big Data poses multiple strategic challenges for governance and legislation, with the final aim of minimising harm and maximising benefit from the use of data. Such challenges require consideration of risks and risk management.

The first issue is related to the practice of the so-called 'dataveillance', where the use of data improves surveillance and security. It refers to the continuous monitoring and collecting of users' online data (data resulting from email, credit card transactions, GPS coordinates, social networks, etc.), including communication and other actions across various platforms and digital media, as well as metadata. This kind of surveillance is partially unknown and happens discreetly. Dataveillance can be individual dataveillance (concerning the individual's personal data), mass dataveillance (concerning data on groups of people) and facilitative mechanisms (without either considering the individual as part of a group, or targeting any specific group).

In the public perception, the idea that one's position and activity might be in some way tracked at most times has become an ordinary fact of life, in conjunction with an increased perception of safety: almost everyone is aware of the ubiquitous use of CCTV[11] circuits, the GPS[12] positioning capabilities inside mobile devices, the use of credit cards and ATM[13] cards and other forms of tracking. On the contrary, this active surveillance might also have an impact on citizens' liberties and might be used by governments (and businesses too) for unethical purposes.

Ethical concerns revolve around individual rights and liberties, as well as on the 'data trust deficit', whereby citizens have lower levels of trust in institutions to use their data appropriately.

Other important tools for accountability to the public should be implemented, in order to avoid the public perception that there are no mechanisms for accountability outside of public outcry. This implies tackling the challenge for Big Data governance. For instance, it would be useful if there were a formulation and upholding of an authoritative ethical framework at the national or international level, drawing upon a wide range of knowledge, skills and interests across the public, private and academic sectors, and confirmed by a wide public consultation.

Alongside this ethical framework an update of the current legislative system would be opportune for minimising harm and maximising benefit from the use of data: in fact, the regulation is developing at a much slower pace than the Big Data technology and its applications. This results in the business community's responsibility to decide how to bridle the insights offered by data from the multiple data sources and devices, according to their respective core ethical values.

DATA OWNERSHIP

Another dimension of the debate on Big Data also revolves around data ownership, which might be considered as a sort of IPR issue separate from technology IPR.

The latter refers to the procedures and technologies used to acquire, process, curate, analyse and use the data. Big Data technology IPRs are mostly covered by the general considerations applicable for software and hardware IPRs and the related business processes, though considered in the Big Data domain. In this view, special IPR approaches are not needed, being covered by existing models and approaches existing for the assertion, assignment and enforcement of copyright, design rights, trademarks and patents for IT technology in general.

On the contrary, data ownership refers to the IP related to the substantive data itself, including both raw data and derived data. The main IP rights in relation to data are database rights, copyright and confidentiality: due to the fact that database rights and copyright protect expression and form rather than the substance of information, the best form of IP protection for data is often considered the one offered by the provisions safeguarding the confidentiality of information, being capable of protecting the substance of data that is not generally publicly known.

IP challenges in the Big Data domain are different from existing approaches and need special care, especially as regards protection, security and liability, besides data ownership. At the same time, addressing the challenges raised by IP issues is essential, considering the expected high incomes due to increased Big Data innovation and technology diffusion.

Data ownership and the rights to use data might be covered by copyright and related contracts which are valid when collecting the data, often including also confidentiality clauses. In case of further processing of big datasets, it has to be explored when and how this creates new ownership: in fact, the acquisition of data, its curation and combination with other datasets, as well as possible analysis of them and resulting insights, creates new rights to the resulting data, which need be asserted and enforced.

Regardless of the considerations stemming from the regulatory perspective, notably Directive 96/9/EC on the legal protection of databases, the main ethical dilemma concerns how to consider user's data. In other words, the question is to whom these data belong: still to the user, or to the company that conducted the analyses, or the company that gathered the original data?[14]

All these issues should not only be specifically addressed by national and European legislation on IPR in relation to data, which is of uncertain scope at the moment, but also investigated by the data ethics debate: best practices for collection, recommendations and guidelines would be very useful. Currently, a key role for addressing this issues is played by contract provisions.

In view of ensuring the fair attribution of value represented in data creation, but, at the same time, considering the multiple, competing interests at stake in B2B[15] data sharing, balancing operations should be conducted between the data producers' interest to remain in control of their data and to retain their rights as the original owners, the public interest in avoiding data monopolies (due to the fact that data still fuel innovation, creativity and research) and data subjects' interest in their personal information collected by a company.

Regarding the first of these interests and the related ownership claims, the legal framework is still uncertain and fragmented. The situation is further complicated by the difficulty of applying legal categories: the data are an intangible good difficult to define and the same legal concept of data ownership is not clearly defined. Many questions arise, such as: does existing EU law provide sufficient protection for data? If not, what more is needed? Are data capable of ownership (sui generis right or copyright law)? Is there a legal basis for claims of ownership of data? Is there the need of enactment of exclusive rights in data? Or is it better to explore alternatives?

Regarding alternatives, an interesting option is to provide the factual exclusivity of data through flexible and pragmatic solutions able to provide certainty and predictability, by combining agile contracting with enabling technological tools. As for the contractual layer of this solution, it consists of ad hoc and on-the-fly B2B data exchange contracts, provided under the well-defined data sovereignty principle to safeguard data producers' control over data generated. For this purpose, access and usage policies or protocols need to be implemented. At the same time, it is necessary to establish a trade-off with other interests, like individual 'interest' over personal data, in this case. On the contrary, the technological layer provides enabling technologies to implement and enforce the terms and conditions set forth by the data sharing agreements. Technologies to be explored include, for instance, sticky policies, Blockchain, Distributed Ledger Technologies and smart contract, Digital Rights Management technologies and APIs.[16]

This kind of solution is well-developed by the International Data Space Association (IDSA),[17] consisting of more than one hundred companies and institutions from various industries and of different sizes from 20 countries collaborating to design and develop a trustworthy architecture for the data economy. Its vision and reference architecture rotate around the concept of 'data sovereignty', defined as 'a natural person's or corporate entity's capability of being entirely self-determined with regard to its data' (IDSA, 2019). Data sovereignty, which is materialised in 'terms and conditions' (such as time to live, forwarding rights, pricing information, etc.) linked to data before it is exchanged and shared. Such terms and conditions are supported and enforced through the technical infrastructure, including tools for the secure and trusted authorisation, authentication and data exchange (such as blockchain, smart contracts, identity management, point-to-point encryption, etc.) to be customised to the needs of individual participants.

In line with the joint benefit approach and with the related user-centric business model based on PDS, a similar path could be further extended also for strengthening the contract provisions underpinning high-value personal data ecosystems leaving the process under the individuals' control, like in the DataVaults Project. This is also the goal of the new Smart Cities Marketplace Initiative within the Citizen Focus Action Cluster: 'Citizen Control of Personal Data',[18] launched on 27 January 2021. Its intention is

> to contribute to speeding up the adoption, at scale, of common open urban data platforms, and ensure that 300 million European citizens are served by cities with competent urban data platforms, by 2025. The potential for citizen's personal data to contribute to data ecosystems will be significantly enhanced by introducing secure, ethical and legal access to this highly coveted and valuable personal data, incorporating citizen-generated data as 'city data'.

Novel contract rights, including IPR provisions, might be further spread in the data-driven economy, in view of confirming users' control over their data, as well as their empowerment, thereby contributing to going beyond possible existing differences between national laws and gaps in the European legislation.

Nevertheless, as in the past, when the IPR development has followed the commercialising of innovation, the growth of the Big Data market is likely to generate also the further renewal of the IPRs' regulatory framework underpinning it and to pave the way to set a coherent system at European level.

CONCLUSIONS

The rise of Big Data and the underlying ability to capture and analyse datasets from highly diversified contexts and generate novel, unanticipated knowledge, as well as AI developments relying on data, are capable of producing economic growth and bringing relevant benefits, both at the social and the individual level. This rapidly sprawling phenomenon is expected to have significant influence on governance, policing, economics, security, science, education, health care and much more.

The collection of Big Data and inferences based on them are sources enabling both economic growth and generation of value, with the potential to bring further improvement to everyday life in the near future. The examples span from road safety, to health services, agriculture, retail, education and climate change mitigation. Possible improvements rely on the direct use and collection of Big Data or on inferences or 'nowcasting' based on them: new knowledge and insights are generated, as well as real-time reports and analyses with alerting purposes can be produced.

At the same time, Big Data practices and techniques put at stake several ethical, social and policy challenges, threats and potential hurdles. They are often interrelated and range from concerns related to data ownership to the 'datafication' of society, to privacy dilemmas and the potential trade-off between privacy and data analytics progress, social cooling, dataveillance, discriminatory practices and the emerging Big Data divide. Such challenges, threats and potential hurdles also include, for instance, the data-driven business ethics violations, the 'data trust deficit', the concerns due to the use of Big Data in the public sector and the desirable role of the government towards the fair policy development and the provision of enhanced public services.

These and similar items need greater ethics engagement and reflection, in the framework of an interdependent ecosystem, composed of different and complementary competences (primarily legislators, data-driven businesses, IT developers and data scientists, civil society organisations and academia) in order to come up with a Big Data market fully respectful of human dignity and citizens' rights and susceptible of further development in an ethically acceptable way.

The fruitful development of this ecosystem might also require the adjustment of familiar conceptual models and archetypes of research ethics, to better align them with the epistemic conditions of Big Data and the data analytics work. The envisioned alignment should reflect also on the shift towards algorithmic knowledge production to identify and address eventual mismatches between the Big

Data research and the extant research ethics regimes. In parallel, inquiry should be moved away from considering only traditional categories of harm (e.g. physical pain and psychological distress) to cover other types and forms (e.g. effects of the perennial surveillance on human behaviour and dignity and group discrimination). Likewise, the concept of the human subject and related foundational assumptions should be revisited to include not only individuals, but also distributed groupings or classifications.

The need to productively re-think some concepts of research ethics and regulations, due to the development of large-scale data analytics, represents an opportunity to reaffirm basic principles and values of human dignity, respect, transparency, accountability and justice. The final aim is to contribute to shaping the future trajectory of the Big Data revolution, with its interplay with AI breakthroughs, in a way that is truly responsive to foundational ethical principles.

NOTES

1. COM (2020b). This communication is part of a wider package of strategic documents, including the COM (2020a), the Communication on Shaping Europe's digital future.
2. The volume of data produced is growing quickly, from 33 zettabytes in 2018 to an expected 175 zettabytes in 2025 in the world (IDC, 2018).
3. European Data Protection Supervisor, Opinion 3/2020 on the European strategy for data. In the same document, the EDPS applauds the EC's commitment to safeguard that European fundamental rights and values, underpinning all aspects of the data strategy and its implementation.
4. A high-value description and classification of the PETs and their role was provided by the e-SIDES project (https://e-sides.eu/e-sides-project) deliverables. In the e-SIDES Deliverable D3.2 and in the related White Paper, the overview of existing PETs is accompanied by an assessment methodology of them for facing legal and ethical implications based on interviews and desk-research: it provides, on the one hand, the technology-specific assessment of selected classes of PETs, and, on the other hand, a more general assessment of such technologies.
5. In particular within the call H2020-ICT-2019-2, topic ICT-13-2018-2019 'Supporting the emergence of data markets and the data economy'. Further information on DataVaults can be retrieved at the following link: https://www.datavaults.eu/.
6. Autonomous and Intelligent Systems.
7. See, for instance, EC's COM (2019) and EFFRA (2013, 2020).
8. An interesting reading on the risk of racial profiling which might be generated by new technological tools and methods, such as Big Data, automated decision making and AI is the 'General recommendation No. 36 (2020) on preventing and combating racial profiling by law enforcement officials' released by the United Nations' Committee on the Elimination of Racial Discrimination (2020) on 17 December.
9. https://www.socialcooling.com/
10. https://cordis.europa.eu/project/rcn/206179_it.html
11. Closed-Circuit Television.
12. Global Positioning System.
13. Automated Teller Machine.
14. An interesting reading on this topic is AA.VV (2016).
15. Business to Business
16. Application Programming Interfaces.
17. https://www.internationaldataspaces.org/
18. https://smart-cities-marketplace.ec.europa.eu/news/new-initiative-citizen-control-personal-data-within-citizen-focus-action-cluster. This initiative is committed to seek to

remove existing constrains and helping to create the conditions and relationships whereby 'the citizen will be willing to share personal data with a city and with other actors in the data economy. The ambition behind this new initiative is to give the smart cities movement a boost by providing cities with access to a rich personal data pool. This pool of data, in turn, would stimulate further activity within the data economy, accelerate the take-up of urban data platforms and contribute to the improvement of mobility, health, energy efficiency and better governance among other'.

REFERENCES

AA.VV. (2016). Data ownership and access to data. Position statement of the Max Planck Institute for Innovation and Competition of 16 August 2016 on the current European debate.

Andrejevic, M. (2014). The Big Data divide. *International Journal of Communication, 8*, 1673–1689.

Bailly, M., & Manyika, J. (2013). *Is manufacturing 'cool' again?*. McKinsey Global Institute. Retrieved from https://www.brookings.edu/opinions/is-manufacturing-cool-again/

BDVA. (2020). Big Data challenges in smart manufacturing industry. A White paper on digital Europe Big Data challenges for smart manufacturing industry. Retrieved from https://bdva.eu/sites/default/files/BDVA_SMI_Discussion_Paper_Web_Version.pdf. Accessed on July 26, 2021.

BDVA Position Paper. (2019, April) Towards a European data sharing space – Enabling data exchange and unlocking AI potential. Retrieved from https://www.bdva.eu/node/1277. Accessed on July 26, 2021.

COM. (2019). 168 final "Building trust in human-centric artificial intelligence". Retrieved from https://eur-lex.europa.eu/legal-content/EN/ALL/?uri=CELEX:52019DC0168. Accessed on July 26, 2021.

COM. (2020a). 65 final "White paper on artificial intelligence – A European approach to excellence and trust". Retrieved from https://ec.europa.eu/info/sites/default/files/commission-white-paper-artificial-intelligence-feb2020_en.pdf. Accessed on July 26, 2021.

COM. (2020b). 66 final "A European strategy for data". Retrieved from https://eur-lex.europa.eu/legal-content/EN/TXT/?uri=CELEX%3A52020DC0066. Accessed on July 26, 2021.

COM. (2020c). 767 final "Proposal for a regulation of the European Parliament and of the Council on European data governance (Data Governance Act)". Retrieved from https://eur-lex.europa.eu/legal-content/EN/TXT/?uri=CELEX%3A52020PC0767. Accessed on July 26, 2021.

DataVaults Project. Retrieved from https://www.datavaults.eu/

EFFRA. (2013). Factories of the future multi-annual roadmap for the contractual PPP under Horizon 2020. Retrieved from https://www.effra.eu/sites/default/files/190312_effra_roadmapmanufacturingppp_eversion.pdf

EFFRA. (2020). Vision for a manufacturing partnership in Horizon Europe 2021–2027.

ENISA. (2015). Privacy by design in Big Data. An overview of privacy enhancing technologies in the era of Big Data analytics. Retrieved from www.enisa.europa.eu. Accessed on July 26, 2021.

e-SIDES Deliverable D3.2 and White Paper. (2018). How effective are privacy-enhancing technologies in addressing ethical and societal issues?. Retrieved from https://e-sides.eu/resources. Accessed on July 26, 2021.

e-SIDES Project. Retrieved from https://e-sides.eu/e-sides-project

European Data Protection Supervisor, Opinion 3/2020 on the European strategy for data. Retrieved from https://edps.europa.eu/sites/default/files/publication/20-06-16_opinion_data_strategy_en.pdf

European Data Protection Supervisor, Opinion 4/2015. Towards a new digital ethics. Data, dignity and technology, 11 September 2015. Retrieved from https://edps.europa.eu/sites/edp/files/publication/15-09-11_data_ethics_en.pdf

Executive Office of the President. (2014). Big Data: Seizing opportunities, preserving values. Retrieved from https://obamawhitehouse.archives.gov/sites/default/files/docs/big_data_privacy_report_may_1_2014.pdf. Accessed July 26, 2021.

Favaretto, M., De Clercq, E., & Elger, B. S. (2019). Big Data and discrimination: Perils, promises and solutions. A systematic review. *Journal of Big Data, 6*(1), 12.

IDSA. (2019). Reference architecture model, version 3.0. Retrieved from https://internationaldata-spaces.org/use/reference-architecture/ Accessed on July 26, 2021.

Kagermann, H., & Wahlster, W. (2013). *Securing the future of German manufacturing industry: Recommendations for implementing the strategic initiative Industrie 4.0.* Final report of the Industrie 4.0 Working Group, AcatechVNational Academy of Science and Engineering, Germany. Retrieved from https://www.academia.edu/36867338/Securing_the_future_of_German_manufacturing_industry_Recommendations_for_implementing_the_strategic_initiative_INDUSTRIE_4_0_Final_report_of_the_Industrie_4_0_Working_Group. Accessed on July 26, 2021.

Meijer, A., & Wessels, M. (2019). Predictive policing: Review of benefits and drawbacks. *International Journal of Public Administration, 42*(12), 1031–1039.

Metcalf, J., & Crawford, K. (2016). Where are human subjects in Big Data research? The emerging ethics divide. *Big Data & Society, 3*(1), 1–14.

Reichert, P. (2014). Comarch EDI platform case study: The advanced electronic data interchange hub as a supply-chain performance booster. In P. Golinska (Ed.), *Logistics operations, supply chain management and sustainability* (pp.143–155). Cham: Springer.

Reinsel, R., Gantz, J., Rydning, J. (2018). *Data Age 2025. The digitization of the World. From Edge to Core. An IDC White Paper*. Retrieved at https://www.seagate.com/files/www-content/our-story/trends/files/idc-seagate-dataage-whitepaper.pdf

Rubinstein, I. S. (2013). Big Data: The end of privacy or a new beginning?. *International Data Privacy Law, 3*(2), 74–87.

Smart Cities Marketplace Initiative within the Citizen Focus Action Cluster. (2021). Citizen control of personal data. Retrieved from https://smart-cities-marketplace.ec.europa.eu/news/new-initia-tive-citizen-control-personal-data-within-citizen-focus-action-cluster

Tene, O., & Polonetsky, J. (2013). Big Data for all: Privacy and user control in the age of analytics. *Northwestern Journal of Technology and Intellectual Property, 11*(5), 237–273.

United Nations' Committee on the Elimination of Racial Discrimination. (2020). General recommendation No. 36 on preventing and combating racial profiling by law enforcement officials. Retrieved from https://digitallibrary.un.org/record/3897913. Accessed on July 26, 2021.

van Brakel, R. (2016). Pre-emptive Big Data surveillance and its (dis)empowering consequences: The case of predictive policing. In B. van der Sloot, D. Broeders, E. Schrijvers (Eds.), *Exploring the Boundaries of Big Data* (pp.117-141). Amsterdam: Amsterdam University

von der Leyen, U. (2019). A union that strives for more. My agenda for Europe. Retrieved from https://ec.europa.eu/info/sites/info/files/political-guidelines-next-commission_en_0.pdf. Accessed on July 26, 2021.

CHAPTER 7

HEALTH DATA, PUBLIC INTEREST, AND SURVEILLANCE FOR NON-HEALTH-RELATED PURPOSES

Mark Taylor and Richard Kirkham

ABSTRACT

A policy of surveillance which interferes with the fundamental right to a private life requires credible justification and a supportive evidence base. The authority for such interference should be clearly detailed in law, overseen by a transparent process and not left to the vagaries of administrative discretion. If a state surveils *those it governs and claims the interference to be in the public interest, then the evidence base on which that claim stands and the operative conception of public interest should be subject to critical examination. Unfortunately, there is an inconsistency in the regulatory burden associated with access to confidential patient information for non-health-related surveillance purposes and access for health-related surveillance or research purposes. This inconsistency represents a systemic weakness to inform or challenge an evidence-based policy of non-health-related surveillance. This inconsistency is unjustified and undermines the qualities recognised to be necessary to maintain a trustworthy confidential public health service. Taking the withdrawn Memorandum of Understanding (MoU) between NHS Digital and the Home Office as a worked example, this chapter demonstrates how the capacity of the law to constrain the arbitrary or unwarranted exercise of power through judicial review is not sufficient to* level the playing field. *The authors recommend 'levelling up' in procedural oversight, and adopting independent mechanisms equivalent*

Ethical Issues in Covert, Security and Surveillance Research
Advances in Research Ethics and Integrity, Volume 8, 93–118

ISSN: 2398-6018/doi:10.1108/S2398-601820210000008008

*to those adopted for establishing the operative conceptions of public interest
in the context of health research to non-health-related surveillance purposes.*

Keywords: Public interest; confidentiality; independent oversight; health-
related surveillance; data protection; privacy

INTRODUCTION

This chapter considers the issue of data sharing in the context of health.
Notwithstanding the highly sensitive interests involved, health data have long
been known to be of public value for the secondary purposes of medical research
and health-related surveillance and can have non-health-related uses as well. This
variable use of health data has raised the prospect of an equivalent variability in
the oversight of data sharing, creating a risk that, in the long-term, public trust
in the security of health data might be undermined. This chapter evidences the
problem and outlines a solution.

To illustrate the risks, we explore the example of the now withdrawn
Memorandum of Understanding (MoU) in the United Kingdom (UK) between
NHS Digital and the Home Office[1] to supply the latter with information obtained
by the health service. One of the purposes of the data sharing was to enable the
Home Office to better locate those suspected of an immigration offence. Here a
decision on the 'public interest' in disclosure was taken without exposure to the
kind of open debate that is typically associated with governance models applied
before data sharing for other purposes. For example, those seeking access to confidential patient information for the purposes of health research, notwithstanding its public value, must normally have a patient's explicit consent or navigate
an approvals process with more independent scrutiny and challenge than was
applied to the Home Office's non-health-related surveillance purposes. Health-
related surveillance may not always be subject to the same intensity of case-by-
case review, and here data disclosure under recent Coronavirus notices may be a
good example of reduced review standards being applied. Nevertheless, health-
related surveillance in the context of health research is typically characterised by
a balance being struck between competing public interests (e.g., between confidentiality and public health protection) that has been relatively precisely articu-
lated in legislation following parliamentary debate and informed by independent
advice. The deficit in process for non-health-related surveillance increases the risk
that a decision on the public interest in disclosure will have shallow roots, run
no deeper than institutional and short-term political interest, and will pay insufficient regard for the interests of all those affected.

We suggest that this situation is problematic for a variety of reasons and
provide a recommendation for the way forward. The main concern is that the
mischief that the law is designed to address is the need to secure the trust of
users of health services, by ensuring that health data is only released, lacking an
individual's consent, according to an applied standard of the public interest. To
make this argument, we adopt the concept of *social legitimacy* and consider the

extent to which current governance arrangements ensure that those subject to governance have reasons to accept the conceptions of public interest applied by decision-makers.

To address the concerns raised in this chapter, we acknowledge that the law in the UK does provide some constraints on arbitrary or unwarranted exercise of power. However, whilst there is some capacity in judicial remedies, its limitations in this context are also laid bare. Given the problems, this chapter concludes with the recommendation that it is necessary to level the playing field between those who would access confidential patient information for the purposes of health surveillance, those who would access the same data for the purposes of non-health-related surveillance, and those who would access it for the purposes of carrying out research to determine the effectiveness and effects of either type of policy. If social legitimacy in the governance framework is to be upheld, then we would recommend levelling up rather than levelling down. At the heart of the solution needs to be either an extension of parliamentary scrutiny or the expansion of the remit of independent advice on patient data.

This chapter takes the following approach. We begin by establishing the current historical and legal basis for the control of health data in the UK. This is followed by a defence of an important normative purpose of legislation in this context and an argument that this is being undermined by practices exemplified by the, now withdrawn, MoU between NHS Digital and the Home Office. Our conclusion is that the withdrawn MoU illustrates the risk of poor legal design, which currently insufficiently allows for oversight and in this instance was reliant on the ad hoc intervention of a Parliamentary select committee to block potentially unlawful practice. A preferable approach which can pre-empt problems before they arise is to strengthen, in the management of patient data, either prospective parliamentary scrutiny or the role of independent advice, as is already the case for health-related research without explicit patient consent.

THE UK LEGAL FRAMEWORK FOR THE USE OF HEALTH DATA

Background and Legal Context

The importance of being able to use health data for health surveillance purposes is longstanding. For instance, when in 1854 John Snow plotted cases of cholera on a map of Soho in London, his work was dependent on data he had gathered from affected households. For health surveillance to maximise its potential to achieve public health benefits through learning and research, it has long been understood that access to confidential health information is often required. For centuries, this practice was not covered by statute, and instead in law was only dealt with tangentially by the common law duty of confidence. This position became politically untenable around the turn of the millennium, when following a series of scandals, such as Alder Hey (Redfern, Keeling, & Powell, 2001), there was a sustained political reaction to using identifiable health data for purposes beyond individual care without individual consent. The subsequent momentum towards requiring the explicit consent of a patient for the use of confidential patient information for secondary purposes, jeopardised some health surveillance purposes. At this point, Parliament stepped in.

The significance of sensitive health data for medical purposes beyond individual care, including medical research and health-related surveillance, is today recognised by statutory provisions that permit the duty of confidence to be set aside. This body of law, which is detailed below, allows confidential patient information to flow from general practitioners (GPs), hospital doctors, and other healthcare professionals to national bodies otherwise equipped to monitor and respond to public health risks.

Recent years have revealed, however, the increasing significance and use that may be attached to health data for secondary purposes beyond medical research and health-related surveillance. Advances in information processing, the underlying technological capacity to transfer and analyse big data sets, and the changing – increasingly national (rather than local) level – data flows associated with a modern health care service, are creating new opportunities to use confidential patient information to achieve other kinds of public benefit and undertake other kinds of surveillance activity. The previous use by the Home Office of data obtained and generated through the provision of health care to identify immigration offenders is a case in point. This 'growth area' raises several legal dilemmas, as the use of confidential patient data for surveillance unrelated to medical purpose is not systematically subject to the same procedural safeguards as is the case in relation to use of data for medical purposes. The processes and principles that for nearly 20 years have been associated with the use of health data for secondary medical purposes, including surveillance, are not routinely applied in the case of surveillance for non-health-related purposes. This contrast in legal regimes is detailed below.

Health Surveillance Using Health Data

The powers to share health data for surveillance programmes are extensive and operate within a legal framework that can authorise disclosure without individual patient consent when that is in the public interest. Further, such power to disclose data operates through in-built procedural safeguards that require decisions to be determined upon public interest, safeguards which have their roots in parliamentary disquiet over the possibility of unchecked political discretion regarding the proper conception of public interest to apply in this context. For nearly 20 years, those safeguards have been interpreted and applied by a body charged with providing independent advice to decision-makers.

The foundation of this approach is S. 251 of the National Health Service Act 2006 (re-enacting S. 60 of the Health and Social Care Act 2001), which makes provision for the Secretary of State to lay Regulations establishing a lawful basis for the disclosure of confidential health information for medical purposes. These Regulations can make provision for the common law duty of confidence to be set aside and provide a lawful basis for the disclosure of confidential patient information where none might otherwise exist. Such provisions can be made for a range of purposes, including for surveillance purposes. In fact, it was a perceived risk to the continued viability of cancer registries in England and Wales that motivated, at least in part, the introduction of the Regulations. When debating them, Lord Hunt of Kings Heath quoted correspondence received from Sir Richard Doll and Sir Richard Peto of the Clinical Trials Service:

> It is, we believe, important for the future health of the people in this country that a legislative framework should exist that ensures that public health surveillance and medical research can continue. (625 Parl Deb HL (5th ser.), 2001, cols. 865–866)

The National Health Service Act 2006 itself, as the parent act, describes the parameters of the Regulations that can be made. It does so widely. Medical purposes are broadly defined to mean the purposes of any of:

> (a) preventative medicine, medical diagnosis, medical research, the provision of care and treatment and the management of health and social care services, and

> (b) informing individuals about their physical or mental health or condition, the diagnosis of their condition or their care and treatment. (National Health Service Act 2006, S. 251(12)(a))

The passage of the legislation was accompanied by continued support for a process to facilitate data sharing, but there was disquiet with the proposal that a Whitehall politician should have the ability to set aside the duty of confidence owed by a health professional to a patient for purposes that were not tightly constrained. The fear was that permitted uses might come to undermine the confidentiality of the health service. This was explicitly recognised by Lord Hunt in debates:

> The breadth of the power sought has been the root of concerns expressed in this House. I fully accept that if such a power did not operate with effective safeguards the potential for misuse might well undermine the trust between patients and the NHS. (625 Parl Deb HL (5th ser.), 2001, col. 866)

The same fear was expressed more forcefully by Earl Howe:

> The mere existence of this power, not to mention the exercise of it, will start the rot. Once doctors and nurses have ceased to be the guardians of the most private information that any of us possess, and once that guardianship has been transferred to a politician in Whitehall, you no longer have a system that will command public trust. That is a process that we should not even countenance. (625 625 Parl Deb HL (5th ser.), 2001, cols. 858–859)

To appease such concerns,[2] the solution was the establishment of an independent body, of broad-based membership, to advise on the purposes for which it was appropriate that any Regulations make provision.[3] As Baroness Northover said when introducing the relevant amendment to the Bill:

> This is simply not an area in which it could ever be appropriate to give such wide powers to the Secretary of State. That is why we propose in the amendment to establish a statutory advisory committee to advise and assist the Secretary of State in this matter ... which does not have to sit muzzled in the background as an earlier incarnation, proposed in the other place, just might have done. It consists of representatives of patients' groups, clinicians, medical researchers, health service researchers and others. (625 Parl Deb HL (5th ser.), 2001, cols. 409–410)

The body was known as the Patient Information Advisory Group (PIAG). The resulting Regulations were known as the Health Service (Control of Patient Information) Regulations 2002.

Subsequently, PIAG became an authoritative voice in the control structure around data sharing law in health, including recommending on the content and scope of Regulations laid under the Parent Act. With the benefit of PIAG's advice, under Reg. 3 (1), provision was made for the processing of confidential patient information for the surveillance of communicable diseases and other risks to public health:

(a) diagnosing communicable diseases and other risks to public health;
(b) recognising trends in such diseases and risks;
(c) controlling and preventing the spread of such diseases and risks;
(d) monitoring and managing –
    (i) outbreaks of communicable disease;
    (ii) incidents of exposure to communicable disease;
    (iii) the delivery, efficacy, and safety of immunisation programmes;
    (iv) adverse reactions to vaccines and medicines;
    (v) risks of infection acquired from food or the environment (including water supplies);
    (vi) the giving of information to persons about the diagnosis of communicable disease and risks of acquiring such disease (Health Service (Control of Patient Information) Regulations 2002, Reg. 3(1)).

The Health Service (Control of Patient Information) Regulations 2002 thus provided a lawful basis for health care professionals to disclose confidential patient information for the purposes of surveilling communicable disease and other risks to public health. The processing of confidential patient information for such purposes can *only* be undertaken by one of a number of specified bodies (specified in Reg. 3(3)). There are additional controls built into permitted data flows by the Regulations.

Additional Requirements

As well as being limited to a specific range of bodies, any processing under Reg. 3 is subject to the more general requirements of Reg. 7. These include that:

(2) No person shall process confidential patient information under these Regulations unless he is a health professional or a person who in the circumstances owes a duty of confidentiality which is equivalent to that which would arise if that person were a health professional. (Health Service (Control of Patient Information) Regulations 2002, Reg. 7(2)[4]

It is important to note that the Regulations permit processing that would otherwise be unlawful but do not usually require bodies to disclose information for this purpose. There is the possibility for the Secretary of State to require the processing of confidential patient information for specified purposes under Reg. 3(4) but, to the authors' knowledge, the only occasion on which 3(4) has been relied on is in response to the Coronavirus. In 2021, the Secretary of State issued a number of notices under Reg. 3(4) requiring organisations to process confidential patient information in the manner set out in the notice for purposes set out in

Reg. 3(1). This is currently time-limited (at the time of writing to 30 September 2021) and when the Coronavirus notices expire all relevant information should be deleted.[5]

The Health Service (Control of Patient Information) Regulations 2002, therefore, establish a specific legal basis for the disclosure of health data for 'public health' surveillance purposes. This sits within a broader legal landscape. There are other longstanding legal requirements associated with the disclosure of confidential patient information for public health and indeed for other surveillance.

Other Statutory Disclosures: Health Protection

Since the nineteenth century, under several pieces of legislation, there has been a statutory responsibility to notify certain authorities where infectious diseases are concerned. A distinguishing feature of these responsibilities is that they are heavily constrained by legislation in terms of the scope in which they can be applied, for example, The Reporting of Injuries, Diseases and Dangerous Occurrences Regulations 2013. They do not represent the same 'breadth of power' that was a cause for concern in relation to the more expansively defined 'medical purposes' in S. 251 of the National Health Service Act 2006.

Perhaps the leading example is the Health Protection (Notification) Regulations 2010 (see also Health Protection (Notification) (Wales) Regulations 2010), which extends the previous responsibility and now adopts an 'all hazards' approach. There is now a responsibility upon a registered medical practitioner (R) to notify the proper officer of a local authority where they have 'reasonable grounds for suspecting' that a patient (P) has (or has died from):

(a) a notifiable disease;
(b) an infection[6] which, in the view of R, presents or could present significant harm to human health; or has (having) been
(c) contaminated[7] in a manner which, in the view of R, presents or could present significant harm to human health. (Health Protection (Notification) Regulations 2010, Reg. 2(1))[8]

A crucial distinction with the powers as typically exercised under the Health Service (Control of Patient Information) Regulations 2002 is that the Health Protection (Notification) Regulations 2010 power is not discretionary. The disclosure power is a requirement. Where a local authority has been so notified that there is a responsibility upon them to disclose the fact and content of that notification to Public Health England, the proper officer in the local authority in which P usually resides, and also the proper officer in the Port Authority or local authority in which P has disembarked (from ship, hovercraft, aircraft, or international train) if known (Health Protection (Notification) Regulations 2010, Reg. 6). Diagnostic laboratories also have a duty to notify Public Health England if they identify any 'causative agent' listed within sch. 2 of the Regulations or evidence of any infection caused by such an agent (Health Protection (Notification) Regulations 2010, Reg. 4).

What is noticeable about these Regulations, besides the clear description of mandatory data flow, is that the Confidential Patient Information disclosed is to be either of a particularly restricted nature (relating to a finite list of notifiable diseases) (Health Protection (Notification) Regulations 2010, sch. 1) or associated with infection or contamination that could present *significant* harm to human health. If a health professional were to disclose information in circumstances where they had no reasonable grounds to consider there to be a risk of *significant* harm, they would not be able to avoid liability for a breach of a duty of confidence.[9] There is no such restriction on the Health Service (Control of Patient Information) Regulations 2002 (Taylor, 2015).

Unlike the Health Service (Control of Patient Information) Regulations 2002, PIAG did not advise on the Health Protection (Notification) Regulations 2010, but the legal framework of the parent legislation, the Public Health (Control of Disease) Act (1984), provided significant constraint on the scope of potential Regulations. Where Regulations can plough only a narrow furrow, as established by parent legislation debated in Parliament, the concerns associated with the opaque exercise of power in furtherance of a particular political or narrow institutional agenda are blunted; at least that is, if the Parliamentary process is doing its job through effective opposition and robust debate of legislative proposals in both Houses. It is where statute appears to offer a subsequent opportunity for the exercise of unconstrained discretion that a check and balance on a conception of the public interest in disclosure is most valuable. It was the concern attached to the broad sweep of 'medical purpose' that was contained in the relevant provisions of the Health and Social Care Act 2001 (re-enacted as National Health Service Act 2006, S. 251) that motivated calls for an independent voice on the appropriate breadth and operation of subsequent Regulations.

To summarise: where health-related data are concerned, in UK law two key control devices have emerged. First, legislation has been drafted in such a way to restrict the circumstances in which data can be shared. On this point, there is variability in the extent to which Parent legislation restricts the permissible scope of Regulations. In particular, the breadth of 'medical purpose' in the National Health Service Act 2006 is more permissive than other legislation. To tackle this broader discretionary power, however, a second control device has been attached to the process: namely the establishment of an independent gatekeeper to patient data and an advisor on regulatory and policy reform. Within the parameters established by the National Health Service Act 2006, the role of the advisory group can be seen to vary according to the specificity of the data flows anticipated by individual Regulations. In particular, there is a significant distinction in the operation of Reg. 3 – which permits processing *only* as described for purposes related to communicable disease such as coronavirus and other risks to public health – and Reg. 5 – which permits processing for a relatively broad range of purposes.[9] It is Reg. 5 that is most open ended in scope. In relation to the former (Reg. 3), the advice of PIAG was sought on the appropriate wording of the Regulation. In relation to the latter, the advisory group was further invited to advise on the interpretation and application (of Reg. 5) on a case-by-case basis.

Surveillance/Research Distinction

The different approach taken towards surveillance (under Reg. 3) and medical research (under Reg. 5) under the Health Service (Control of Patient Information) Regulations 2002 may be explainable by the extent to which it was considered possible, at the point in time that the Regulations were being debated, to evaluate the mix and significance of private and public interests engaged. With Reg. 3, the purpose of the surveillance, the nature of the data needed, and the relative importance of the public interest served by such surveillance when compared with the public interest in a confidential health care service could all be taken into consideration during parliamentary debate even if specific public health risks, such as COVID-19, were unknown at the time. As a result, Parliament felt able to say – *in the light of independent advice* – that so far as communicable diseases and other risks to public health to be disclosed under Reg. 3 were concerned, the public interest in disclosure trumped the public interest in confidentiality. Parliament did not feel in a position to make the same sweeping statement in relation to *all* medical research potentially supportable under Reg. 5. Here it was felt more appropriate to put in place a process to enable ongoing, granular, independent scrutiny, and advice.

Before support was given to an activity in pursuit of a medical purpose under Reg. 5, the opinion of PIAG would be sought. PIAG was disbanded in 2008 but at that time the Ethics and Confidentiality Committee (ECC) of the National Information Governance Board took over this advisory function (Health and Social Care Act 2008, S. 157). When the NIGB was itself abolished in 2013, then the advisory role of the ECC transferred to a newly established Confidentiality Advisory Group (CAG). CAG, as part of the Health Research Authority (HRA), continues to offer advice on the use of Reg. 5. In fact, CAG's role in relation to individual decisions on the use of Reg. 5 was put on a statutory footing for the first time by the Care Act 2014 (sch. 7(8)). At that time, the authority for decisions on medical research (as opposed to other non-research-related medical purposes) was passed from the Secretary of State to the HRA. The Secretary of State retains responsibility for making decisions in relation to non-research-related medical purposes.

There are three reasons to draw attention to the Reg. 5 requirement for the scrutiny of applications for the disclosure of confidential information by an independent body, made up of a broad representation, extending to include significant lay membership. First, to highlight the process that has been put in place in the health research context, where there would otherwise be a broad discretion to set aside the duty of confidence and permit disclosure of confidential information without independent advice. Second, to recognise that the advisory group (currently CAG) follows a regular and systematic practice of transparent advice on individual cases of disclosure where the Regulations are most open ended. All minutes, recording advice and reasoning, are published. (The relevance of this will become clear shortly.) Third, to distinguish the process that would need to be undertaken – and the safeguards associated with that process – if a researcher wanted access to confidential patient information (without explicit patient consent) in order to challenge the validity of claims being made in support of a particular use of data for surveillance purposes.

Non-health Surveillance Using Health Data

Up to this point, the focus of the chapter has been on the use of confidential health data for health-related purposes, including what might be described as health surveillance. We will argue shortly that the legal structure put in place is broadly robust, consistent with the purposes of the legislative scheme, and normatively defensible. By contrast, the use of health data for non-health surveillance purposes is less satisfactory.

The Health and Social Care Act 2012 established NHS Digital (originally known as the Health and Social Care Information Centre). The Health and Social Care Act 2012 also established a new legal framework for the flow of confidential information within England and Wales. Under the 2012 Act, NHS Digital not only has the power to require confidential patient information, and other information, from health and social care bodies but also has power to disclose data for both health and non-health related purposes. Although the Health and Social Care Act 2012 impacted significantly upon the legal basis and operational flow of much NHS Data, one thing it did not change was the importance of the Health Service (Control of Patient Information) Regulations 2002 for those seeking access to confidential patient information for secondary 'medical purposes' (as defined by the National Health Service Act 2006, S. 251) without patient consent. If data are disclosed by NHS Digital on the basis of Reg. 5 of the Health Service (Control of Patient Information) Regulations 2002, whether for medical research or health-related surveillance purposes, then independent advice is injected into the process by operation of the arrangements described above. Further to this, due to a change in legislation introduced by the Care Act 2014, CAG now also has a role advising NHS Digital directly on its data dissemination policy. This is further discussed below and is additional to CAG's involvement in the processes associated with operation of the Health Service (Control of Patient Information) Regulations 2002. As we will see though, the operation of this advisory role in practice is quite different from the role of CAG in relation to the Health Service (Control of Patient Information) Regulations 2002. The governance model does not operationally provide equivalent intensity of independent scrutiny prior to a disclosure for non-health-related surveillance purposes.[10]

NHS Digital has the power to require information where it is considered 'necessary or expedient' (Health and Social Care Act 2012, S. 259(1)(a)) for the purposes of any of its statutory functions. As a public body, NHS Digital may only disseminate or publish information where it has specific power to do so. Its powers are set out in the Health and Social Care Act 2012 (S. 261, 262). This includes a range of circumstances set out in S. 261(5)(e). The power of disclosure under S. 261(5)(e) does not set aside the common law duty of confidence and so, where no other legal basis is available, disclosure must be in the public interest. NHS Digital is, as the non-executive public body responsible for collecting, processing, and disseminating significant volumes of confidential patient information across the NHS, accountable for ensuring those data flows are not only lawful but also consistent with its own data publication and dissemination policy. NHS Digital is responsible for any operational decision on disclosure and thus must determine, in cases where disclosure is only lawful if in the public interest, whether the relevant public interest test is satisfied.

As indicated above, in exercising any function of publishing or otherwise disseminating information, NHS Digital must have regard to any advice given to it by the CAG as the committee appointed by the HRA under sch. 7 Para. 8(1) of the Care Act 2014 to give such advice (Health and Social Care Act 2012, S. 262A (as amended)). However, there is no established process – as there is under the Health Service (Control of Patient Information) Regulations 2002 – for NHS Digital to routinely seek advice in relation to dissemination for specific purposes, and this includes in relation to dissemination for non-health-related surveillance. There is facility for issues to be raised unilaterally by the CAG but, in order to do so, it is necessary for the CAG to be aware that there is an issue to raise (Health Research Authority, 2018). In other words, therefore, issues can be raised with the CAG for advice at the discretion of NHS Digital but there is no *requirement* to do so; and even though the CAG can raise an issue with NHS Digital, it is possible it will not do so due to its lack of prior notification.

There are a number of non-health disclosures that have been made by NHS Digital since its establishment. By way of illustration, this chapter considers disclosures made under a now withdrawn MoU with the Home Office. Consideration of this example demonstrates the variability in oversight and independent advice that accompanies disclosure for different purposes. In relation to secondary *medical* purposes, discretion is exercised following *prior* independent advice on the public interest in *permitting* health professionals to disclose, for example, health research (e.g., Health Service (Control of Patient Information) Regulations 2002, Reg. 5) or communicable disease surveillance (e.g., Health Service (Control of Patient Information) Regulations 2002, Reg. 3). In relation to *non-health*-related purposes (e.g., served by disclosure under Health and Social Care Act 2012, S. 261(5)(e)) discretion may be exercised with *no independent advice*[11] or equivalent consultation on the public interests and yet health professionals may be *required* to provide the information that is disclosed. It also demonstrates the imbalance in regulatory burden felt by those who would use patient data for non-health-related surveillance and those who would access the same data for research purposes (including, potentially, research that might challenge the health impacts of the surveillance).

Disclosure to Home Office Under MOU

NHS Digital entered into a MoU for the purpose of processing information requests from the Home Office to NHS Digital to (re)establish contact between the Home Office and immigrants. This included tracing those suspected of immigration offences and where re-contact would enable their removal from the UK. The MoU was published late in 2016 and came into effect on 1 January 2017, although the practice of providing information to the Home Office had been undertaken before that (House of Commons, Health and Social Care Committee, 2018a, pp. 3–4).

The data requested by the Home Office were limited to demographic/administrative details covering name (or change of name), date of birth, gender, address, and the date of NHS registration. It did not include any clinical information or information relating to the health, care, or treatment of the individual (Gordon, 2017), but NHS Digital processes still, appropriately in our view (although more on this later), treated the information as confidential (House of Commons, Health and Social Care Committee, 2018a).[12] NHS Digital is empowered to disclose confidential information under S. 261(5)(e) where

> [...] the disclosure is made in connection with the investigation of a criminal offence (whether or not in the United Kingdom). (Health and Social Care Act 2012, S. 261(5)(e))

In a letter from Noel Gordon (2017), Chair of NHS Digital, to Dr Sarah Wollaston, Chair of the Health and Social Care Committee, NHS Digital asserted that it was the understanding of NHS Digital that:

> The s261 gateways do not constrain [NHS Digital] to considering only serious offences or harm to the person.

Thus, although NHS Digital acknowledged that where information is confidential and is to be disclosed under S. 261(5)(e), the duty of confidence in such information must still be considered, it suggested a lower threshold may be applied than for other uses of health data. Here, the distinction with the 2010 Regulations (see also Health Protection (Notification) (Wales) Regulations 2010) discussed above is telling, where it is only where there are grounds to consider there to be a risk of *serious* harm that disclosure is required.

According to the letter to the Health and Social Care Committee, the policy of NHS Digital (at the time) was that prior to exercising the power to disclose confidential information under S. 261(5)(e), NHS Digital carried out an assessment which 'weighed the public interest in favour and/or against a disclosure' (Gordon, 2017) in order to avoid an unjustifiable breach of confidence. It was asserted by NHS Digital that 'a public interest test is carried out in each individual case' (Gordon, 2017). The process by which such a test was carried out appears, however, to have been an entirely internal assessment, opaque, and without the benefit of external or independent advice. This individual case consideration was also apparently carried out in the context of not inconsiderable numbers. The Health and Social Care Committee report on the policy noted that there were 10,275 requests for disclosure across the period 2014–2016 (House of Commons, Health and Social Care Committee, 2018a, p. 6).

In terms of retaining the integrity of the overall legal approach towards handling patient data there are several problematic features to this policy. Fundamentally, our concern is with the systemic failure it demonstrates to require equivalent checks and balances on the operative conception of public interest. The lack of independent contribution to an understanding of how the public interest test might operate was strongly criticised by the Health and Social Care Committee (House of Commons, Health and Social Care Committee, 2018a, pp. 9, 18). Following scrutiny by the Health and Social Care Committee, the MoU between NHS Digital and the Home Office was withdrawn (NHS Digital, 2018c).[13] According to NHS Digital's (2018b) website:

> The Home Office can still request non-medical information to locate an individual where this is in the interests of safeguarding an individual and necessary to protect a person's welfare. Any

such request would be considered by NHS Digital's Welfare Assessment Panel. As at 31 March 2021, NHS Digital has not released any information to the Home Office on these grounds since the MOU was suspended in May 2018.

On the face of it, this may seem to be a success story. An unduly one-sided interpretation of 'public interest' was course-corrected following parliamentary scrutiny. However, our argument is that the need for the *ex post facto* adjustment of the conditions under which the public interest test was understood to be met illustrates the weakness of the process. It is a weakness that persists for so long as decisions on disclosure for non-health surveillance can be made without robust, open, and independent, scrutiny prior to a decision on disclosure being made. The situation is illustrative of the varying intensity of independent challenges to a conception of public interest across the context of health- and non-health-related surveillance due to systemic inconsistencies in review processes across the two contexts.

PROTECTING THE SOCIAL LEGITIMACY OF HEALTH DATA SHARING THROUGH INSTITUTIONAL DESIGN

The example of the MoU and the discussion around health research and surveillance illustrates the potential for the sharing of health data to be managed through very different processes and according to the application of variable, and unevenly applied, law and principle. Of particular concern, is that this example illustrates that in relation to *non-health* surveillance, there is the potential for wide-ranging and discretionary release of confidential information on the basis of an internal assessment of 'public interest' without independent input or review; at least, not prior to a disclosure decision. There is, of course, the possibility of recourse to the courts after sharing, and we consider this further below.

One way to defend a more 'relaxed' policy towards the sharing of health data for the purposes of non-health-related surveillance might be to argue that the data that are being shared, such as basic demographic information about the individual, are not health data for the purposes of the law – and hence not covered by the duty of confidence. To be clear, NHS Digital did state in their evidence to the Health and Social Care Committee that it treated the demographic information as confidential (Gordon, 2017). Nevertheless, at the same time, there is a suggestion in the published material that NHS Digital were of the view that they did not *need* to treat the information as confidential. In a letter to Dr Sarah Wollaston (Chair of the Health and Social Care Committee) the Chair of NHS Digital, Noel Gordon (2017), remarked that:

> It should be noted that the [NHS Digital] treats the administrative information as subject to the duty of confidentiality, notwithstanding that [the Department of Health] considers that such purely demographic/administrative information does not attract the duty of confidence.

Can Demographic Information Be Subject to a Duty of Confidence?

There is good reason to consider demographic/administrative information obtained or generated through the delivery of health care to be covered by the duty of confidence. In *R (W)* v. *Sec'y of State for Health* (2016), the Court of Appeal found even data that 'falls at the least intrusive end of the spectrum of medical information' may be 'private' (p. 707 [27]). When deciding whether privacy rights are engaged it is necessary to have regard to the 'reasonable expectations' of the subject of the data in question (*Campbell* v. *MGN Ltd.*, 2004). In *R (W)* v. *Sec'y of State for Health* (2016), the Court noted the tendency in all authoritative guidance published to

> [...] articulate the same approach to the issue of confidentiality: all identifiable patient data held by a doctor or a hospital must be treated as confidential. The documents have been drafted in expansive terms so as to reflect the reasonable expectations of patients that all of their data will be treated as private and confidential. These publicly available documents inform the expectations of patients being treated in the NHS. (p. 710 [39])

This is consistent with other developments in law which support taking *all* factors into account as part of a broader contextual consideration of whether a reasonable expectation of privacy attaches to the use and disclosure of information in all the circumstances. This points against taking any single factor as determinative, including whether data are purely demographic, even if – such as an individual's name – it is already in the public domain. As Lord Nicholls put it in *OBG Ltd.* v. *Allan* (2008):

> As the law has developed breach of confidence, or misuse of confidential information, now covers two distinct causes of action, protecting two different interests: privacy, and secret ("confidential") information .... In some instances information may be in the public domain, and not qualify for protection as confidential, and yet qualify for protection on the grounds of privacy. (p. 72 [255])

Where the courts find that an individual has a reasonable expectation of privacy, taking *all* circumstances into account – including expectations attached specifically to the health care context, then duties will follow even if the information is entirely demographic or administrative and has no clinical detail attached. This may be considered necessary if public trust in the confidentiality of the information provided to a health service is to be protected.

Legislative Purpose and (Social) Legitimacy

If the above argument is correct, then the disclosure of demographic data needs to be considered through the same legal regimes that deal with other categories of health data. On the detail of those legal regimes, evidently Parliament possesses the legal authority to enable discretionary disclosure for the purposes it sees fit. Even so, both a legal and a normative claim can be made about the principles of law that should underpin the design of the processes that manage the control of the sharing of health data. First, processes that manage health data should continue to respect the concerns that motivated Parliamentary debate of S. 251 of the National Health Service Act 2006 (originally enacted as S. 60 of the Health and Social Care Act 2001) and the subsequent Health Service (Control of Patient Information) Regulations 2002. This means that where there is a broad discretion to disclose for purposes beyond individual care, it is necessary to design institutions for health data sharing that will protect public confidence in a confidential healthcare system. In relation to the processes attached to Regulations laid under S. 251, it was accepted that there needs to be a check on the conception of public interest employed to ensure that it does not slip the moorings of public trust. Whilst the Health and Social Care Act 2012 has established new reasons, and powers through which, to share health data, it does not adjust the importance of preserving public trust as an underpinning purpose of this area of law. If anything, it reiterates that purpose, with NHS Digital being placed under a duty, under S. 253(1) (ca) of the Health and Social Care Act 2012, to have regard to 'the need to respect and promote the privacy of recipients of health services'.

Additionally, there is a deeper normative claim to be made in favour of incorporating a strong public interest element into the legal system where individual rights and collective interests overlap, as they clearly do with health data. This concerns the importance of promoting and protecting the social legitimacy of a process that permits confidential patient information to be used for purposes beyond individual care. As Curtin and Meijer (2006) remark, legitimacy, as a concept, has been variously defined and described:

> First of all purely formal (legal) legitimacy in the sense of the manner in which a particular structure of authority was constituted and acts according to accepted legal rules and procedures. Although many political scientists and lawyers focus on formal legitimacy, some stress the primordial importance of what is termed social (empirical) legitimacy. Social legitimacy refers to the affective loyalty of those who are bound by it, on the basis of deep common interest and/or strong sense of shared identity. (p. 112)

Here it is the latter sense of legitimacy that is considered: social (empirical) legitimacy. We are associating the concept of social legitimacy with 'the capacity of the system to engender and maintain the belief that the existing political institutions are the most appropriate ones for the society' (Lipset, 1981). This approach mirrors thicker accounts of procedural fairness which strive not only to secure in decision-making processes what is formally necessary for lawful public authority, but additionally integrate within them either effective opportunities for participation (Mashaw, 1985) or safeguards which protect the regulated communities involved (Rosanvallon, 2011).

Ultimately, what drives shifts and re-designs to a decision-making process is the need to maintain qualities 'that provide arguments for the acceptability of its decisions' (Mashaw, 1983, p. 24; see also Taylor & Whitton, 2020). This may be a political decision but it is not just the backdrop to the Health Service (Control of Patient Information) Regulations 2002 that suggests that the social legitimacy of the public use of health data should not be taken for granted. In her foreword to the 2016 *Review of Data Security, Consent and Opt-outs* Dame Fiona Caldicott, National Data Guardian for Health and Social Care (2016), remarked that:

> People should be assured that those involved in their care, and in running and improving services, are using such information appropriately and only when absolutely necessary. Unfortunately, trust in the use of personal confidential data has been eroded and steps need to be taken to demonstrated trustworthiness and ensure that the public can have confidence in the system. (p. 2)

This statement was made even before the media reports were released of NHS patient data being handed to the Home Office in an 'immigration crackdown'

(Forster, 2017). The central contention of this chapter is that institutional design of a process that incorporates transparent and open debate of the relative merits of disclosure for surveillance purposes *prior* to a decision being taken is better suited to form a conception of public interest that will meet the demands of social legitimacy. It will promote the principle that data are only released under conditions where this is *acceptable* to those whose data are being used.[14] This is less likely to be achieved through reliance upon the courts to intervene after the fact.

THE LAW AND JUDICIAL CONTROL

One response to demands for social legitimacy and securing the integrity of patient data might be to argue that the strength of the law that surrounds administrative discretion in this area is sufficient to prevent abuse. Indeed, the grounds of administrative law (e.g., *Council of Civil Serv. Unions* v. *Minister for the Civil Serv.*, 1985) have gradually evolved over the years to the point where it is widely accepted that a series of good administration standards are expected of decision-makers, albeit the exact parameters of those standards are a matter of some contention and highly context-specific in application. However, on a number of levels, the saga of the MoU and NHS Digital's subsequent decision making cautions against assuming that by themselves legal safeguards are, or could be, sufficient.

Room for Conflicting Legislative Purposes to Broaden the Use of Disclosure Powers

A first shortfall in the protective value of judicial review is that the lack of specificity within legislation that confers discretionary power can, without further checks and balances, reduce the scope for judicial scrutiny of administrative decision making. To address this problem, a basic test of administrative power is that even if a body possesses a broad power, it needs to be conducted in accordance with the purposes of legislation (*Roberts* v. *Hopwood*, 1925). On this point, the Health and Social Care Act 2012 (S. 261(5)) clearly envisages that NHS Digital has the power to release information for non-health purposes in the following circumstances:

(a) the information has previously been lawfully disclosed to the public,

(b) the disclosure is made in accordance with any court order,

(c) the disclosure is necessary or expedient for the purposes of protecting the welfare of any individual,

(d) the disclosure is made to any person in circumstances where it is necessary or expedient for the person to have the information for the purpose of exercising functions of that person conferred under or by virtue of any provision of this or any other Act,

(e) the disclosure is made in connection with the investigation of a criminal offence (whether or not in the United Kingdom), or

(f) the disclosure is made for the purpose of criminal proceedings (whether or not in the United Kingdom).

Even where the legislator provides a purpose for discretionary action, however, in a context where strong individual interests are impacted, that power is constrained by a further limiting principle of administrative law, that of 'legality'.

> Fundamental rights cannot be overridden by general or ambiguous words. This is because there is too great a risk that the full implications of their unqualified meaning may have passed unnoticed in the democratic process. In the absence of express language or necessary implication to the contrary, the courts therefore presume that even the most general words were intended to be subject to the basic rights of the individual. (*R* v. *Sec'y of State for the Home Dep't, Ex parte Simms*, 2000, p. 131)

The test of legality has become an increasingly powerful tool within the judicial armoury when interpreting the scope of primary legislation and case law has confirmed that this obligation for clarity in legislation for rights-infringing powers goes beyond those rights that are squarely captured by Convention rights.[15] With regard to S. 261(5), some of the listed circumstances are specific and would appear to meet the test of legality but it is at the very least arguable that, in their specificity, none of these criteria unambiguously sanction a *general* policy of releasing a whole class of data, as opposed to specifically individualised data requests as might be necessary, for instance, to pursue criminal proceedings. The closest we get to a general power to disclose patient data is contained in S. 261(5)(d), but this section appears to possess all the ambiguity of open discretion that the 'legality' test is designed to block.

The argument of legality, therefore, is a powerful weapon against an unchecked general discretionary power to share patient data. Our concern, however, is that there is sufficient specificity to allow for a certain degree of discretionary disclosure in individual cases in circumstances where the legislation is otherwise silent on any subsidiary checks that might be used to control or limit that discretion's operation.

Limits to the Ability to Scrutinise the Merits of Individual Decisions

A second shortfall with relying upon legal rectification of errors in the disclosure of information is that the room for the courts to scrutinise individual decisions is narrow. Through the common law, when considering whether a public body was justified in introducing a policy, such as a policy of surveillance, the courts may be invited to consider the quality of the reasoning or evidence underlying or supporting the decision:

> Courts, under judicial review, rather than appeal, will not normally interfere with a public authority's assessment of the evidence or facts of a case. However, interference has been permitted where the decision is unsupported by substantial evidence, sometimes called a perverse decision. Recently the courts have been prepared also to intervene where there has been a misdirection, disregard or mistake of a material fact. (Jowell, 2015, pp. 51–52)

Nevertheless, albeit a limited form of rationality review of the substance of decisions may be available, where the duties owed towards affected individuals are left undetailed in legislation the intensity of review will be light. Further, even if the process by which such standards is made is left underdeveloped, the common law only partially fills the void. Ideally, if an *individual* is to be deprived of a benefit, such as control over their personal data, then as well as notice of the decision they should have opportunity to make representation and have individualised reasons provided. The 2012 Act, though, does not require NHS Digital to notify individuals that their health data have been shared or to provide reasons for the sharing of information. Plausibly, the strength of interest involved might establish a ground for arguing that common law procedural fairness requires some input of individuals before decisions are made (*McInnes* v. *Onslow-Fane*, 1978), or that reasons should be provided (*R* v. *Sec'y of State for the Home Dep't, Ex parte Doody*, 1994). Along these lines, one of us has previously argued that a respect for human rights will require an organisation to *consult* prior to adopting a policy that impacts negatively upon an individual's fundamental rights and freedoms (Grace & Taylor, 2013). This may be as close as a court would be willing to get to requiring the kind of input into a decision-making process that has taken place in the context of health surveillance and in the exercise of discretion in relation to health research. It is also highly likely that the intensity of the scrutiny of the substance of the decision would be restricted by the deferential nature of the *Wednesbury* reasonableness test, particularly where a powerful competing public interest, such as security, can be appealed to.

Stronger tests through which to challenge individual decisions are available under the Human Rights Act 1998. Under the Human Rights Act 1998 decisions must be compatible with Convention rights and tested against a more intensive test of proportionality review. The most obvious human right that surveillance will engage is the right to respect for a private and family life. The Human Rights Act 1998 makes it unlawful for a public authority to act in a way that is incompatible with the right to respect for private and family life, home and correspondence, protected by art. 8 of the Convention for the Protection of Human Rights and Fundamental Freedoms (European Convention on Human Rights, or ECHR). Under Art. 8(2):

> There shall be no interference by a public authority with the exercise of this right except such as is in accordance with the law and is necessary in a democratic society in the interests of national security, public safety or the economic well being of the country, for the prevention of disorder or crime, for the protection of health and morals, or for the protection of the rights and freedoms of others. (Convention for the Protection of Human Rights and Fundamental Freedoms, 1950)

Disclosure of confidential patient information, for the surveillance purposes, will constitute a prima facie interference with Article 8 unless disclosure was authorised by the patient. The Human Rights Act 1998 does then provide an action by which the *necessity* of an interference, even if in pursuit of a legitimate aim, may be challenged.

In the case of *de Freitas* v. *Permanent Sec'y of Ministry of Agric., Fisheries, Lands and Hous.* (1999), the Privy Council considered the meaning of the phrase 'reasonably necessary' and adopted a three-stage test:

> whether: (i) the legislative objective is sufficiently important to justify limiting a fundamental right; (ii) the measures designed to meet the legislative objective are rationally connected to it; and (iii) the means used to impair the right or freedom are no more than is necessary to accomplish the objective. (p. 80, citing *Nyambirai* v. *Nat'l Soc. Sec. Auth.*, 1996, p. 75)

This test has been subsequently adopted by British Courts when determining if an interference with a convention right is necessary, with recognition that analysis of these three elements introduces questions of proportionality (*Huang* v. *Sec'y of State for the Home Dep't*, 2007; *R (Daly)* v. *Sec'y of State for the Home Dep't*, 2001, p. 547). It is through the concept of necessity, and the associated concept of proportionality, that the courts could subject a policy of surveillance to – what might approach –merit based review:[16] determining whether the objective of the surveillance was 'sufficiently important', whether surveillance was a rational approach to achieving the objective, and whether the interference that the surveillance represents is necessary (read 'proportionate') to achievement of that objective.

Although there is the possibility, through the concept of proportionality, for a closer review of the merits of a decision than would ordinarily be associated with judicial review, there is still classically, a 'margin of appreciation' afforded national authorities when it comes to reasonable disagreement regarding what is understood be 'necessary' (*Handyside* v. *U.K.*, 1976, p. 754). A domestic equivalent, affording the executive a margin of appreciation relative to the court's own assessment, must be understood to operate at least consistently with respect for the separation of powers.[17]

Judicial Review Is a Retrospective Solution Only

A third risk with relying upon judicial oversight is that judicial review is a remedy of last resort. Certainly, judicial review is a potentially powerful process, and the latent prospect of judicial review should discourage arbitrary decision making and encourage a public body to ensure a decision-making process will bring relevant issues into consideration. But, there is now a wealth of literature that demonstrates that it operates very much as a reserve remedial route and is informally set up to filter out many more cases than it filters in (Bondy & Sunkin, 2009). It is, in other words, a process that can provide some assurance as to the quality of decision making in NHS Digital but only an intermittent assurance check, and arguably a disproportionately legal form of assurance at that. For most decision-making processes alternative safeguards are often better equipped either to provide efficient redress or in preventing administrative error before it occurs. More importantly, judicial review is a process that need not promote the social legitimacy discussed earlier, nor challenge the *relative* value attached to the interests of a confidential health care system and identification of immigration offenders.

THE WAY FORWARD: EXPANDING THE REMIT OF THE INDEPENDENT ADVISORY BOARD

The context of state sponsored surveillance of data collected by the health service for the purposes of supporting immigration policy is one that well-illustrates the risks of non-health-related use of health data. This policy demonstrates an embedded inconsistency in the manner in which health data are currently being managed, which in turn risks undermining the integrity of the system and user confidence in the health sector.

The above section has argued that there are grounds upon which the legality of the use of health data for non-health-related surveillance may be challenged. However, neither the prospect of challenge for unjustified interference with human rights, nor judicial review, are likely to provide the long-term fix to the risks that the former use of the MoU gave rise to. A further solution might be for Regulations to be introduced, or better still the Health and Social Care Act 2012 to be amended, to stipulate more detailed restrictions on the sharing of health data by NHS Digital for non-health-related purposes. Within such legislation, the process of balancing competing interests could be made transparent and consultative, and the relevant factors upon which such balancing exercises are based (such as seriousness of offences for which data are sought) could be outlined.

However, although more guidance on the relevant factors for developing policies on disclosure would be a step forward in terms of clarifying the legal authority of NHS Digital and the lawfulness of such administrative practices as the MoU, it would not address many of our wider concerns. Judicial review would continue to operate as a safeguard, but almost certainly an insufficient one which could only intermittently introduce into the decision-making process the kinds of challenge, independent advice, or transparency that can be offered by the processes associated with a specialised independent advisory body, such as CAG or the National Data Guardian (Health and Social Care (National Data Guardian) Act 2018). To provide this ongoing scrutiny there needs to be an additional process put in place prior to a decision on release of data, either on a case-by-case basis (e.g., Health Service (Control of Patient Information) Regulations 2002, Reg. 5) or before new policies are struck.

The institutional solution of an independent advisory body, or watchdog, is one that has been adopted across governance in circumstances where, for a variety of reasons, an element of independence is seen as necessary to ensure that the decision-making process retains loyalty to the full set of values underpinning the scheme (Vibert, 2007). Independence is promoted as a safeguard needed to establish trust in the use of public power by facilitating a process through which certain exercises of public power can be either blocked or 'fire-alarms' raised as to potentially arbitrary or otherwise undesirable decision making (McCubbins & Schwartz, 1984). Reasons for the advisory body solution might also include the lack of time, knowledge, skill, and possibly inclination of other options (in particular, the courts or Parliament) for performing a monitoring role.

Taking all this together, in the context of considering whether a request for surveillance is justified *prior* to a decision being made, extending the requirement for independent review prior to disclosure would have five clear advantages to relying upon judicial oversight alone:

1. *Method*: A body offering independent advice on public interest prior to a decision being taken can adopt an inquisitorial approach and reflect the results of broad consultation within its advice. It can request evidence on relative effectiveness prior to implementation or alongside implementation as part of

an evaluation of implementation. A court is more constrained by the adversarial nature of the judicial process and the limited range of opportunities it has to instigate independent investigation, revisit a position over time, or request evidence of impact be gathered after its decision.

2. *Skill-set:* Independent advice can draw on a range of relevant expertise to the function on hand, including but not exclusively so, legal expertise. Such input is unlikely to be incorporated into standard judicial review proceedings.

3. *Operability:* A claim for unlawful interference with an individual's interests or rights is subject to an individual's disposable resource (in terms of both time and money) and motivation. An independent body established for the purpose and part of an established process is subject to no such constraint. Independent bodies can also operate in circumstances where the affected individuals may not be well aware of their loss of rights.

4. *Timeliness:* Judicial determination can only follow sometime after a decision has been made – and a policy has been implemented. The harm to public trust and confidence may already be done. Advisory bodies can operate more flexibly both before and after decisions are made.

5. *Challenging:* Those invited to provide independent advice, as opposed to making a decision, on the merits of an issue need not worry – in the same way that a court might – about inappropriately overstepping the separation of powers. Its accountability function is as much one of providing transparency and moral suasion, as it is determining outcomes. Advisory bodies can also operate as 'disrupters', challenging institutional biases.

Many of these advantages are also possessed by Parliamentary select committees but, as in the case of the MoU discussed in this chapter, Parliament is a powerful but generally reactive and randomly triggered safeguard. Parliament can work well for crisis moments in administrative malpractice but is less likely to be effective, or as prompt, as a regular monitor of administrative policy making (Flinders, 2008, pp. 184–189).

CONCLUSION

Decisions taken by those with the authority to interfere with fundamental rights and freedoms *ought* to be based on evidence. For this reason, one might expect a policy of surveillance which interferes with the fundamental right to a private life, to require credible justification and an evidence base. It should also be one that is clearly detailed in law and not left to the vagaries of administrative discretion. If a state surveils those it governs and claims the interference to be in the public interest, then the evidence base on which that claim stands should be subject to critical examination.

This volume explores many aspects of the rapidly changing and evolving surveillance landscape. This chapter has considered just one aspect of this: the regulatory framework relevant to public policy decisions on surveillance, the efficacy of which may be informed by health research in England and Wales. The chapter has addressed just two questions in this context: (1) Is any inconsistency in regulatory burden associated with access to confidential patient information for non-health-related surveillance purposes and access for health-related surveillance purposes justified? (2) Is any inconsistency in regulatory burden associated with surveillance and the research necessary to inform, or challenge, that policy of surveillance consistent with the promotion of evidence-based decision making?

The suggestion is that the regulatory framework is deficient in this regard: there is an uneven playing field occupied by those seeking access to data for health- or non-health-related surveillance purposes and also policymakers and researchers when it comes to accessing the data needed to evaluate the efficacy of public policy. Unless we are able to independently interrogate the quality of the data on which public policy decisions on surveillance are based, we cannot challenge any justification for a surveillance policy. Further, a failure to allow researchers access to the data under the same conditions as policymakers is a failure to promote evidence-based decisions, as the decision-makers are not readily challenged.

Clinicians see themselves as gatekeepers, fiercely protective of the sensitive data entrusted to them. Without a patient's explicit consent there will be only a very limited range of circumstances under which health professionals will disclose confidential health information for purposes beyond individual care. Health researchers have long complained of the difficulties they face in obtaining confidential health information for research purposes. Besides the legal constraints, there are systems of approval and a culture of caution to be navigated. Where pursuit of statutory purposes involves surveillance of health data, the process by which such data can be lawfully accessed is different from those processes that health researchers must navigate. This results in a different regulatory burden. This is not consistent with promotion of social legitimacy and public trust in a confidential healthcare service.

If society is to be able to challenge the quality of a decision to surveil the population, then there must be independent research access to the data underpinning a decision to surveil. Such access should bear an equivalent regulatory burden to the access for surveillance purposes. Otherwise, we introduce systemic obstruction to access the data necessary to hold government action to account. Put simply, it should not be easier to get the data for surveillance purposes than to get the data to carry out research on the impacts of such surveillance.

NOTES

1. The Home Office is one of the largest government departments in the UK, with a wide range of security-related responsibilities, including border control, immigration, citizenship, policing, prisons, law and order, and tackling terrorism.

2. It should be recognised that the suggestion of a statutory committee did not in fact satisfy Earl Howe, who thought the risk to public confidence by the breadth of the power insufficiently contained. It was enough, however, to enable the Bill to make progress through both Houses.

3. The responsibility to consult the Patient Information Advisory Group (PIAG) was originally contained in S. 61 of the Health and Social Care Act 2001. The responsibility to consult its successor body, the Ethics and Confidentiality Committee (ECC) (as part of the National Information Governance Board (NIGB)) was under S. 252 of the National

Health Service Act 2006 prior to amendment. When the NIGB was abolished, the relevant body to consult became the Care Quality Commission (see Health and Social Care Act 2012, S. 280(5)).

4. For the purposes of Health Service (Control of Patient Information) Regulations 2002, art. 7 ¶ 2, 'health professional' has the same meaning as in S. 69(1) of the Data Protection Act 1998.

5. Coronavirus (COVID-19): Notification to organisation to share information. Department of Health and Social Care. (Last updated 10 February 2021.)

6. Any reference to infection or contamination is 'a reference to infection or contamination which presents or could present significant harm to human health' (Public Health (Control of Disease) Act 1984, S. 45A(2)).

7. Contamination includes radiation (Public Health (Control of Disease) Act 1984, S. 45A(2).

8. The duty in relation to the living is contained within art. 2 (Health Protection (Notification) Regulations 2010). The duty in relation to the dead is within art. 3 (Health Protection (Notification) Regulations 2010)).

9. Subject to art. 7, confidential patient information may be processed for medical purposes in the circumstances set out in the Schedule to these Regulations provided that the processing has been approved –

(a) in the case of medical research, by both the Secretary of State and a research ethics committee, and

(b) in any other case, by the Secretary of State.

10. NHS Digital has an internal committee, established for the purpose of independent advice, known as the committee on Independent Group Advising on the Release of Data (IGARD) (NHS Digital, 2018a). There is no mention in the minutes of IGARD of any request to comment on dissemination in relation to the Home Office for immigration offender tracing. A matter commented upon by the Health and Social Care Committee: 'We also find it disturbing that the matter has not been considered by NHS Digital's own Independent Group Advising on the Release of Data (IGARD)' (House of Commons, Health and Social Care Committee, 2018, p. 23). For NHS Digital's explanation on non-consultation with IGARD, see Health and Social Care Committee (2018, Q116–Q118).

11. NHS Digital hosts an independent advisory board, known as IGARD (Independent Group Advising (NHS Digital) on the Release of Data), but the Health Select Committee found that data sharing with the Home Office under the MoU had not been considered by IGARD. A fact that the Chair of the Committee described as 'disturbing'. House of Commons, Health and Social Care Committee (2018c, January 29).

12. Note that the continued operation of the duty of confidence led the National Data Guardian to comment that NHS Digital may have drawn too much from the fact that S261(5)(e) does not constrain disclosure to only serious offence or harm (House of Commons, Health and Social Care Committee, 2018, p. 14).

13. For discussion of announcement see blog post by Understanding Patient Data (2018).

14. On the difference between acceptable and preferable see Taylor and Taylor (2014). On the significance of acceptability to public interest decision making, see Taylor and Whitton (2020). For an interesting discussion of the significance of public engagement to public interest decision making see Sorbie (2020).

15. This test goes beyond the Human Rights Act 1998. See, for example, the use of the test in *R* v. *Hughes* (2013) and *R (UNISON)* v. *Lord Chancellor (Equal. and Human Rights Comm'n) (Nos. 1 and 2)* (2017).

16. For discussion of the extent to which the intensity of such review may vary in difference ways, according to the exigencies of judicial deference and judicial restraint, see Rivers (2006).

17. For more on why assessment of proportionality must respect separation of powers see Rivers (2006).

REFERENCES

625 Parl Deb HL (5th ser.) (2001) (UK).

Bondy, V., & Sunkin, M. (2009). The dynamics of judicial review litigation: The resolution of public law challenges before final hearing. Retrieved from https://publiclawproject.org.uk/resources/the-dynamics-of-judicial-review-litigation/

Campbell v. *MGN Ltd.* (2004) 2 AC 457 (HL) (appeal taken from Eng.).

Care Act 2014, c. 23 (Eng.).

Convention for the Protection of Human Rights and Fundamental Freedoms. (1950, November 4), 213 U.N.T.S. 221.

Coronavirus (COVID-19). (2020 [updated 2021]). Notification to organisation to share information. Department of Health and Social Care. Retrieved from https://www.gov.uk/government/publications/coronavirus-covid-19-notification-of-data-controllers-to-share-information

Council of Civil Serv. Unions v. *Minister for the Civil Serv.* (1985) AC 374 (HL) (appeal taken from Eng.).

Curtin, D., & Meijer, A. J. (2006). Does transparency strengthen legitimacy? A critical analysis of European Union policy documents. *Information Polity, 11*(2), 109–122.

Data Protection Act. (1998), c. 29 (Eng.).

de Freitas v. *Permanent Sec'y of Ministry of Agric., Fisheries, Lands and Hous.* (1999) 1 AC 69 (appeal taken from Eastern Caribbean CA).

Flinders, M. (2008). *Delegated governance and the British state: Walking without order*. Oxford: OUP. doi:10.1093/acprof:oso/9780199271603.001.0001

Forster, K. (2017, January 25). NHS patient data handed to Home Office in immigration crackdown. *The Independent*. Retrieved from https://www.independent.co.uk/

Gordon, N. (2017, March 6). Letter to Sarah Wollaston. Publications: Health and Social Care Committee, UK Parliament. Retrieved from https://www.parliament.uk/globalassets/documents/commons-committees/Health/Correspondence/2016-17/Correspondence-Memorandum-Understanding-NHS-Digital-Home-Office-Department-Health-data-sharing.pdf

Grace, J., & Taylor, M. J. (2013). Disclosure of confidential patient information and the duty to consult: The role of the Health and Social Care Information Centre. *Medical Law Review, 21*(3), 415–447. doi:10.1093/medlaw/fwt013

Handyside v. *U.K., 24 Eur. Ct. H.R. (ser. A)* (1976).

Health and Social Care Act 2001, c. 15 (Eng.).

Health and Social Care Act 2008, c. 14 (Eng.).

The Health Protection (Notification) Regulations 2010, SI 2010/659 (Eng.)

The Health Protection (Notification) (Wales) Regulations 2010 W.S.I. 2010/1546 (W. 144).

The Health Service (Control of Patient Information) Regulations 2002, SI 2002/1438 (Eng.).

Health Research Authority. (2018). CAG advice to NHS Digital. Retrieved from https://www.hra.nhs.uk/about-us/committees-and-services/confidentiality-advisory-group/cag-advice-nhs-digital/

House of Commons, Health and Social Care Committee. (2018a). Memorandum of Understanding on data-sharing between NHS Digital and the Home Office: Fifth report of session 2017–19. Retrieved from https://publications.parliament.uk/

House of Commons, Health and Social Care Committee. (2018b, March 15). Oral evidence: Memorandum of Understanding on data-sharing, HC 677. Retrieved from http://data.parliament.uk/writtenevidence/committeeevidence.svc/evidencedocument/health-and-social-care-committee/memorandum-of-understanding-on-datasharing-between-nhs-digital-and-the-home-office/oral/80609.html

House of Commons, Health and Social Care Committee. (2018c, January 29). Letter from the Chair of the Committee to the Chief Executive of NHS Digital. Retrieved from https://publications.parliament.uk/pa/cm201719/cmselect/cmhealth/677/67709.htm

Huang v. *Sec'y of State for the Home Dep't* (2007) 2 AC 167 (HL) (appeal taken from Eng.).

Human Rights Act. (1998), c. 42 (Eng.).

Jowell, J. (2015). Proportionality and unreasonableness: Neither merger nor takeover. In H. Wilberg & M. Elliott (Eds.), *The scope and intensity of substantive review: Traversing Taggart's rainbow* (pp. 41–60). London: Hart Publishing. doi:10.5040/9781474202701

Lipset, S. M. (1981). *Political man: The social bases of politics.* Baltimore, MD: Johns Hopkins University Press.

Mashaw, J. L. (1983). Bureaucratic justice: Managing social security disability claims. Retrieved from https://www.jstor.org/stable/j.ctt1dt009d

Mashaw, J. L. (1985). *Due process in the administrative state.* New Haven, CT: Yale University Press.

McCubbins, M. D., & Schwartz, T. (1984). Congressional oversight overlooked: Police patrols versus fire alarms. *American Journal of Political Science, 28*(1), 165–179. doi:10.2307/2110792

McInnes v. *Onslow-Fane* (1978) 1 WLR 1520 (ChD).

National Data Guardian for Health and Care. (2016). Review of data security, consent and opt-outs. Retrieved from https://www.gov.uk/government/publications/review-of-data-security-consent-and-opt-outs

National Health Service Act 2006, c. 41 (Eng.).

NHS Digital. (2018a). Independent group advising on the release of data. Retrieved from https://digital.nhs.uk/about-nhs-digital/corporate-information-and-documents/independent-group-advising-on-the-release-of-data

NHS Digital. (2018b). National back office for the personal demographics service. Retrieved from https://digital.nhs.uk/services/national-back-office-for-the-personal-demographics-service#home-office-tracing-service

NHS Digital. (2018c). Memorandum of Understanding (MOU) on processing information requests from the Home Office to NHS Digital to be able to trace immigration offenders. Retrieved from https://www.gov.uk/government/publications/information-requests-from-the-home-office-to-nhs-digital

Nyambirai v. *Nat'l Soc. Sec. Auth.* (1996) 1 LRC 64 (SC) (Zim.).

OBG Ltd. v. *Allan* (2008) 1 AC 1 (HL) (appeal taken from Eng.).

Public Health (Control of Disease) Act 1984, c. 22 (Eng.).

R (Daly) v. *Sec'y of State for the Home Dep't* (2001) 2 AC 532 (HL) (appeal taken from Eng.).

R (UNISON) v. *Lord Chancellor* (Equal. and Human Rights Comm'n) (Nos. 1 and 2) (2017) 3 WLR 409 (SC) (appeal taken from Eng.).

R (W) v. *Sec'y of State for Health* (2016) 1 WLR 698 (CA).

R v. *Hughes* (2013) 1 WLR 2461 (SC) (appeal taken from Eng.).

R v. *Sec'y of State for the Home Dep't*, Ex parte *Doody* (1994) 1 AC 531 (HL) (appeal taken from Eng.).

R v. *Sec'y of State for the Home Dep't*, Ex parte *Simms* (2000) 2 AC 115 (HL) (appeal taken from Eng.).

Redfern, M., Keeling, J. W., & Powell, E. (2001). The Royal Liverpool children's inquiry: Report. Retrieved from https://www.gov.uk/government/publications/the-royal-liverpool-childrens-inquiry-report

The Reporting of Injuries, Diseases and Dangerous Occurrences Regulations (2013), SI 2013/1471 (Eng.).

Rivers J. (2006). Proportionality and variable intensity of review. *Cambridge Law Journal, 65*(1), 174–207. doi:10.1017/S0008197306007082

Roberts v. *Hopwood* (1925) AC 578 (HL) (appeal taken from Eng.).

Rosanvallon, P. (2011). Democratic legitimacy: Impartiality, reflexivity, proximity. Retrieved from https://www.jstor.org/stable/j.ctt7stdc

Sorbie, A. (2020). Sharing confidential health data for research purposes in the UK: Where are the 'publics' in the public interest?. *Evidence & Policy: A Journal of Research, Debate and Practice, 16*(2), 249–265. doi:10.1332/174426419X15578209726839

Taylor, M. J. (2015). Legal bases for disclosing confidential patient information for public health: Distinguishing between health protection and health improvement. *Medical Law Review, 23*(3), 348–374. doi:10.1093/medlaw/fwv018

Taylor, M. J., & Taylor, N. (2014). Health research access to personal confidential data in England and Wales: Assessing any gap in public attitude between preferable and acceptable models of consent. *Life Sciences, Society and Policy, 10*(15), 1–24. doi:10.1186/s40504-014-0015-6

Taylor, M. J., & Whitton, T. (2020). Public interest, health research and data protection law: Establishing a legitimate trade-off between individual control and research access to health data. *Laws, 9*(1), 6. doi:10.3390/laws9010006

Understanding Patient Data. (2018). Changes to the Home Office – NHS Digital Memorandum of
    Understanding. Retrieved from https://understandingpatientdata.org.uk/news/memorandum-
    understanding-changed
Vibert, F. (2007). *The rise of the unelected: Democracy and the new separation of powers*. New York, NY:
    Cambridge University Press. doi:10.1017/CBO9780511491160

CHAPTER 8

PRIVACY AND SECURITY: GERMAN PERSPECTIVES, EUROPEAN TRENDS AND ETHICAL IMPLICATIONS

Hartmut Aden

ABSTRACT

Since the European Union's (EU) Charter of Fundamental Rights became binding in 2009, data protection has attained the status of a fundamental right (Article 8) throughout the EU. This chapter discusses the relevance of data protection in the context of security. It shows that data protection has been of particular relevance in the German context – not only against the backdrop of rapidly evolving information technology, but also of the historical experiences with political regimes collecting information in order to oppress citizens.

Keywords: Germany; security; surveillance; transparency; privacy; social movements

INTRODUCTION – THE RELEVANCE OF PRIVACY IN GERMANY AND IN EUROPE

Over the past few decades, privacy has become an important issue in many countries, evolving in parallel with the rapid development of information technologies

Ethical Issues in Covert, Security and Surveillance Research
Advances in Research Ethics and Integrity, Volume 8, 119–129

ISSN: 2398-6018/doi:10.1108/S2398-601820210000008009

and the internet. This chapter discusses how historically unique and specifically German perspectives on privacy and data protection have shaped the relationship between privacy and security, and how privacy and data protection have gained relevance as fundamental rights and as ethical requirements in Europe. The chapter shows that the European Union's (EU) Charter of Fundamental Rights (CFR) and the recently introduced EU framework for data protection have contributed to the growing importance of data protection in everyday life, as well as for security agencies.

The EU's CFR became binding with the Treaty of Lisbon in 2009. In 2016, the General Data Protection Regulation (GDPR) 2016/679[1] and the Directive (EU) 2016/680[2] on data protection in the area of law enforcement (policing and criminal justice) laid down detailed rules on the implementation of data protection. When the CFR and the GDPR became directly binding, they established a solid legal framework for *privacy* and *data protection* everywhere in Europe. This includes binding rules for companies from outside the EU processing the personal data of individuals who are physically in the EU zone, as long as the processing activities are related to the monitoring of the individuals' behaviour or to the offering of goods or services (Art. 3(2) GDPR).

This chapter takes a trans-disciplinary historical-institutionalist perspective in discussing path dependencies between the misuse of knowledge about citizens by former German regimes, and the importance that many German citizens attribute to privacy in relation to the state's security agencies. These issues are related to the broader question about to what extent specific characteristics of a political system influence the relationship between security, ethics, and privacy.

The chapter uses the terms *data protection* and *privacy* not as synonyms, but rather as complementary aspects of the same right (see Tzanou, 2017, pp. 21–24 on the relationship between these terms). The term *privacy* is laid down in newer fundamental rights catalogues such as the EU's CFR. *Privacy* guarantees that private life is protected against attempts by state agencies and private parties to obtain and retain information related to an individual's private sphere. *Data protection* (guaranteed as a fundamental right by Article 8 CFR) is somewhat more broad. *Data protection* includes self-determination with respect to any information on individuals. Since *privacy* and *data protection* are complementary in relation to each other, courts tend to refer to both of them in conjunction.

GERMAN EXPERIENCES OF SECURITY AGENCIES COLLECTING EXCESSIVE INFORMATION ON CITIZENS

Over the last 90 years, German citizens have been confronted with two political regimes that based and enforced their abuse of power on information collected about their own citizens and, particularly, about their political opponents. The first of these was the *Geheime Staatspolizei* (commonly known as the *Gestapo* – Secret State Police) during the Nazi regime. The second was the *Ministerium für Staatssicherheit* (the '*Stasi*' – Ministry for State Security) in Eastern Germany. It is always a delicate exercise to compare these political regimes – they both oppressed sections of their citizenry, however, they did so for very different reasons and to different extents. With this in mind, in the context of this chapter, it is relevant that both political regimes misused information collected by the *Gestapo* and the *Stasi* for further surveillance purposes. From a security ethics perspective, it is clear that these historical cases demonstrate the risks related to (mass) surveillance by powerful security agencies.

The *Gestapo*, established in 1933, quickly developed into one of the backbones of the Nazi's racist prosecution strategies. At that time, modern technological surveillance, as it is known today in the era of information technology, did not yet exist. The information collected about Jewish citizens, political opponents, and members of other groups targeted by racist prosecution mostly stemmed from denunciation – citizens providing evidence to security agencies for a variety of reasons knowing well that this would lead to prosecution, imprisonment and even murder – and other information provided by citizens (see Gellately, 1992).

The *Stasi* was established in early 1950 soon after the eastern zone of Germany, occupied by the Soviet Union's forces at the end of World War II, became the *German Democratic Republic* (*Deutsche Demokratische Republik*, the DDR) in 1949. Until the end of the DDR regime in 1989, the *Stasi* employed more than 91,000 full time staff and a large number of informants in order to conduct surveillance of the country's 16 million inhabitants, with a particular focus on citizens suspected of being opposed to the DDR regime (see Macrakis, 2008).

Inferring a relationship between the *Gestapo* and the *Staatssicherheit (Stasi)* on one hand, and the specific sensitivity of German citizens towards privacy on the other, seems plausible; however, is difficult to prove based on the available empirical data. More than in most other countries, data collection by public administration and security agencies and more recently also by private companies has triggered powerful social movements in Germany that forced policy-makers to take privacy seriously. For example, a social movement successfully stopped the 1983 census before the German Constitutional Court (see Section 2). In 2008, more than 34,000 citizens signed a constitutional complaint against the retention of telecommunication meta data by security agencies for future criminal investigation – what was a step towards the annulment of the relevant EU Directive by the Court of Justice of the EU a few years later (cf. Aden, 2016, p. 56f.).

It should not be overlooked that, in any society, significant differences in the attitudes towards privacy exist and persist. Some citizens are worried about state agencies and private companies collecting their personal data, while others look at these practices in a more favourable manner. However, in all countries, opposition to excessive data collection by state agencies and private companies goes beyond specific small groups of civil liberties activists.

These issues, resituated to the current state of technology, are pertinent to the currently very high level of information on individuals now accessible to public security agencies as well as some private companies. In the cases of the *Gestapo* and the *Stasi*, this level of information would have made them incalculably more powerful; the abuse of state power would have become even more effective and broad.

With online communication and mobile devices such as smartphones and laptop computers becoming parts of everyday life, state agencies nowadays can easily track current and past movements and communication. The mass-data collection practices of the US *National Security Agency* (NSA), disclosed by whistle-blower Edward Snowden in 2013, and the surveillance system that the Chinese government established in order to supervise the behaviour of Chinese citizens, demonstrate that states are already able and willing to submit their citizens to a regime of mass surveillance and 24/7 monitoring if no solid ethical culture and rule of law framework prevent them from doing so.

DATA PROTECTION AND PRIVACY: THE 1983 GERMAN CENSUS CASE

In the specific German variant of a continental rule-of-law system, the recognition of privacy as a fundamental right means that any kind of data processing by a public authority needs an explicit and proportionate legal basis. Since the 1980s, this has significantly impacted the legal framework for data processing, initially by the former West German security agencies, and now for a united Germany.

The specific privacy regime that characterises the relationship between privacy and security in Germany goes back to a landmark judgement by the German constitutional court (*Bundesverfassungsgericht*, BVerfG). The BVerfG enjoys a strong position in the German political system, including the power to annul laws disproportionally encroaching upon the citizens' fundamental rights.

In 1983, the then West German government planned to renew the basis for statistical data collection in a general population census. The government intended to combine this census data collection with a renewal of the citizens' registers, in order to verify whether all citizens had correctly declared their residence to the local authorities – a legal obligation (*Meldepflicht*) under German law. However, West German civil liberties groups raised concerns, claiming that the combination of the census with updating the citizens' registers would lead to the existence of the 'transparent citizen' in West Germany. These concerns quickly spread outside the civil liberties groups. Protests developed into a social movement, and some lawyers involved in the growing movement brought a case before the BVerfG. This was possible because, similar to applications before the European Court of Human Rights, German citizens are able to bring fundamental rights cases directly before the BVerfG as constitutional complaints (*Verfassungsbeschwerden*). In exceptional cases, if serious harm to fundamental rights is seen as directly derived from a German law, citizens do not even have to go to the ordinary courts and through the stages of appeal before bringing a case to the BVerfG.

In response to the constitutional complaints brought before it, the BVerfG, in its judgement, annulled the 1983 census law. The reasons given by the court at that time now sound somewhat prophetic at a distance of almost 40 years, and several rounds of technological innovations later.

1. In the context of modern data processing, the general right of personality [*Allgemeines Persönlichkeitsrecht*] under Article 2.1 in conjunction with Article 1.1 [Human Dignity – *Menschenwürde*] of the Basic Law encompasses the protection of the individual against unlimited collection, storage, use and sharing of personal data. The fundamental right guarantees the

authority conferred on the individual to, in principle, decide themselves on the disclosure and use of their personal data.

2. Limitations of this right to 'informational self-determination' are only permissible if there is an overriding public interest. They require a statutory basis that must be constitutional itself and comply with the principle of legal clarity under the rule of law. The legislator must furthermore observe the principle of proportionality. It must also put in place organisational and procedural safeguards that counter the risk of violating the general right of personality.[3]

Essentially, the BVerfG judgement established a new fundamental right through the interpretation of two already existing rights. Since then, this new fundamental right has had a significant impact upon the way in which public authorities and private entities process personal data. In the security sector, federal laws governing criminal procedure, the federal police agencies, and the federal intelligence services had to be adapted to this new fundamental right. As policing is one of the core tasks of the 16 States (*Länder*) in the German federal system, the *Länder* had to include data processing rules in their policing laws (cf. Aden & Fährmann, 2019).

In 2008, the BVerfG even established an additional fundamental right: the *guarantee of the confidentiality and integrity of information technology systems*,[4] again, equally deduced from Articles 2.1 and 1.1 of the German constitution (*Grundgesetz*). The establishment of this new fundamental right in Germany recognises the relevance of the essential role of personal electronic devices as they are used today and the potential threat to privacy if state surveillance is not effectively limited through legislation. This has become even more relevant since then. People use their smartphones and computers all day long, and therefore these devices 'know' much about their users, in many cases including information on the core of private life, such as communication between family members.

PRIVACY AND THE CURRENT STATE OF TECHNOLOGICAL DEVELOPMENT

The rapid development of information technology during the past decades (cf. Aden, 2019; Nogala, 1989, 2019) creates additional challenges for the relationship between privacy and security as well as for security ethics.

The Internet, since the 1990s, has facilitated information sharing and communication worldwide – it has also enabled security agencies to intercept and retain detailed information on every citizen. In one sense, this approach is understandable from the perspective of requirements of state agencies to protect their citizens, and, indeed, to avoid criticisms of not doing so. Accordingly, in reaction to the terrorist attacks in New York City and Washington DC on 11 September 2001, many state security agencies developed mass surveillance strategies. In 2013, whistleblower Edward Snowden revealed the extent to which the US NSA retained huge quantities of data, not justifiably related to any specific security purpose. Although Snowden's revelations led to a controversial debate on the legitimacy of mass surveillance, and, in some jurisdictions, to certain legal limitations, untargeted surveillance by security agencies was not substantially restricted (see Lyon, 2015).

Rapid technological advances have contributed to making mass surveillance even more intrusive and in contention with fundamental rights. Carrying a smartphone in everyday life means that users produce passive data that security agencies and private parties, such as providers of smartphone applications, can easily access. Smartphones therefore have become auto-surveillance tools enabling security agencies to monitor individuals and to track their movements. German security agencies frequently use stealth pings ('stille SMS') in order to secretly detect the location of a device and its user. They also use their legal authority to claim data on all mobile devices (and their owners) present in a specific area at a given time from mobile communication providers in order to find potential suspects following a crime (see Fährmann, Aden, & Bosch, 2020, p. 141; Monroy, 2019).

The growing relevance of other devices connected to the internet in everyday life ('internet of things' or IoT) is likely to make mass surveillance even easier for security agencies. Security research is developing new search and identification technology, mostly based on the use of biometric data such as fingerprints and facial recognition, often combined with automated searches of large quantities of data (see Kühne & Schlepper, 2018 for a critique).

During police stops, biometric data stored in ID cards and passports enable police officers to use newly introduced mobile devices to compare the personal data of the legitimate holder to the data of the individual present at the stop – in order to be sure that the passport is not counterfeit or stolen. In German state and federal police laws, the legal requirements for background checks in police databases tend to be low – mostly the only requirement is that the information is necessary to carry out a police task. German police officers therefore routinely carry out background checks in police databases: mobile devices enable them to collect fingerprints or photographs – they can use this biometric data to check if the stopped individual has entries in police databases (cf. Fährmann et al., 2020, p. 142f.). The quantity of data accessible in police databases is rapidly growing, accelerated not only by a new generation of technology, but also by recent initiatives to make the EU's policing and migration databases interoperable: the *Schengen Information System*, the *Visa Information System, Eurodac*, the newly established EU *Entry Exit System*, and other databases (cf. Aden, 2020 for a critique).

In the German rule of law system, state action that restricts the citizens' use of their fundamental rights requires a legal basis and proportionate safeguards in order to prevent excessive restrictions. Therefore, if German security agencies wish to use new technologies, for example, body-worn cameras or facial recognition, this requires a specific legal basis, defining the extent to which these technologies may restrict the right to data protection. Technological development can also lead to more performant technologies that make already existing legal bases more intrusive to fundamental rights. For example, video technology has rapidly become more performant over the past decades. With older video cameras, it was often impossible to identify individuals in a crowd on video footage. Recent technological development allows a comparatively high level of resolution, and individuals can be more easily detected. Therefore, laws authorising video surveillance (Closed Circuit

Television, CCTV) have become much more intrusive upon the citizens' right to data protection, even if the relevant laws have not been amended in their wording (see Fährmann et al., 2020, p. 143ff.).

The use of machine learning and artificial intelligence tools by security agencies is also likely to trigger further mass surveillance in the future (cf. Golla, 2020). As a result, the fast development of information technology that enables security agencies to potentially collect detailed information about all citizens including core aspects of their private life will require clear ethical standards and legal limitations that protect the individuals' fundamental rights.

TRANSPARENCY, ACCOUNTABILITY AND DATA PROTECTION

Data protection can only be effective if it is integrated into a solid accountability framework. The obligation to explain and justify conduct is a core element of accountability (Bovens, 2007, p. 450). As major parts of electronic data processing are invisible for the individuals concerned, independent data protection authorities play a crucial role as accountability forums (cf. Aden, 2021, p. 35f.).

In addition to independent oversight, transparency is another key factor involved in the accountability of data processing (cf. Raab, 2012, p. 24ff.). Transparency means, in this case, that only if citizens understand the purposes for which security agencies will use and process their data, they are able to decide if these purposes are acceptable to them. Article 5(1) GDPR mentions transparency as one of the core principles for data protection, along with principles such as the legality and fairness of data processing and purpose limitation. Directive 2016/680 on data protection for policing and criminal justice purposes does not explicitly mention transparency as a data protection principle (Article 4(1)). However, transparency is referenced as part of the fairness principle laid down in Article 4(1) (cf. Johannes & Weinhold, 2018, p. 65; Tzanou, 2017, p. 26). Transparency and fairness are closely connected. Only if the use and application of a technology is transparent, and therefore understandable for the citizens, may they perceive it as fair and legitimate – and therefore accept it.

In the digital era, the accountability of data processing and principles of fairness and transparency are confronted by new challenges. Even if citizens wish to understand how state agencies and private companies process their personal data, mounting quantities of data and complex technologies make this increasingly difficult. Both security agencies and private companies are not necessarily interested in making data processing transparent. In their eyes, transparency may lead to critical questions and unwanted monitoring and oversight. More generally, the availability of information leads to an asymmetric power relationship (cf. Aden, 2004, 2018). Power is based on access to and understanding of information and knowledge; power can be more easily exerted upon someone who does not understand the data landscape. In this respect, accountability of operators and transparency for citizens are crucial elements of lawful and ethical data processing.

PRIVACY AND SECURITY – NEW SYNERGIES?

In political debates, privacy and security are often framed in opposition to each other, with data protection preventing enforcement agencies from collecting, retaining, and analysing data necessary for combating criminal behaviour effectively.

However, political debates, and sometimes also arguments by security practitioners, tend to overestimate this conflict and to underestimate synergies between data protection and effective law enforcement. Collecting large quantities of data alone does not guarantee effective law enforcement. With increasing quantities and types of 'big data', quality management, in order to turn it into effective intelligence, becomes an ever more demanding task. False or outdated information may misguide law enforcement and lead to a loss of precious investigative time. Therefore, keeping databases and other information used by security agencies up-to-date is a major issue. In contrast to paper archives, electronic information nowadays needs very little space to be stored. Searches in databases have become easy and fast, even with vast quantities of data. Therefore, the instances of paper files or stacks being full and difficult to manage that forced security agencies to trash outdated information in the analogue world are not applicable in the digital age.

Thus, one impact and result of privacy regulation can be more effective investigation and enforcement. Data protection laws prohibit the use of false or outdated personal data, in the interest of the individuals concerned, but also in the interest of the quality of investigations and effective management of resources. According to CFR Article 8 (2), 'everyone has the right of access to data which has been collected concerning him or her, and the right to have it rectified'. False or outdated data may have far-reaching consequences for the individuals concerned; for example, an unjustified arrest. Therefore, developing effective tools to assure high quality data used for security purposes creates synergies between privacy and security. It follows that when privacy laws prevent security agencies from collecting a wide swath of data, they are forced to create and use a more focussed investigative strategy.

Privacy by design and by default, required by EU data protection law (Article 25 GDPR and Article 21 Directive 2016/680), also aims to ensure effective consideration of privacy issues at the development and implementation stages of new technologies. This is a strategy to prevent the dependency of effective data protection on the 'human factor' at the end user stage. Data protection solutions that depend upon their application by individual users are likely to be circumvented or simply forgotten by negligence. Designing technology in a way that only allows its use in a way that is data protection friendly is therefore a relevant strategy to create synergies between privacy, ethics, and security (see Aden & Fährmann, 2019, 2020 on the growing importance of *privacy by design* solutions). Data protection laws only define *privacy by design and by default* as a general obligation. Therefore, specific technological standards will have to be developed in order to implement *privacy by design and by default* for technology used by security agencies. Data protection impact assessments (as foreseen by

Article 35 GDPR and Article 27 Directive 2016/680) and trans-disciplinary cooperation between lawyers, engineers and social scientists can be adequate loci for the development of new technologies implementing the ideas of *privacy by design and by default* (cf. Aden & Fährmann, 2020).

TOWARDS EUROPEAN LEGAL AND ETHICAL STANDARDS FOR THE PROTECTION OF THE CITIZENS' PRIVACY?

In June 2020, two years after the GDPR (EU) 2016/679 entered into force, the European Commission drew a generally positive picture.

> In an economy increasingly based on the processing of data, including personal data, the GDPR is an essential tool to ensure that individuals have better control over their personal data and that these data are processed for a legitimate purpose, in a lawful, fair and transparent way. (European Commission, 2020, p. 1)

However, additional harmonisation efforts remain on the agenda with respect to GDPR rules requiring adaptation to specific issue areas, to opening clauses left to the member states' legislators and to the transposition of the data protection directive (EU) 2016/680 for law enforcement into the member states' laws.

This chapter has shown that Germany has been a forerunner for establishing data protection and privacy as fundamental rights. Bad experiences with political regimes that built their power on surveillance may have contributed to make this topic more relevant in Germany compared to other countries. Surveillance strategies by public authorities repeatedly triggered social movements that successfully forced policy-makers to take privacy seriously. Through the EU's CFR, binding since 2009, the GDPR and the law enforcement data protection directive, similar standards now govern the relationship between security and data protection in all EU countries. While most areas are covered by the directly binding GDPR, data protection standards for security agencies in the area of policing and criminal justice have been separately regulated in the law enforcement data protection directive – this means that the member states have to transpose the directive and establish binding standards in their own laws. However, the wording and the substantive data protection standards tend to be similar to those covered by the GDPR. Further standards that the European Data Protection Board – a coordinating body including the member states' Data Protection Authorities and the European Data Protection Supervisor – and upcoming judgments of the Court of Justice of the EU interpreting the GDPR and the directive are likely to influence data protection standards for law enforcement as well. Thus, it can be forecasted that even in Germany, where policing is one of the core authorities of the 16 *Länder*, improved European standards for data protection will influence the security sector as well.

Sociologists of law claim that law has an impact on the behaviour of most people (Friedman, 2016). In the digital era, data protection laws that establish ethical rules oriented towards the protection of fundamental rights can play a crucial role for security ethics. In Germany, and the EU in general, the increasingly rapid development of information and surveillance technology continues to make the relationship between security and privacy an important issue for security ethics and for the protection of citizens' fundamental rights against exaggerated intrusion into private life for security purposes.

NOTES

1. Regulation (EU) 2016/679 of the European Parliament and of the Council of 27 April 2016 on the protection of natural persons with regard to the processing of personal data and on the free movement of such data, and repealing Directive 95/46/EC (GDPR), OJ EU L 119 of 4.5.2016, p. 1.

2. Directive (EU) 2016/680 of the European Parliament and of the Council of 27 April 2016 on the protection of natural persons with regard to the processing of personal data by competent authorities for the purposes of the prevention, investigation, detection, or prosecution of criminal offences or the execution of criminal penalties, and on the free movement of such data, and repealing Council Framework Decision 2008/977/JHA, OJ EU L 119 of 4.5.2016, p. 89.

3. BVerfG judgement of 15 December 1983 BVerfGE 65, 1; official English summary: https://www.bundesverfassungsgericht.de/SharedDocs/Entscheidungen/EN/1983/12/rs19831215_1bvr020983en.html;jsessionid=87B3C7425DE662A7E1A31F91729C4D70.2_cid377 (accessed 20.12.2020).

4. BVerfG, judgement of 27 February 2008, BVerfGE 120, 274; official English summary: https://www.bundesverfassungsgericht.de/SharedDocs/Entscheidungen/EN/2008/02/rs20080227_1bvr037007en.html (accessed 20.12.2020).

REFERENCES

Aden, H. (2004). Herrschaft und Wissen. In H. Aden (Ed.), *Herrschaftstheorien und Herrschaftsphänomene* (pp. 55–70). Wiesbaden: Verlag für Sozialwissenschaften.

Aden, H. (2016). Die Beteiligung von Bürgerrechtsverbänden an Gerichtsverfahren. Politisierung von Rechtsfragen oder Entpolitisierung durch Verrechtlichung?. In M. Plöse, T. Fritsche, M. Kuhn, & S. Lüders (Eds.), *„Worüber reden wir eigentlich?" Festgabe für Rosemarie Will* (pp. 556–565), Berlin: Humanistische Union.

Aden, H. (2018). Information sharing, secrecy and trust among law enforcement and secret service institutions in the European Union. *West European Politics (WEP)*, *41*(4), 981–1002.

Aden, H. (2019). Polizei und Technik zwischen Praxisanforderungen, Recht und Politik. *Vorgänge, no. 227*, *58*(3), 7–19.

Aden, H. (2020). Interoperability between EU policing and migration databases: Risks for privacy. *European Public Law*, *26*(1), 93–108.

Aden, H. (2021). Financial accountability in the broader framework of accountability studies. In P. Stephenson, M.-L. Sánchez-Barrueco, & H. Aden (Eds.), *Financial accountability in the European Union. Institutions, policy and practice* (pp. 25–40). London: Routledge.

Aden, H., & Fährmann, J. (2019). Defizite der Polizeirechtsentwicklung und Techniknutzung. *Zeitschrift für Rechtspolitik*, *52*(6), 175–178.

Aden, H., & Fährmann, J. (2020). Datenschutz-Folgenabschätzung und Transparenzdefizite der Techniknutzung. Eine Untersuchung am Beispiel der polizeilichen Datenverarbeitungstechnologie. *TATuP – Zeitschrift für Technikfolgenabschätzung in Theorie und Praxis*, *29*(3), 24–29.

Bovens, M. (2007). Analysing and assessing accountability: A conceptual framework. *European Law Journal*, *13*(4), 447–468.

European Commission. (2020). Communication [...]: Data protection as a pillar of citizens' empowerment and the EU's approach to the digital transition – Two years of application of the General Data Protection Regulation. COM(2020)264 final, Brussels.

Fährmann, J., Aden, H., & Bosch, A. (2020). Technologieentwicklung und Polizei: intensivere Grundrechtseingriffe auch ohne Gesetzesänderung. *Kriminologisches Journal, 52*(2), 135–148.

Friedman, L. M. (2016). *Impact. How law affects behavior*. Cambridge, MA: Harvard University Press.

Gellately, R. (1992). *The Gestapo and German society: Enforcing racial policy, 1933–1945*. Oxford: Oxford University Press.

Golla, S. J. (2020). Lernfähige Systeme, lernfähiges Polizeirecht Regulierung von künstlicher Intelligenz am Beispiel von Videoüberwachung und Datenabgleich. *Kriminologisches Journal, 52*(2), 149–161.

Johannes, P. C., & Weinhold, R. (2018). *Das neue Datenschutzrecht bei Polizei und Justiz. Europäisches Datenschutzrecht und deutsche Datenschutzgesetze*. Baden-Baden: Nomos.

Kühne, S., & Schlepper, C. (2018). Zur Politik der Sicherheitsversprechen. Die biometrische Verheißung. In J. Puschke & T. Singelnstein (Eds.), *Der Staat und die Sicherheitsgesellschaft* (pp. 79–99). Wiesbaden: Springer VS.

Lyon, D. (2015). *Surveillance after Snowden*. Cambridge: Polity Press.

Macrakis, K. (2008). *Seduced by secrets: Inside the Stasi's Spy-tech World*. Cambridge: Cambridge University Press.

Monroy, M. (2019). Die Ortungswanze in der Hosentasche Maßnahmen nach §§ 100 StPO zum Ermitteln des Aufenthaltsorts und der Kennung von Mobiltelefonen. *Vorgänge, no. 227, 58*(3), 85–93.

Nogala, D. (1989). *Polizei, avancierte Technik und soziale Kontrolle*. Pfaffenweiler: Centaurus.

Nogala, D. (2019). Polizei, avancierte Technik und soziale Kontrolle. Wie geht's dem Frosch heute? *Vorgänge, no. 227, 58*(3), 21–30.

Raab, C. (2012). The meaning of 'accountability' in the information privacy context. In D. Guagnin, L. Hempel, C. Ilten, I. Kroener, D. Neyland, & H. Postigo (Eds.), *Managing privacy through accountability* (pp. 15–32). Basingstoke: Palgrave Macmillan.

Tzanou, M. (2017). *The fundamental right to data protection*. Oxford: Hart Publishing.

CHAPTER 9

A FRAMEWORK FOR REVIEWING DUAL USE RESEARCH

Simon E. Kolstoe

ABSTRACT

'Dual use research' is research with results that can potentially cause harm as well as benefits. Harm can be to people, animals or the environment. For most research, harms can be difficult to predict and quantify, so in this sense almost all research could be seen as having dual use potential. This chapter will present a framework for reviewing dual use research by justifying why the responsibility for approving and conducting research does not sit with Research Ethics Committees (RECs) alone. By mapping out the wider research landscape, it will be argued that both responsibility and accountability for dual use research sits on the shoulders of broader governance structures that reflect the philosophical and political aspirations of society as a whole. RECs are certainly still important for identifying potential 'dual use research of concern', and perhaps teasing out some of the details that may be hidden within research plans or projects, but in a well-functioning system should never be the sole gate keepers that determine which research should, and should not, be allowed to proceed.

Keywords: Dual use; dual use research of concern; Research Ethics Committee; Institutional Review Board; research governance; research integrity

'Our need will be the real creator'. Plato

Ethical Issues in Covert, Security and Surveillance Research
Advances in Research Ethics and Integrity, Volume 8, 131–143

ISSN: 2398-6018/doi:10.1108/S2398-601820210000008010

INTRODUCTION

The general response that humans have to hardship is to be innovative. Nature, in the sense of environment and disease, has been a strong driver of innovation, but so too has human conflict. As research is often the foundation for innovation, it is no surprise to find that research agendas are often based upon addressing threats, be they viral pandemics or conflict between nations. While it is no bad thing that the narrative of scientific humanism (either secular or religious) is broadly optimistic, it is naïve to think that research agendas can be separated from the context of conflict. Understanding and making sense of this context is an important role for research ethics.

Perhaps the most obvious, or at least well known, manifestation of research ethics comes from the activities of Research Ethics Committees (RECs), also known as Institutional Review Boards (IRBs) in US-influenced countries. These committees are made up of scientists, lawyers, philosophers and lay-members, whose role is to analyse research plans and come to judgements on ethical issues. Historically, the need for these committees (henceforth referred to as RECs) has been driven by the need to protect participants, especially following atrocities committed during the Second World War. Their establishment in the medical sciences is most famously described in the Declaration of Helsinki (WMA, 2013), but over the last 50 years or so RECs have also become well established in most other research areas. This has brought about challenges especially in fields where methodologies, culture and sometimes philosophy differ from the 'medical model' of research. However, although still viewed as a problem by some in the humanities (Lincoln & Tierney, 2004), the issues highlighted by the expansion of RECs have been broadly positive as it has helped to move the philosophy of research ethics beyond just considering the physical protection of research participants, to also encompass the support of researchers and good research practice (Trace & Kolstoe, 2018).

While this has been a broadly positive development, it has created overlap, and sometimes conflict, between the role and contribution of RECs and other structures within the research community (such as professional bodies, peer review, grant committees, etc.) (Kolstoe & Carpenter, 2019). For instance, in recent years concerns relating to 'research culture' (Wellcome Trust, 2020) and 'research integrity' (Vitae, 2020) have become important. Likewise concerns relating to results reproducibility, publication practices and quality control (through peer review or otherwise) have increasingly been raised (Munafò et al., 2017). Is it feasible or desirable for RECs to play a role in governing such things? If not who should be responsible?

These issues have provided a strong catalyst for attempts to plot out the social and institutional structures that underpin research so as to better understand where accountability and responsibility lie, or should be made to lie (Science and Technology Committee – House of Commons, 2018). This process has also forced greater clarity in understanding who within society is responsible for different aspects of research agendas, and likewise defines the limits of all groups, structures and organisations that are engaged with research – including RECs (Moore & Donnelly, 2018).

A case in point is the development of offensive Chemical, Biological, Radiological and Nuclear (CBRN) weapons (sometimes euphemistically referred to as 'deterrents' or 'capabilities'). The indiscriminate destruction caused by such offensive technologies created the need for internationally enforced treaties and agreement prohibiting many aspects of research that might lead to the refinement of such weapons. These agreements are codified in law, and thus become a formal, legally enforced, charter adhered to by most institutions and others involved in research activities (NTI, n.d.). While the socially or scientifically aware REC member may remain alert to the possibilities of research in these areas, it is seldom the formal role of RECs to identify and form judgements on such research, simply because such research is limited by treaty, law or policy well before it gets anywhere close to a REC review.

However, CBRN research focussed on offensive weapon capabilities, and subject to international agreement, presents an overly simplistic case. There are plenty of other research projects that are not directly focussed on creating new weapons, but which may develop technologies or knowledge that could be applied in multiple ways – both helpful and harmful. Such technology may be psychological, biological, cyber or other types of research with the so-called 'dual use' capacity (Kavouras & Charitidis, 2019). Who, or what structure, within the research landscape should be responsible for reviewing the underlying research activities and determining whether they should or shouldn't be allowed to proceed? Is this a role for RECs?

In the following, I will argue that making judgements on so-called 'dual use' is not a role for RECs. While I will concede that REC members should remain alert for *any* potential ethical issues that may arise from a specific research protocol, I will present a framework that places accountability for 'dual use' applications well upstream of the REC review. In order to justify this framework, the chapter will first define research ethics, and then map out how RECs fit into the broader research approvals landscape. This is important because researchers (and often even REC members) find the research approvals landscape confusing and often repetitive, especially when it comes to identifying who has responsibility and accountability for different aspects of research. This is particularly pertinent for considering dual use issues that could be argued as representing some of the most harmful results of research. Following this mapping exercise, the chapter will provide some practical advice for RECs who may be concerned about potential applications of the research they review by briefly considering (using examples) how RECs can better expand the idea of 'dual use research of concern' (DURC) (EPA, 2016).

A FRAMEWORK FOR DEFINING ACCOUNTABILITY AND RESPONSIBILITY IN RESEARCH

The term 'research ethics' is generally used quite broadly to encompass all ethical considerations pertaining to research, but the remit of RECs is often significantly narrower. According to the Declaration of Helsinki, the role of a REC is to specifically consider research protocols:

> The research protocol must be submitted for consideration, comment, guidance and approval to the concerned research ethics committee before the study begins. (WMA, 2013)

And according to the World Health Organisation (2009):

> The main responsibility of a research ethics committee is to protect potential participants in the research, but it must also take into account potential risks and benefits for the community in which the research will be carried out.

These declarations make it clear that REC review is situated at a particular point of time within the research process: RECs consider research plans once detailed protocols have been developed, but prior to the start of data collection. This is the reason why RECs are referred to as IRBs in many countries, perhaps trying to distinguish between committees that are established specifically to review research protocols in this defined way, and those that are set up to discuss wider ethical issues that may impinge upon multiple research protocols. This distinction is important because the review of detailed protocols is a complex task requiring specific technical or methodological expertise (or at least insight), while the review of wider ethical issues is often more abstract and less immediate. For this reason, it is important to distinguish clearly between the role of RECs reviewing protocols and the role of other groups within the research landscape that have been established to consider wider ethical issues framed in terms of which types of research 'should', or 'should not', be allowed to occur.

Asking this latter question of what research 'should' or 'should not' occur is a complicated matter that touches on other areas including politics, philosophy and law. As research is essentially a community effort to discover more about the world, or address specific problems, it should be no surprise that communities of experts play an important role in establishing the priorities within their areas of interest. This may happen in a number of different ways, but primarily occurs through the distribution of research funds in the form of research grants. The effect of this is to essentially remove the ultimate accountability for the topic of research from the researchers themselves, in favour of placing it upon the community that commissions the research through deciding the funding allocation. This works in different ways in different contexts (both national and scientific), but does mean that the decision of what should or shouldn't be the subject of research becomes heavily influenced by the wider value-forming processes that specific nations or cultures choose to employ when making funding allocations. However, it is important to note that while this ultimate accountability rests with society, from a pragmatic perspective the responsibility for making decisions about specific research projects as they are subsequently (often following funding decisions) developed and implemented lie with others in the system.

To better understand how these more detailed responsibilities are distributed it is helpful to consider three related, but distinct, concepts that are common to many research systems: (1) research integrity, (2) research governance and (3) the role of the REC. Understanding these three roles is key to understanding how dual use research should ideally be handled.

Research Integrity

Should an individual researcher ever create something, or do something, that may harm others or the environment? It is helpful to consider the issues surrounding this question under the heading of research integrity, or more specifically the moral integrity of the researchers themselves.

However, in doing so, it needs to be acknowledged that the word integrity is often used in two senses in relation to research. Integrity of *research* refers to issues of trustworthy methods and reproducibility of results, while integrity of *researchers* refers to the character traits of the individual(s) conducting research. But, on reflection, these two uses can be collapsed into a single practical definition wherein a researcher, who shows the character traits of integrity, will produce research that also has both methodological and structural integrity. Thus, the best way to understand research integrity is to simply consider the attitudes and values of researchers themselves because if they are appropriate, the outcome of the research can also be considered to have integrity. This is clearly important when considering dual use research because it suggests that researchers themselves, if showing integrity, may draw lines as to what they will, or will not, be prepared to do.

Surveys of researchers and research stakeholders have listed the key traits of a researcher as being rigorous, accurate, original, honest and transparent (Joynson & Leyser, 2015). Ongoing empirical work has sought to further define, refine or even weigh these desirable traits (Wellcome Trust, 2020), but for the purposes of this chapter, research integrity will be taken to mean the *character traits of researchers that allow the production of reliable and trustworthy research results*. Given this definition, it becomes clear that research integrity is developed through research training and experience. Such training commences in school science lessons, continues through undergraduate study, and then perhaps most critically, is informed by the mentorship that is provided while studying for higher research degrees and subsequently working within professional research teams, often subject to the principles and values of membership in professional research associations.

While such specialist experience is probably the main driver for developing the traits required for research integrity, wider personal experience based upon upbringing and other psychological factors also need to be considered as influential to the attitudes and traits shown by researchers. As a consequence, and as with any other population of humans, while there may well be some traits that are common to all or most researchers (perhaps rigorous, accurate, original, etc.), there are also likely to be legitimate differences of opinion between researchers who may equally be considered to be acting with integrity so far as their actual research conduct is concerned.

One area of difference concerns the reasons or motivations behind why an individual may be conducting research in the first place. Here, some people may be driven by a strong desire to create research that helps others, others may be driven by curiosity, others by competition or the search for novelty (Joynson & Leyser, 2015) and still others perhaps by a feeling of loyalty towards their society or way of life. Such differences are to be expected, but do mean that they may manifest as different opinions as to what research is, and is not, acceptable. In this sense, for any given researcher to act with integrity, they must also act in line with their wider values, thus creating a legitimate difference between researchers.

Given this definition of research integrity, it is entirely reasonable for research-ers to disagree with each other as to the appropriateness of different research projects. But, the important thing to note, is that it is not 'research integrity' itself that prohibits certain types of research, but rather how research integrity is manifest in different individuals due to the complex interaction between specific research values and then wider personal or cultural values.

These differences are broadly positive because healthy debate protects against extremism. In general, researchers and scientific communities are particularly strong at convening conferences, forums and other fora to discuss (often heatedly) differences of opinion. This is the reason why professional societies exist. Their influence is particularly important because they lead to the development of codes, declarations and even the laws through which research is governed.

However, one critical observation is that while such discussions are often referred to as 'research ethics', they often occur within the context of broad pro-fessional and even political debate. Committees may well be set up to examine specific issues and create specific 'ethical' guidance, but these are not RECs in the sense described above. While it is entirely reasonable that REC members may want to get involved with such broader ideological discussions, especially if estab-lishing precedence based on research protocols that have been reviewed, the main role of RECs is to keep their focus quite narrow, focussing specifically on the spe-cific project protocols they are given to review. Confusing this specific role with wider issues regarding research or researcher integrity detracts from the value that RECs add to the research ecosystem.

Research Governance

Distinct from research integrity that, as argued in the previous section, focusses on the moral values of researchers themselves, research governance is the name given to the processes, policies and laws that govern research programmes and projects (Kolstoe & Carpenter, 2019). In this broad sense, review by a REC is a necessary part of the research governance process, but RECs are not the whole research governance process, and nor do they give final 'approval' for research to occur. Although research can often not occur unless a REC favourable opinion has been granted, it is in actual fact the employer/research sponsoring organisation that gives the final go ahead or approval for activities conducted by their researchers. This is not well understood and causes confusion for many researchers who think (mistakenly) that the role of a REC is to provide overall approval for research. Viewing RECs in this way is inaccurate because it obscures the important point that in order to provide a balanced ethical opinion, RECs should have a degree of independence from both the researcher and the establishment that is funding/ conducting the research. While of course bias will always creep in to any decision making process, one of the aims for a REC is to try to acknowledge, and therefore address, as many biases as possible. A helpful analogy may be that RECs should be to institutions as peer reviewers are to journal editors. Similarly while editors, not peer reviewers make the final decision as to whether a manuscript can be published, it is research governance systems, not RECs, that make the final decision as to whether a research project can go ahead. This is true even if in practice an unfavourable opinion from a REC will often stop most research projects from proceeding.

Maintaining this independence does not mean that institutions should not play a role in establishing and supporting RECs, but rather that this support should be mainly procedural and administrative. Institutions must support the *REC process* without interfering with the REC's *freedom* to review and come to opinions on research protocols. Quite often this can be achieved by ensuring a certain proportion of members are 'independent', meaning not otherwise employed, or subject to direct line management, from authority structures within the institution or organisation seeking to conduct the research. How independent 'independent enough' is, and how many of such members there are on a committee, is a matter of opinion and perhaps policy. While it would clearly be a problem if independent members were directly antagonistic towards researchers or the research organisation, at the same time it would defeat the object of independent review if REC members always approved every idea that came before them because of close ties with the sponsoring institution, company or organisation.

The next section will discuss the role of RECs in detail, but for the purpose of understanding research governance, the key point is that REC review may be mandated by governance policy, and RECs may well be supported or directed within governance structures specifically through guidance created for them, but RECs should always be one step removed from these governance structures so as to allow freedom in ethical decision making (Iphofen, 2017). This independence is critical particularly if the subject or topic of the research is contentious.

But why have this independence? Surely it will speed up research preparation if RECs are forced to follow the lead from the institution that they support? While this is undoubtedly the case, the main argument for REC independence comes from a 'due diligence' perspective. Insurers, trustees, donors and independent funders are keen to ensure that institutions, be they universities, government departments or private companies, are trustworthy and adhere as close as possible to their established mission, business task or objective. Where this involves research, given the high propensity for waste (Chalmers et al., 2014), it is very much within the interests of the organisation to build in as many independent checks as possible, one of these being independent REC review. A good research governance policy will therefore provide clear guidance as to how a sufficiently independent REC can be established, alongside perhaps the framework within which it is expected to function.

Establishing a governance framework coupled with guidance for REC review is absolutely critical especially when considering potential dual use research. For instance, if the REC is established within an organisation – such as the military – where the overall aims and objectives are defence related, this framework and guidance should make it absolutely clear to the REC that they should expect to review military related research. Likewise, RECs in organisations that have a stated non-military aim should not expect to receive research that has direct military application. While projects may, from time to time, slip through, it is actually a governance responsibility upstream of the REC review to decide what projects are broadly within the remit of the specific organisation. RECs can then be free to focus on the details of the research protocol itself, rather than worry about whether or not the organisation should be carrying out this type of research in the first place.

Role of RECs/IRBs

So far in this chapter, I have argued that the ethical and moral debates surrounding dual use research belong upstream of the REC review – primarily as part of the discussions surrounding funding allocation, broader subject level research integrity considerations (often at a funding or professional society level), but then supported by governance processes and guidance that should be screening out, or making decisions about, which potential research projects should not proceed well prior to review by RECs. But even with these processes in place, how should RECs consider or at least approach potential dual use research?

The first thing that RECs need to do is have a clear idea of the policies and guidance produced by their hosting organisation, along with the governance structures within which they are expected to operate. If, for instance, the organisation hosting the REC has a remit for defence research – such as in a defence establishment – it would be inappropriate for the REC to object to such research on principle. This does not mean that the REC shouldn't feel free to raise concerns, but rather that such concerns should be pursued at a relatively high level perhaps as a parallel process to the review of specific research protocols, with the aim of creating or modifying guidance so as to deal with future occurrences of the situation at hand (more details of how this might work are provided in the final section). While policy level decisions are under consideration, RECs need to ensure they comply with extant policy and guidance as a matter of due process. If individual members of RECs find this difficult from an integrity perspective they should discuss this with the committee, and potentially abstain from decisions or even resign their positions if they feel morally unable to agree with the overall governance structure and guidance within which the REC is expected to operate. To summarise, it is not the RECs role to determine the governance structures within which they operate, although they can feedback their views on whether current policy is effective and thus hopefully engage constructively to review and improve policy over time.

Secondly, the REC role is not to judge the personal integrity of the researchers. Whereas the competency of researchers to conduct the proposed study is clearly an issue for the REC, wider judgements on the integrity of the researchers themselves are not a matter for the REC. This is because, and as mentioned above, research integrity is a complex mix of personal, professional, societal and even political values. RECs need to understand that researchers may hold a wide range of views as to the types of research that should (or should not) be conducted. If the REC is concerned by these broader opinions or attitudes (in contrast to specific concerns regarding the protocol under review) these should again be raised parallel to the reviewing of research protocols with professional bodies, or by pursuing dialogue with specific research communities or governance structures.

This distinction between making a decision on a protocol using extant governance policy and guidance, and raising broader integrity or governance concerns at a higher level can feel like a very limiting compromise imposed upon REC members especially if they have specific concerns about the application of research programmes or ideas. However, it must be acknowledged that predicting the ultimate use of research findings, and also making character/integrity judgements about specific researchers, is a very difficult task. If RECs were expected to do this for every project that they reviewed it is unlikely that they would come to any decision or have time to consider other important aspects within their remit (such as the protection of research participants). As a consequence, the REC must make the pragmatic decision to focus on the concerns raised by the specific project at hand so as to come to an expedient decision and then, if REC members still feel strongly inclined, pursue any wider concerns about issues of dual use or similar with those who can influence or change both governance policy and/or professional guidelines.

In this respect the membership, and attitude of the members of RECs is critically important. Alongside having the requisite (as defined by the relevant governance policy) mix of expert and lay members, the members also need to understand that their role is not to create new policy directly, or influence the values of research communities on the fly as they review specific projects. While of course REC members will pick up key experience that will be valuable in the subsequent creation or modification of policies, guidelines and in some cases even laws, this input should be saved for the correct time, which is seldom during the REC review of a specific project protocol.

The only exception may be when REC members, due to their experience, note a legal issue. While the responsibility for ensuring legality and obtaining legal opinions is a research governance issue (as this is where the accountability ultimately sits), it can be helpful for a REC to flag to the research team that they may need to look into the legality of some aspects of the proposed work. A good example of this comes from data protection legislation (and particularly confusions cause by the EU's General Data Protection Regulation) wherein RECs may be more familiar than the researchers as to the best ways for the required information to be presented.

DUAL USE RESEARCH OF CONCERN

The complexities of trying to determine the potential for research specifically within the biological sciences in relation to the creation of potentially weaponisable biological organisms has recently led to the term Dual Use Research of Concern or 'DURC' being used (EPA, 2016). Although the term has primarily come from the life sciences, it is useful more broadly as it distinguishes between a set of research that may potentially have more than one use which, as mentioned in the introduction, could include almost any research, and the set of research that causes specific concerns *due to* this dual use. Since some research may move in and out of the category of DURC depending on the way that it is governed, or alternatively it may not be clear until after the protocol has been developed exactly what the concerns might be, it is not unreasonable for RECs to play a legitimate role in highlighting DURC to both the governing institution and more widely if necessary. However, while playing an important role in initiating such conversations (with individuals from RECs perhaps legitimately becoming involved in subsequent debates) it must be reiterated that the REC role is very much to initiate these discussions, not develop ad hoc policy or guidance. The REC will therefore often need to accept that there is no policy reason why a specific project under consideration should not go ahead at that time, even if the REC has broader concerns that the extant policy environment is not suitably dealing with the specific DURC. The REC does, however, have an important subsequent duty to flag the issue so as to initiate policy change.

One, perhaps fairly straightforward, example where a REC might play an important role in identifying DURC would be the situation where, when reviewing a protocol, the REC considers that some of the information being gathered by the researchers (if put in the public domain) might be useful for planning or implementing a terrorist attack. In this situation, the REC would be acting well within its remit to ask the research team whether they had considered this possibility, and perhaps ask for a written response detailing how the research team will mitigate against this risk in much the same way as the REC would ask for details of the mitigation of any other risk. If the REC is not satisfied with the subsequent response it could provide an unfavourable opinion (again in the same way as when unsatisfied by responses on any other topic) and then feed its reasoning back to the organisation responsible for the research. While not directly proposing solutions, by serving as a blocker to the research the REC would be flagging the issue as a serious, research stopping, concern that requires further thought by others within the research system and perhaps the development of new guidance/policy.

A second, more complex, example of DURC might be in the development and testing of a novel technology (such as a radar system) that alongside civilian applications may also be used to increase the lethality of a weapons system. Here, the REC would initially need to consider whether the support for such research was allowed under the governance framework within which both the REC and the research team operated. If, for instance, the REC was situated within a university that had a clear commitment not to engage with research that has a clear lethal potential, the REC would be acting well within its remit to provide an unfavourable opinion for such a project on the grounds of governance policy. In this case, the REC would also need to flag to its appointing authority that this research should not have been allowed to reach the REC in the first place. Conversely, if the REC was instead situated within a governance structure and organisation/institution with a clear military or defence remit, it would be unreasonable for the REC to provide an unfavourable decision on the same grounds. This is not to say that REC members should not express specific concerns about how the research may be conducted and/or applied, but rather that such concerns should be based upon the premise that there was no reason, per se, that lethal research should not be conducted due to it being acceptable under current policy/governance arrangements. The REC may well still decide to provide an unfavourable opinion on other grounds such as risk to participants, or even concerns that the resulting technology may cause unacceptable injuries to enemy combatants, but the justification for this unfavourable opinion would need to be specific to the protocol/application rather than based upon a blanket disapproval for research of this kind.

In these examples, presuming unfavourable opinions from the REC, what happens next would be down to the actions of the research or governance team. While these teams may well be frustrated by the REC decision, they are in a much better position to initiate further discussions within the research integrity and governance realms, simply because as researchers in the field they are both members of the relevant communities and also (hopefully) experts in the scientific/methodological area. As a consequence, they are far better positioned to raise the issue, participate in discussions, and hopefully come up with an acceptable solution that could subsequently be supplied to the REC in the form of guidance should another, similar, protocol be presented for review. The solution could, for instance, take the form of a new policy, process or procedure endorsed by the field (or at least sponsoring institution), demonstrating how they acknowledge the original issue flagged by the REC, and detailing an agreed course of action. While individual members of the REC may still feel uneasy, and of course the REC would still be able to ask further questions if needed, demonstrating that the research fits within formal guidance endorsed by the sponsoring organisations, and even potentially the field of research, should go at least some way to allaying the RECs concerns.

If, however, a REC continued to feel strongly about certain types of research (either methodologies or programmes), and the solution did not seem to evolve through the process outlined above, the onus would then be on the chair of the REC to raise the issue with the authority appointing the REC, perhaps directly asking for guidance for how to deal with the issue should/when it occurs in future protocols. As a consequence, the solution for both the REC and the researchers would be improved guidance ideally agreed by both researchers and the authority governing the REC.

CONCLUSION

Almost all research has the possibility for dual use, some of which may also cause legitimate concern. Considering this potential is primarily a role for research communities, or at least the communities that are responsible for commissioning, funding and governing the research in the first place. Arrangements can then be made through the use of guidance in the form of professional (integrity) standards, and more explicit governance policies or arrangements. Ideally any potential for DURC would be identified and dealt with long before a research protocol was presented to a REC. However, should a REC have concerns regarding DURC in a protocol under review, they should first look to see whether this DURC was considered acceptable under the committee's terms of reference. If not, the REC should seek clarification with the researchers as they would any other concern before providing an unfavourable opinion. As with any other unfavourable ethics opinion this should give the researcher cause to discuss the concern within their research field and governance contacts. If the research field or governing institution/sponsor disagreed with the REC, such discussions should lead to new or better guidance that could be presented to the REC alongside any future applications of a similar nature. Although the REC should not formally take part in these discussions (as such discussions are not within the remit of the REC reviewing specific protocols) it would be well within the responsibility of the REC chair and other members to take part in subsequent debates in a personal capacity, so as to help provide new guidance on the DURC in question that could be then be applied during future REC reviews.

REFERENCES

Chalmers, I., Bracken, M. B., Djulbegovic, B., Garattini, S., Grant, J., Gülmezoglu, A. M., ... Oliver, S. (2014, January). How to increase value and reduce waste when research priorities are set. *The Lancet*, *383*(9912), 156–165. https://doi.org/10.1016/S0140-6736(13)62229-1

EPA. (2016). EPA Order 1000.19: Policy and procedures for managing dual use research of concern. Retrieved from https://www.epa.gov/research/policy-and-procedures-managing-dual-use-research-concern

Iphofen, R. (2017). Governance and ethics: Maintaining the distinction. *TRUST Enewsletter*, *1*, 5.

Joynson, C., & Leyser, O. (2015). The culture of scientific research. *F1000Research*, *4*(66), 1–11. https://doi.org/10.12688/f1000research.6163.1

Kavouras, P., & Charitidis, C. A. (2019). Dual use in modern research. In R. Iphofen (Eds.), *Handbook of research ethics and scientific integrity* (pp. 1–21). Cham: Springer International Publishing. https://doi.org/10.1007/978-3-319-76040-7_7-1

Kolstoe, S. E., & Carpenter, D. (2019). Research approvals iceberg: Helping it melt away. *BMC Medical Ethics*, *20*(1), 1–4. https://doi.org/10.1186/s12910-019-0434-2

Lincoln, Y. S., & Tierney, W. G. (2004). Qualitative research and institutional review boards. *Qualitative Inquiry*, *10*(2), 219–234. https://doi.org/10.1177/1077800403262361

Moore, A., & Donnelly, A. (2018). The job of "ethics committees." *Journal of Medical Ethics*, *44*(7), 481–487. https://doi.org/10.1136/medethics-2015-102688

Munafò, M. R., Nosek, B. A., Bishop, D. V. M., Button, K. S., Chambers, C. D., Percie du Sert, N., ... Ioannidis, J. P. A. (2017). A manifesto for reproducible science. *Nature Human Behaviour*, *1*(1), 0021. https://doi.org/10.1038/s41562-016-0021

NTI. (n.d.). List of biological, chemical, and nuclear treaties. Retrieved from https://www.nti.org/learn/treaties-and-regimes/treaties/

Science and Technology Committee – House of Commons. (2018). Research integrity. Retrieved from https://publications.parliament.uk/pa/cm201719/cmselect/cmsctech/350/35002.htm

Trace, S., & Kolstoe, S. (2018). Reviewing code consistency is important, but research ethics committees must also make a judgement on scientific justification, methodological approach and competency of the research team. *Journal of Medical Ethics*, *44*(12), 874. https://doi.org/10.1136/medethics-2018-105107

Vitae. (2020). Research integrity: A landscape study. Retrieved from https://www.vitae.ac.uk/vitae-publications/research-integrity-a-landscape-study

Wellcome Trust. (2020). Time for change: What researchers think about the culture they work in. *The Biochemist*, *42*(3), 70–72. https://doi.org/10.1042/bio20200032

WMA. (2013). WMA declaration of Helsinki – Ethical principles for medical research involving human subjects. – WMA – The World Medical Association. Retrieved from https://www.wma.net/policies-post/wma-declaration-of-helsinki-ethical-principles-for-medical-research-involving-human-subjects/. Accessed on August 20, 2018.

World Health Organization. (2009). *Research ethics committees: Basic concepts for capacity-building* (pp. 5–12). Geneva: WHO Production Services.

CHAPTER 10

SECURITY RISK MANAGEMENT IN HOSTILE ENVIRONMENTS: COMMUNITY-BASED AND SYSTEMS-BASED APPROACHES

Daniel Paul and Alex Stedmon

ABSTRACT

In recent years, there has been a growing dialogue around community-based and systems-based approaches to security risk management through the introduction of top-down and bottom-up knowledge acquisition. In essence, this relates to knowledge elicited from academic experts, or security subject-matter experts, practitioner experts, or field workers themselves and how much these disparate sources of knowledge may converge or diverge. In many ways, this represents a classic tension between organisational and procedural perspectives of knowledge management (i.e. top-down) versus more pragmatic and experience focussed perspectives (i.e. bottom-up).

This chapter considers these approaches and argues that a more consistent approach needs to address the conflict between procedures and experience, help convert field experience into knowledge, and ultimately provide effective training that is relevant to those heading out into demanding work situations. Ultimately, ethics and method are intricately bound together in whichever approach is taken and the security of both staff and at-risk populations depends upon correctly managing the balance between systems and communities.

Ethical Issues in Covert, Security and Surveillance Research
Advances in Research Ethics and Integrity, Volume 8, 145–157

ISSN: 2398-6018/doi:10.1108/S2398-601820210000008011

Keywords: Security risk management; hostile environments; community-based approaches; systems-based approaches; knowledge management; humanitarian workers

INTRODUCTION

The last two decades have seen a rise in security issues around the world. In the wake of growing insecurity, organisations have looked to improve their security risk management frameworks, developing concepts which originated in the health and safety field to deal with more pressing risks such as terrorist acts, abduction, and piracy. Risks that were previously exclusive to the battlefield are now prevalent in situations affecting a range of overseas workers, from frontline humanitarian workers, oil and gas executives, media reporters and journalists, government officials, business travellers, and even regular tourists. For example, research indicates that one in five humanitarian workers experienced intentional violence (Buchanan & Muggah, 2005) and that this high rate supported Claus's (2011, 2015) observations that humanitarian organisations face more risks than other sectors.

The literature on security studies has traditionally focussed on states as the main actors (Browning & McDonald, 2011). Security studies as an academic field have neglected the individual as a viewpoint, attempting to understand broader security issues on why states go to war and how military power is projected (Buzan & Hansen, 2009). A shift in this approach occurred at the end of the Cold War in 1991 with the emergence of critical security studies, which shifted the focus to individuals, considering human rights, effects of non-state conflict (such as terrorism), and the effects of criminal activity (Williams, 2013).

Early academic sources in humanitarian security began to appear in the late 1990s when three articles were published in the journal *Humanitäres Völkerrecht* (*International Humanitarian Law*), discussing security practices within the United Nations, the International Committee of the Red Cross, and humanitarian non-governmental organisations in general (Connelly, 1998; Dind, 1998; Van Brabant, 1998a, respectively). The articles addressed the changing nature of what they termed the 'humanitarian space', or the environments in which humanitarian programmes occur, stating that there was an increase in attacks against humanitarian workers.

This prompted the first statistical review into humanitarian worker deaths (Bolton et al., 2000). The study concluded that attacks against humanitarian workers were on the rise caused by an increase in conflicts between non-state actors, such as rival militias, and lawlessness as the main driver (Bolton et al., 2000). However, there was a greater range of risks that workers were exposed to, such as being caught in the crossfire between warring groups, landmines, abduction and kidnapping, and crime related to lawlessness, such as muggings and carjacking (Bolton et al., 2000; Martin, 1999).

An important document was released in 2000 titled *Good Practice Review 8: Operational Security in Violent Environments* (Van Brabant, 2000). This built on earlier work by Van Brabant (1998a), Martin (1999), and through consultation with a range of humanitarian sector staff, to pose a new model for security management. This document was the first true work to draw together thinking in the sector (Harmer & Schreter, 2013). It emphasised the need for humanitarian organisations to take more responsibility for staff security, provide training to ensure staff are prepared, as well as foster the acceptance of the organisation's presence and work with the communities they help (Van Brabant, 2000). This created the community-based approach as a school of thought within the sector (Brunderlein & Grassmann, 2006).

APPROACHES TO SECURITY RISK MANAGEMENT

The impetus to change security management in the sector led to the development of community-based and systems-based approaches (Brunderlein & Grassmann, 2006). The community-based approach views security from the bottom-up, with the individual humanitarian worker and their unique perspective as the focal point, while the systems-based approach is top-down, which puts security advisors and their procedures at the centre of design and implementation (Schneiker, 2015).

Community-based, Bottom-up Approach

The community-based approach began to gain traction around the turn of the twenty-first century (Martin, 1999; Van Brabant, 1998a, 1998b, 2000). The approach relies on local communities to trust and support the organisation and their work, thus reducing risks to humanitarian workers (Martin, 1999). As it relies on the community to accept the presence of the humanitarian organisation, it is also referred to as the 'acceptance' approach (Van Brabant, 1998a). In this approach, security is effectively cultivated at the field level (Schneiker, 2015), with the organisational level providing support and resources (Van Brabant, 2000). Successful acceptance also required organisations to gain acceptance from potentially aggressive actors (Van Brabant, 1998b), with organisations needing to 'obtain credible security guarantees' (Brunderlein & Grassmann, 2006, p. 71). Where strong acceptance exists, the community is likely to protect humanitarian workers if possible or warn them of potential danger (Van Brabant, 2000).

With this approach it is necessary for workers to meet with local community members, though doing this they are exposed to possible risks (Van Brabant, 2001). The approach emphasises the need for workers' training, such as on mine awareness, communications, and how to survive an abduction (Bollentino, 2006). Brunderlein and Grassmann (2006) identified four weaknesses with the community-based approach:

- The approach relies on the community trusting the humanitarian workers.
- Communities can be unaccepting of organisations because of their resentment to the country they are from.

- Communities need to provide security for the humanitarian workers, but in some circumstances cannot provide their own security.
- Relies on individuals who have the necessary experience to build relationships with key stakeholders.

The approach is also reliant on humanitarian workers who can develop relationships with others and build trust (Van Brabant, 2001). The approach requires humanitarian workers to have close relationships with the community and face the same risks they face (Martin, 1999; Schneiker, 2015). This promotes 'emotional decision making' where risks may not be assessed realistically (Daudin & Merkelbach, 2011, p. 7), resulting in workers staying with the community when they should leave (Neuman & Weissman, 2016, p. 16). The context of decision making is therefore extremely complex and humanitarian staff represent a large area of risk themselves, who can take a 'negligent attitude towards their own security' (Brunderlein & Grassmann, 2006, p. 67). The wealth of literature in the field of anthropology, ethnography, and indigenous studies points up the diverse ethical and methodological challenges that can arise when taking such an approach (George, MacDonald, & Tauri, 2020; Iphofen, 2011–2013).

Systems-based, Top-down Approach

The systems-based approach emerged from a review of the 2003 attacks in Iraq, which emphasised the need for more organisational oversight of field security (Ahtisaari, 2003). This approach favours 'top-down' management of security (Schneiker, 2015), focussing on enforcing standardised procedures (Brunderlein & Grassmann, 2006), including manuals, guidelines, and rules (Harmer, Haver, & Stoddard, 2010). Danger is seen as a quantitative measure, relying on mathematics to determine risk levels so that it can be avoided altogether (Neuman & Weissman, 2016). In this way, it replaces the subjective nature of awareness with more scientific methods (i.e. based on empirical approaches) to elicit knowledge from security experts who are used to decide and design procedures (Brunderlein & Grassmann, 2006), and attempting to move away from the gut-feeling responses which were often of importance in the community-based approach (Harmer et al., 2010). Training focusses on following these procedures, rather than helping staff develop risk awareness (Barnett, 2004).

Unlike the community-based approach, the systems-based approach views security as a functional entity that can be modelled, predicted, and controlled (Collinson & Duffield, 2013; Neuman & Weissman, 2016). In this way, the influence of the individual humanitarian worker is minimised or eliminated (Beerli & Weissman, 2016), as individual decision making is seen as too unpredictable to manage effectively (Daudin & Merkelbach, 2011).

Brunderlein and Grassmann (2006) identified four weaknesses to the systems-based approach:

- It relies on the quality of risk assessments and therefore the security intelligence.
- It is reactive and based on generic risks and responses, which oversimplifies the complex nature of political, social, and economic risks.

- To be effective, it needs an effective response capability, such as that provided by the military.
- It skews the long-term outlook for programmes, instead of putting more emphasis on immediate security.

This rigid nature of security systems, where experts are relied on to provide advice and staff are given rules and procedures to follow, can create a false sense of security where individual responsibility for security awareness is removed (Barnett, 2004; Daudin & Merkelbach, 2011). The role of security experts may give other staff a belief that the experts alone are responsible for security, thus 'everybody's business becomes nobody's business' and overall security capability is reduced (Fast, Freeman, O'Neill, & Rowley, 2013, p. 236). Furthermore, quantifying risk can answer where, when, and how questions, but does not provide answers on why risks occur which further reduces general understanding and awareness (Brooks, 2016).

RELATIONSHIP BETWEEN TOP-DOWN AND BOTTOM-UP APPROACHES

The community-based and systems-based approaches should, in theory, be complementary to each other (Brunderlein & Grassmann, 2006): effective risk-analysis can inform when community-based approaches are safe to implement, which allows staff to build acceptance which in turn provides greater access to information to inform risk-analysis (Bollentino, 2008). However, the community-based approach has not been largely adopted by many organisations (Brunderlein & Grassmann, 2006) and is poorly supported by literature or studies of how it works in practice (Bollentino, 2008; Grassmann, 2005). Not long after it was proposed, the attacks in Iraq occurred, which prompted many organisations to believe that the community-based approach did not work (Grassmann, 2005).

The attacks revealed the difficulty in building acceptance, which is critical for the community-based approach, as it is required from all parties, including those who are potential aggressors (Van Brabant, 2001). There are some countries where this is not possible however (Collinson & Duffield, 2013) since in some contexts there are groups that promote anarchy and do not want humanitarian organisations helping the local community (Childs, 2013; Egeland, Harmer, & Stoddard, 2011). As with the ongoing conflict in Syria, extremist groups explicitly seek a lack of stability and promote violence. Such conflicts are likely to continue worldwide, which are typified by guerrilla warfare, terrorism, and a rise in lawlessness, meaning the groups from whom acceptance is needed are likely to be opposed to humanitarian goals (Burkle, 2005; Fast & Wille, 2010; Kaldor, 2012). This presents a considerable challenge to the ethical demands of ethnographic and indigenous research.

Arguably the community-based approach cannot be effective with humanitarian work, which has become increasingly politicised (Bollentino, 2008; Brunderlein & Grassmann, 2006; Duffield, 2014; Fast et al., 2013). Duffield (2014) discusses how many humanitarian organisations have started to move away from impartial approaches, in which assistance is given to all based on their need, even where such groups could be partial to and fuelling conflicts. Organisations instead become peacebuilders, planning programmes to bring about an end to conflict (Duffield, 2014). Programmes with such aims are often better funded by donors, which also include government institutions, which limits what community groups the funding can support and ultimately makes humanitarian aid political in nature (Egeland et al., 2011; Fast et al., 2013), therefore limiting how effective the community-based approach can be.

Considering both the politicisation of aid as well as the perceived need to professionalise security, the sector has largely adopted systems-based approach over a community-based approach (Claus, 2011; Collinson & Duffield, 2013; Daudin & Merkelbach, 2011; Egeland et al., 2011).

The systems-based approach allows investment in a central system which can be implemented in other communities, while the community-based approach means investment is in one local area (Brunderlein & Grassmann, 2006; Childs, 2013). Investment into local acceptance is seen as financially risky as the approach does not always ensure security (Collinson & Duffield, 2013). Furthermore, the systems-based approach also allows an organisation to document how it meets its legal Duty of Care obligations; or their obligations to take necessary measures to protect staff (Kemp & Merkelbach, 2011). Organisations are becoming more aware of their legal obligations in comparison to before the 2003 attacks (Kemp & Merkelbach, 2011; Klamp, 2007) and implement systems to protect their staff and reputation, which in turn allows them to compete for further funding (Bollentino, 2008).

Lastly, the systems-based approach is easier to achieve as a strategy (Neuman & Weissman, 2016), where management can mark progress by identifying what measures have been implemented and how many staff have received training (Barnett, 2004). The measures implemented are also more objective at keeping staff safe (Daudin & Merkelbach, 2011; Schneiker, 2015), whereas community-based approaches are subjective in their effect on improving security (Brunderlein & Grassmann, 2006). Therefore, the systems-based approach is preferred to the community-based approach in terms of finance, documenting legal obligations as well as management oversight.

Though the systems-based approach seeks to replace individual judgement with standardised procedures (Brunderlein & Grassmann, 2006; Collinson & Duffield, 2013; Neuman & Weissman, 2016), intuitive decision making still occurs with field workers who undervalue the need to collect and analyse data on security (Buchanan & Muggah, 2005). Several authors note that field staff often resist standards imposed from the top-down (Brunderlein & Grassmann, 2006; Daudin & Merkelbach, 2011; Neuman & Weissman, 2016). One explanation is that security objectives are prioritised over programme activities, therefore hindering field staff completing their work (Daudin & Merkelbach, 2011; Fast, Freeman, O'Neill, & Rowley, 2014; Schneiker, 2015).

Another explanation is that a disparity exists between what field workers and security experts believe is necessary to ensure operational security (Adams, 2003;

Barnett, 2004; Brunderlein & Grassmann, 2006; Collinson & Duffield, 2013; Daudin & Merkelbach, 2011). Where this conflict in knowledge management exists, staff are likely to follow their own understandings and beliefs over the instruction of security experts, either passed through training or through procedures (Brunderlein & Grassmann, 2006; Daudin & Merkelbach, 2011). Issues in knowledge mismanagement can mean that systems implemented to keep staff safe are not followed, staff are ill-prepared for the environments they deploy to and the organisation is unable to achieve its goal. This conflict highlights an area of significance not yet fully explored in the literature.

CONFLICT OF KNOWLEDGE BETWEEN TOP-DOWN AND BOTTOM-UP APPROACHES

The top-down systems-based approach emphasises the role of the security expert as the knowledge creator, responsible for designing the system and the supporting material for its implementation (Barnett, 2004; Brunderlein & Grassmann, 2006; Burns, Burnham, & Rowley, 2013). In doing so, the knowledge and experience of field workers is neglected (Bollentino, 2008; Buchanan & Muggah, 2005; Neuman & Weissman, 2016). There are three areas where the literature outlines how this conflict in knowledge has a negative impact: a conflict between procedures and what field workers know to be true, the inability to convert experience into knowledge to improve security systems and training being ineffective at improving staff security.

Conflict between Procedures and Experience

Multiple authors note the disregard many field workers have for the security procedures imposed on them to keep them safe (Ahtisaari, 2003; Collinson & Duffield, 2013; Daudin & Merkelbach, 2011; Neuman & Weissman, 2016; Van Brabant, 2000). Daudin and Merkelbach (2011) state that there is a tendency for field staff to only follow rules that reflect their own beliefs and experience. Adams (2003) makes the point that this is a natural behaviour of people, using the everyday example of crossing the road to frame the issue: though the experts designed the system so that people wait until the red light shows before crossing, many people will use their own judgement to see if it is clear and cross even when the light is not red. Adams (2003) used this example to frame his discussion on how people ignore systems where they believe they have a better understanding of the solution 'in context'.

Security procedures lose even more buy-in from staff when they do not directly reflect the situation field workers find themselves in (Barnett, 2004; Collinson & Duffield, 2013). One example of this is a rule commonly imposed that prevents those with weapons using organisation vehicles (e.g. People in Aid, 2008, p. 17), so the organisation remains neutral. In reality, if an armed person wants to get into the vehicle the humanitarian workers have no way of refusing them carriage. Though such a rule ignores the local context (Barnett, 2004; Collinson & Duffield,

2013), Beerli and Weissman (2016) state that humanitarian workers are likely to face disciplinary action if rules are broken, rather than be commended for their individual judgement. In one study, such an approach was documented to reduce the reporting of incidents by field staff for fear of losing their jobs (Donnelly & Mazurana, 2017). This reduces the ground-truth-reality of how many incidents occur, weakening a systems approach which is reliant on statistics for risk assessments (Bollentino, 2008).

Field Experience is Not Converted into Knowledge

Underlying the disparity between procedures and experience is the inability for organisations to utilise staff experience effectively (Bollentino, 2008; Buchanan & Muggah, 2005). The systems-based approach downplays the role of individual knowledge, which is seen as too diverse and incoherent to be of use (Daudin & Merkelbach, 2011). However, those workers who have amassed experience of working in high-risk environments are likely to be able to rectify procedural and training issues and help review the security systems in use (Barnett, 2004; Bollentino, 2008; Buchanan & Muggah, 2005; Collinson & Duffield, 2013; Darby & Williamson, 2012).

Nonetheless, there is an 'inability to institutionalise staff experience' (Bollentino, 2008, p. 265) and a largely ad hoc approach to its use (Burns et al., 2013; Persaud, 2014). Where staff experience has been utilised to improve security, it has been at the expense of formal training: a study conducted on security issues in Darfur found that new workers had not been given basic training and experienced staff had been expected to guide and look after novice workers, even though their experience was from other countries and not necessarily appropriate (Eckroth, 2010).

The need to capture this knowledge is important for humanitarian organisations, which suffer a high staff turnover compared to other lines of work (Richardson, 2006). This has been identified as a general weakness in knowledge sharing across multiple areas in the sector, including security (Darby & Williamson, 2012; Emmens, Hammersley, & Loquercio, 2006; Richardson, 2006). In a study conducted on reasons staff leave, one of the reasons highlighted was not the risk itself but the lack of training and inappropriate preparations to face such dangers (Emmens et al., 2006). Therefore, if experience is not effectively converted into knowledge it cannot be used by humanitarian organisations to improve security training and preparations, which will itself continue causing a high staff turnover and loss of knowledge.

Training is Ineffective at Improving Staff Security

The systems-based approach has reduced training so that it focusses more on how to follow the procedures, rather than how staff can effectively assess and respond to risks themselves (Barnett, 2004; Burns et al., 2013; Persaud, 2014). As such, field-based training is largely replaced with classroom activities (Barnett, 2004; Persaud, 2014) and many staff deploy into the field unprepared (Barnett, 2004), with many not receiving any training at all (Egeland et al., 2011). Furthermore, training has generally become focussed on hard measures, such as how to respond to gunfire, grenades, or minefields (Bollentino, 2006; Daudin & Merkelbach, 2011) at the expense of 'soft' measures, such as communication skills, situation awareness, and leadership which are likely to be more effective in some settings (George et al., 2020; Persaud, 2014). This results in staff being unable to assess the likelihood and risk of harm themselves, nor elicit information from local communities, therefore becoming reliant on their organisation's security experts (Barnett, 2004). This further reduces the ability of those in the field to be able to think dynamically about risk themselves, instead being reliant on the system to protect or guide them (Bollentino, 2008; Daudin & Merkelbach, 2011). In this sense, security becomes seen as a technical problem which can only be solved with technical expertise (Daudin & Merkelbach, 2011) and training becomes introductory in nature (Bollentino, 2006; Brunderlein & Grassmann, 2006).

The difference in view is often made worse when organisations use external suppliers for training, which is increasingly common (Burns et al., 2013; Collinson & Duffield, 2013; Persaud, 2014). These external providers are only able to give generic training which does not draw upon and incorporate staff experience (Barnett, 2004; Persaud, 2014), and the training often excludes any focus on the specific risks workers may face (Brunderlein & Grassmann, 2006; Eastman, Evert, & Mishori, 2016). There has also been a critique of how effective such training is, with security experts varying in experience level, many of whom have experience from military or police roles that do not necessarily translate into the humanitarian context (Persaud, 2014).

KNOWLEDGE MANAGEMENT IN SECURITY

The triad of conflict areas highlight fundamental aspects surrounding the mismanagement in knowledge within the two approaches. The shift to the top-down approach has minimised the role of the individual (Beerli & Weissman, 2016) and has made field workers dependent on the security systems, rather than able to think flexibly and independently (Barnett, 2004; Bollentino, 2008; Daudin & Merkelbach, 2011). However, a lack of focus on the knowledge of humanitarian workers has had three marked impacts:

- There is a conflict between what workers know to be effective and the procedures in place (Adams, 2003; Collinson & Duffield, 2013; Daudin & Merkelbach, 2011).
- Field experience is not converted into knowledge for use within the organisation (Bollentino, 2008; Buchanan & Muggah, 2005; Darby & Williamson, 2012).
- Training is introductory in nature and does not effectively improve security (Barnett, 2004; Burns et al., 2013; Persaud, 2014).

This inability to utilise experience and knowledge of field workers weakens the overall system (Bollentino, 2008; Brunderlein & Grassmann, 2006; Buchanan & Muggah, 2005).

When top-down and bottom-up knowledge does not align, the systems in place to support users are weakened (Wilson, 2005). Daudin and Merkelbach (2011) stated that this is the case in the humanitarian sector where there is little input from the field level. They discussed issues around security procedures, stating that there was little input from those on the ground, and therefore the content of the procedures diverges. However, from recent research (Paul, 2018) there is evidence that knowledge, in the form of requirements, converges more than it diverges.

This seems to contradict what has been observed in previous research, in which several authors found a misalignment between the organisational and field levels in terms of security thinking (Barnett, 2004; Brunderlein & Grassmann, 2006; Egeland et al., 2011; Martin, 1999; Persaud, 2014; Van Brabant, 2001). Field workers classed as practitioner experts (Burton & Shadbolt, 1995) will have had the opportunity to internalise knowledge, through repeated exposure and experience of utilising security in practical situations (Nonaka & Takeuchi, 1995).

The argument posed in the literature that top-down and bottom-up knowledge does not align may be more relevant for less experienced workers. This is potentially supported through studies on humanitarian worker deaths that show inexperienced workers are more at risk (Bolton et al., 2000; Buchanan & Muggah, 2005; Burnham & Rowley, 2005). Bolton et al.'s (2000) study, which is the only one accounting for length of service, concluded that out of the 382 deaths studied, 31% occurred within the first three months of service, with 17% occurring within the first month, with a median of eight months. This is also backed up by observations and reflections of experienced field workers (Paul, 2018). Further study is needed to identify at what stage field workers adopt and demonstrate more expert skill levels and stop showing qualities identified as those demonstrated by novice workers.

Further research using simulated training scenarios has demonstrated that training in itself was not effective in ensuring novice workers are able to effectively operate in high-risk environments (Paul, 2018). Those who were classed as inexperienced (i.e. less than five years' experience) were not able to effectively apply the explicit knowledge learnt on the day to the scenarios encountered. This largely reflects what is stated in the literature, that training is only introductory, generic, and cannot fully prepare staff for high-risk environments (Brunderlein & Grassmann, 2006; Darby & Williamson, 2012; Egeland et al., 2011; Persaud, 2014).

Organisations sometimes view training as a means of meeting their 'Duty of Care' requirements (Barnett, 2004; Daudin & Merkelbach, 2011; Kemp & Merkelbach, 2011). However, training itself cannot be the end state. This is supported by Claus (2015), an expert on Duty of Care and legal obligations of organisations, who states that organisations are responsible to ensure not only the systems in place but also that staff are effectively trained for the environments they deploy into. Addressing these concerns will allow a better understanding of where knowledge diverges, which in turn would allow organisations to ensure that staff receive the right training to ensure they are prepared for high-risk environments (Claus, 2015). Furthermore, this would allow organisations' Human Resources departments to ensure that only those who are able to demonstrate the required skills are selected for projects in high-risk environments (Darby & Williamson, 2012).

The lack of engaging field workers in developing solutions (Barnett, 2004; Collinson & Duffield, 2013) means that 'bottom-up' community-based knowledge is rarely elicited. Organisations that fail to do this lose knowledge which could improve systems and give them a competitive advantage, either over others or more pertinently for this domain over the problem (Nonaka, 1991; Nonaka & Takeuchi, 1995). This mission-critical information is lost over time in many sectors due to an ageing workforce (Dzekashu & McCollum, 2014). This is even more prevalent in the humanitarian sector due to an above average rate of staff turnover (Balbo, Heyse, Korff, & Wittek, 2015; Darby & Williamson, 2012; Emmens et al., 2006; Richardson, 2006). There is a need to continually capture this knowledge so that it can be passed on through explicit means to other, less experienced workers, who in turn are able to internalise the knowledge and refine it in relation to the problems they might face.

CONCLUSION

This chapter has presented a discussion and critical comparison of community-based and systems-based approaches to security risk management through the introduction of top-down and bottom-up knowledge acquisition. There is still some debate about how much knowledge elicited from academic experts, or security subject-matter experts, and practitioner experts, or the field workers themselves may converge or diverge. However, it is apparent that a more consistent approach needs to address the conflict between procedures and experience, help convert field experience into knowledge, and ultimately provide effective training that is relevant to those heading out into demanding work situations. Evidently it is not enough to argue for the 'ethical' strength of community-based approaches as promoted by ethnographers and indigenous researchers – ethics and method are intricately bound together in such an approach. It is equally unethical to neglect the organisational responsibilities and the duties of care organisations hold towards staff being placed in critical and risky situations. The security of both staff and at-risk populations depends upon correctly managing the balance between systems and communities.

REFERENCES

Adams, J. (2003). Risk and morality: Three framing devices. In A. Doyle & R. Ericson (Eds.), *Risk and morality* (pp. 87–104). Toronto: University of Toronto Press.

Ahtisaari, M. (2003). Report of the independent panel on the safety and security of UN personnel in Iraq. [Online] Retrieved from https://reliefweb.int/report/iraq/report-independent-panel-safety-and-security-un-personnel-iraq. Accessed on May 24, 2021.

Balbo, N., Heyse, L., Korff, V., & Wittek, R. (2015). The impact of humanitarian context conditions and individual characteristics on aid worker retention. *Disasters, 39*(3), 522–545.

Barnett, K. (2004). *Report on security of humanitarian personnel: Standards and practices for the security of humanitarian personnel and advocacy for humanitarian space*. New York, NY: United Nations Office for the Coordination of Humanitarian Affairs.

Beerli, M., & Weissman, F. (2016). Humanitarian security manuals: Neutralising the human factor in humanitarian action. In M. Neuman & F. Weissman (Eds.), *Saving lives and staying alive: Humanitarian security in the age of risk management* (pp. 71–81). London: C. Hurst & Co.

Bollentino, V. (2006). *Designing security: Methods for improving security management practices and security coordination among humanitarian organisations.* Cambridge, MA: Harvard University.

Bollentino, V. (2008). Understanding the security management practices of humanitarian organisations. *Disasters, 32*(2), 263–279.

Bolton, P., Burnham, G., Gutierrez, M., Sheik, M., Spiegel, P., & Thieren, M. (2000). Deaths among humanitarian workers. *British Medical Journal, 321*(7254), 166–168.

Brooks, J. (2016). *Protecting humanitarian action: Key challenges and lessons from the field.* Cambridge, MA: Harvard Humanitarian Initiative.

Browning, C., & McDonald, M. (2011). The future if critical security studies: Ethics and the politics of security. *European Journal of International Relations, 19*(2), 235–255.

Brunderlein, C., & Grassmann, P. (2006). Managing risks in hazardous missions: The challenges of securing United Nations access to vulnerable groups. *Harvard Human Rights Journal, 19*(1), 63–94.

Buchanan, C., & Muggah, R. (2005). *No Relief: Surveying the effects of gun violence on humanitarian and development personnel.* Geneva: Centre for Humanitarian Dialogue and the Small Arms Survey.

Burkle, F. (2005). Anatomy of an Ambush: Security risks facing humanitarian assistance. *Disasters, 29*(1), 26–37.

Burnham, G., & Rowley, E. (2005). *Mortality and morbidity of humanitarian worker narrative report.* Baltimore, MD: John Hopkins Bloomberg School of Public Health.

Burns, L., Burnham, G., & Rowley, E. (2013). Research review of nongovernmental organisations: Security policies for humanitarian programs in war. Conflict and post-conflict environments. *Disaster Medicine and Public Health Preparedness, 7*(3), 241–250.

Burton, M., & Shadbolt, N. (1995). Knowledge elicitation: A systematic approach. In N. Corlett & J. Wilson (pp. 406–440). *Evaluation of human work: A practical ergonomics methodology.* London: Taylor and Francis.

Buzan, B., & Hansen, L. (2009). *The evolution of international security studies.* Cambridge: Cambridge University Press.

Childs, A. (2013). Cultural theory and acceptance-based security strategies for humanitarian aid workers. *Journal of Strategic Security, 6*(1), 64–72.

Claus, L. (2011). *Duty of care and travel risk management global benchmarking study* [White Paper]. London: AEA International Holdings Pte. Ltd.

Claus, L. (2015). *The world of aid is changing: Understanding unique challenges and duty of care best practices for NGOs.* London: AEA International Holdings Pte. Ltd.

Collinson, S., & Duffield, M. (2013). *Paradoxes of presence: Risk management and aid culture in challenging environments.* London: Overseas Development Institute.

Connelly, M. (1998). Security and humanitarian space: The UNHCR perspective. *Humanitares Volkerrecht, 1*(1), 6–9.

Darby, R., & Williamson, C. (2012). Challenges to international human resource management: The management of employee risk in the humanitarian aid and security sectors. *International Journal of Resources Development and Management, 12*(2), 159–186.

Daudin, P., & Merkelbach, M. (2011). *From security management to risk management: Critical reflections on aid agency security management and the ISO risk management guidelines.* Geneva: Security Management Initiative.

Dind, P. (1998). Security and humanitarian space: The ICRC perspective. *Humanitares Volkerrecht, 1*(1), 9–13.

Donnelly, P., & Mazurana, D. (2017). *Stop the sexual assault against humanitarian and development aid workers.* Somerville, MA: Feinstein International Centre.

Duffield, M. (2014). *Global governance and the new wars: Merging of development and security* (rev. ed.). London: Zed Books Ltd.

Dzekashu, W., & McCollum, W. (2014). A quality approach to tacit knowledge capture: Effective practice to achieving operational excellence. *International Journal of Applied Management, 13*(1), 52–63.

Eastman, A., Evert, J., & Mishori, R. (2016). Improving the safety and security of those engaged in global health travelling abroad. *Global Health: Science and Practice, 4*(4), 522–528.

Egeland, J., Harmer, A., & Stoddard, A. (2011). *To stay and deliver: Good practices for humanitarians in complex security environments.* New York, NY: United Nations Office for the Coordination of Humanitarian Affairs.

Eckroth, K. (2010). Humanitarian principles and protection dilemmas: Addressing the security situation of aid workers in Darfur. *Journal of International Peacekeeping, 14*(1), 86–116.

Emmens, B., Hammersley, M., & Loquercio, D. (2006). *Understanding and addressing the staff turnover in humanitarian agencies.* London: Overseas Development Institute.

Fast, L., Freeman, F., O'Neill, M., & Rowley, E. (2013). In acceptance we trust? Conceptualising acceptance as a viable approach to NGO security management. *Disasters, 37*(2), 222–243.

Fast, L., Freeman, F., O'Neill, M., & Rowley, E. (2014). The promise of acceptance as an NGO security management approach. *Disasters, 39*(2), 208–231.

Fast, L., & Wille, C. (2010). *Is terrorism an issue for humanitarian organisations?.* Geneva: Geneva Centre for Security Policy.

George, L., MacDonald, l., & Tauri, J. (2020). *Indigenous research ethics.* Bingley: Emerald.

Grassmann, P. (2005). Rethinking humanitarian security. *Humanitarian Exchange, 30*(1), 32–34.

Harmer, A., Haver, K., & Stoddard, A. (2010). *Good practice review 8: Operational security management in violent environments* (rev. ed.). London: Overseas Development Institute.

Harmer, A., & Schreter, L. (2013). *Delivering aid in highly insecure environments: A critical review of literature, 2002–2012.* London: Humanitarian Outcomes.

Iphofen, R. (2011–2013). *Research ethics in ethnography/anthropology.* Commissioned Discussion Document, DG Research and Innovation, European Commission, Brussels.

Kaldor, M. (2012). *New and old wars: Organised violence in a global era.* Cambridge: Polity Press.

Kemp, E., & Merkelbach, M. (2011). *Can you get sued? Legal liability of international humanitarian aid organisations toward their staff.* Geneva: Security Management Institute.

Klamp, C. (2007). Legal Liability in the humanitarian sector. *Red-R Safety and Security Review, 7,* 2–5.

Martin, R. (1999). NGO field security. *Forced Migration Review, 4*(1), 4–7.

Neuman, M., & Weissman, F. (2016). *Saving lives and staying live: Humanitarian security in the age of risk management.* London: Hurst & Company.

Nonaka, I. (1991). The knowledge creating company. *Harvard Business Review, 69,* 96–104.

Nonaka, I., & Takeuchi, H. (1995). *The knowledge-creating company: How Japanese companies create the dynamics of innovation.* New York, NY: Oxford University Press, Inc.

Paul, D. (2018). *A knowledge elicitation approach to improving security management systems in the humanitarian sector.* Unpublished Ph.D. Thesis, Coventry University.

Persaud, C. (2014). *NGO safety and security training project: How to create effective training for NGOs.* London: The European Interagency Security Forum.

People in Aid. (2008). Policy guide and template: Safety and security. [Online] Retrieved from https://codeofgoodpractice.com/wp-content/uploads/2019/05/People-in-Aid-Safety-and-Security-Policy-Guide-and-Template.pdf. Accessed on May 25, 2021.

Richardson, F. (2006). Meeting the demand for skilled and experienced humanitarian workers. *Development in Practice, 16* (3–4), 334–341.

Schneiker, A. (2015). *Humanitarian NGOs, (in)security and identity: Epistemic communities and security governance.* Oxon: Routledge.

Van Brabant, K. (1998a). Security and humanitarian space: Perspective of an aid agency. *Humanitares Volkerrecht, 1*(1), 14–24.

Van Brabant, K. (1998b). Cool ground for aid providers: Towards better security management in aid agencies. *Disasters, 22*(2), 109–125.

Van Brabant, K. (2000). *Good practice review 8: Operational security management in violent environments.* London: Overseas Development Institute.

Van Brabant, K. (2001). *Mainstreaming the organisational management of safety and security.* HPG Report 9. Overseas Development Institute, London.

Williams, P. (2013). *Security studies: An introduction* (2nd ed.). Oxon: Routledge.

Wilson, J. (2005). Methods in the understanding of human factors. In N. Corlett & J. Wilson (Eds.), *Evaluation of human work: A practical ergonomics methodology* (3rd ed., pp. 1–31). London: Taylor and Francis.

CHAPTER 11

CONDUCTING ETHICAL RESEARCH IN SENSITIVE SECURITY DOMAINS: UNDERSTANDING THREATS AND THE IMPORTANCE OF BUILDING TRUST

Alex Stedmon and Daniel Paul

ABSTRACT

In many security domains, the 'human in the system' is often a critical line of defence in identifying, preventing and responding to any threats (Saikayasit, Stedmon, & Lawson, 2015). Traditionally, such security domains are often focussed on mainstream public safety within crowded spaces and border controls, through to identifying suspicious behaviours, hostile reconnaissance and implementing counter-terrorism initiatives. More recently, with growing insecurity around the world, organisations have looked to improve their security risk management frameworks, developing concepts which originated in the health and safety field to deal with more pressing risks such as terrorist acts, abduction and piracy (Paul, 2018). In these instances, security is usually the specific responsibility of frontline personnel with defined roles and responsibilities operating in accordance with organisational protocols (Saikayasit, Stedmon, Lawson, & Fussey, 2012; Stedmon, Saikayasit, Lawson, & Fussey, 2013). However,

Ethical Issues in Covert, Security and Surveillance Research
Advances in Research Ethics and Integrity, Volume 8, 159–176

ISSN: 2398-6018/doi:10.1108/S2398-601820210000008012

understanding the knowledge that frontline security workers might possess and use requires sensitive investigation in equally sensitive security domains.

This chapter considers how to investigate knowledge elicitation in these sensitive security domains and underlying ethics in research design that supports and protects the nature of investigation and end-users alike. This chapter also discusses the criteria used for ensuring trustworthiness as well as assessing the relative merits of the range of methods adopted.

Keywords: Ethical research; sensitive security domains; establishing trust; knowledge elicitation methods; deductive and inductive reasoning; stakeholders and end-users

INTRODUCTION: RESEARCH IN SENSITIVE DOMAINS

The lack of literature on security is not only down to the relative youth of the field as an academic discipline ('critical security studies' only really becoming a field in the 1990s, Buzan & Hansen, 2009), but also due to the way organisations protect such information and the difficulties in openly sharing it (Williams & McDonald, 2018). Organisations working in the security sector will carefully protect what data and information are publicly available both to ensure the safety of their staff and operations, and also because the reality is that processes are often far from optimal and could reveal potential shortcomings in management and practice (Harmer & Schreter, 2013). Such issues underpin research in sensitive domains by impacting the quality of data that can be collected in primary research and limiting the information available for meta-analyses (Barnard, Geber, & McCosker, 2001).

Though sensitive domains are often associated with health and safety research or specific investigations with vulnerable populations (Cowles, 1988; Sieber & Stanley, 1988), Lee (1993) uses an extended definition to include any domain that possesses three specific characteristics:

- *An intrusive threat* – where the research may cause strong emotional responses from participants. An intrusive threat is any subject which is highly personal to participants and has the potential to cause a negative emotional response (Cowles, 1988). Such typology is fitting to topics in which death and traumatic experiences are discussed, especially if the participant has been directly involved or has emotional links to those involved (Lee, 1993). To highlight the prevalence of death and trauma, between 2007 and 2016 there was a mean of 104 deaths a year in the humanitarian sector (Czwarno, Harmer, & Stoddard, 2017). It is not just death itself or major attack against a field worker, but the experience of being in a developing country, hostile environment or post-disaster setting that can have a negative emotional effect (Brewer, 2017). Such emotions can be re-experienced during the conduct of research and likely to pose an intrinsic threat as it may deal with concepts such as death and trauma by nature of the subject.

- *The threat of sanctions* – where participants fear that in revealing information there will be repercussions on them. For example, this may include situations where participants may have broken rules or committed wrongdoings and with the threat of sanctions this can limit what participants might want to openly say or admit to (Lee, 1993). As the security management has moved to a systems-based approach, a greater number of rules have been imposed on workers (Brunderlein & Grassmann, 2006). These rules give managers the power to impose disciplinary procedures on staff who go against the security measures (Harmer, Haver, & Stoddard, 2010). However, these remove the human aspect of decision making, meaning staff could face discipline for taking actions that were appropriate for the time and place but were contrary to the established rules (Beerli & Weissman, 2016). This is even more likely, where those in the field have little input into the rules imposed (Daudin & Merkelbach, 2011). Therefore, where participants admit to situations where they went against rules, there can be the underlying threat of sanction in the form of disciplinary action.
- *Political threat* – in the broadest sense where data collected might be used for negative purposes by powerful people or organisations (Lee, 1993). This is particularly the case where the research may reveal flaws in security measures which can then be exploited by aggressive actors (Brewers, 1990). For example, with the rise in the kidnapping threat, where aggressive actors conduct surveillance against targets to identify weaknesses (Harmer, Stoddard, & Toth, 2013) and any useful intelligence gleaned from research could be used against security workers themselves. Another aspect of political threat is the loss of funding from donors, for which many humanitarian organisations are critically dependent (Martin, Metcalfe, & Pantuliano, 2011). Humanitarian organisations may limit the information they share about their capabilities and weaknesses, so that donors are more likely to support them (Bollentino, 2008). Such competition for funding means that organisations often obscure the risks they are exposed to and may be reluctant to be fully transparent in the information they do share. Revealing information on security weaknesses can therefore cause a political threat, limiting transparency and producing a culture where participants are less likely to reveal information on operational weaknesses (Lee, 1993).

These characteristics help keep researchers aware of key issues associated with accessing and collecting data within sensitive domains. In doing so, it provides critical reflection on acceptability and ethics – whether the methods are acceptable to the participants and fit for the purpose of the research, and how the methods limit any potential negative effects on those involved in the research (Wilson, 2005).

DEDUCTIVE AND INDUCTIVE REASONING

Research in this domain usually takes an inductive, rather than a deductive, approach. Whilst there are merits to choosing a deductive approach, it suffers from the assumption that the solution lies within the problem and therefore the problem statement must be known to all involved in some way (Wilson, 2010). In simple terms, if a statement cannot be known, then it is seen to be 'deductively' untrue. This is based on 'closed-world assumptions' where any statement which is true is there to be discovered and known to be true, and vice versa (Fox, 2008; Kelly, 2014).

Deductive research can produce strong and reliable conclusions, best suited to quantitative research methods where theories, hypotheses and specific variables can be tested and investigated (Lewis, Saunders, & Thornhill, 2009). However, it is problematic employing deductive reasoning when there are many unknowns (Babbie, 2011). This is often the case in security investigations, especially when investigating the effects of knowledge management on operational security (where established theories and foundational assumptions are lacking).

Inductive research is more suited to new or unexplored fields, as its greatest strength is that it can 'generate theory' where little data exist (Babbie, 2011). Inductive reasoning allows for, and helps to foster, emergent designs and grounded theory approaches (Given, 2008a; Pailthorpe, 2017). Although a theory may be disproven later, it can stimulate discussion and provide a basis for new theories to arise, or for the original theory to be refined through future deductive reasoning (Kelly, 2014). It is therefore important that inductive reasoning remains flexible and open to re-interpretation so that emergent themes can develop freely (Merriam & Tisdell, 2016).

Inductive research often begins with a specific focus and through data gathering identifies patterns and generates new understandings for why particular patterns exist (Bryman & Bell, 2011). In this way, general principles are developed from specific observations (Babbie, 2011). The starting point for inductive research often lies in collecting relevant data, employing mixed methods such as interviews or observations (Fox, 2008). Mixed methods allow the phenomenon to be viewed and tackled from multiple, complementary, angles and triangulated for greater scientific rigour (Milton, 2012).

Inductive reasoning is often employed within the discipline of human factors, which seeks to understand the interactions between humans and the systems they operate within (Stanton, Salmon, Walker, Baber, & Jenkins, 2005; Wilson, 2005). Human factors takes a user-centred perspective when investigating complex socio-technical systems that are typical of security settings (Stanton et al., 2013; Stedmon et al., 2013). By focussing on the individual, and employing knowledge elicitation methodologies, it is possible to identify and capture knowledge necessary for systems to work more effectively (Hoffman, 1987).

DEVELOPING AN ETHICAL RESEARCH APPROACH

Safeguarding those involved in research is paramount in any investigation. It is crucial that critical reflection of the methodologies to be used is applied to the research in order to help identify the inherent risks and how complementary methods can be used (Wilson, 2005). It can also help identify, at an early stage, how the inductive approach can be developed to provide better results (Stanton et al., 2005). A primary concern in sensitive security domains is gaining access and promoting open and transparent data collection processes. This improves the critical reflection on the dependability, and therefore trustworthiness, of the approach and data collected in any investigation (Shenton, 2004). Several techniques can be applied to gain access to sensitive security domains and promote openness from participants:

- *Relationships and building rapport* – it is common for researchers to act as external observers, staying separated and not divulging personal lives to participants (Creswell, 2003). This builds into the concept of non-reactivity in that the researcher has as small an impact as possible on participants and the research (Wilson, 2005). Sensitive domain research requires an alternative approach where researchers develop trusting relationships and a trusted rapport with participants (Clark & Kotulic, 2004). This is often done by demonstrating a shared identity and purpose (Cowles, 1988) and sharing personal accounts relevant to the area of inquiry (Lee & Renzetti, 1990). In doing so, participants can identify the researcher who can promote more open and honest exchanges (Barton, 2015; Dickenson-Swift, James, & Liamputtong, 2007).
- *Recording data and alternatives to recording/transcribing* – both Clark and Kotulic (2004) and Cowles (1988) state that the use of digital recording can often deter participants from feeling open to answer sensitive questions. Therefore, alternative methods of recording data are necessary (Clark & Kotulic, 2004). Cowles (1988) suggests that whilst alternatives may be available, fully explaining the use of any data recorder, and making it known that the recorder can be turned off at any point allows the data to be captured for analysis, but also for the participant to maintain control of the exchange and to state things 'off the record' where appropriate (Cowles, 1988). Where this might occur, for accuracy and ethical reassurance, close written transcripts should be written at the time, reflecting both what is said as well as the context in which it was said.
- *Ensuring confidentiality and non-reactivity* – in any research, it is ethically vital that issues of confidentiality are dealt with sympathetically. It is important to take steps to remove the possibility of deductive-disclosure (i.e. identification of any data and/or individuals from what participants say or through job details) (Kaiser, 2009). In order for data to keep its rich description whilst ensuring privacy to those involved, techniques such as paraphrasing over verbatim transcribing may be necessary. In this way, researchers have a duty and participants have control in the way data are interpreted. Before data are collected, the protocols need to be explained to participants in order to allow them to decide what data can be used, and ensuring they are fully aware of how their data will be used, who will have access to it and how identities may be kept confidential (Adams & Cox, 2008). For a more detailed discussion of privacy in research see Chapter 3 in this volume.
- *Purposive sampling* – Clark and Kotulic (2004) suggest that limiting the number of participants involved in research allows greater time to be spent developing

relationships and trust. Purposive sampling is a common technique in qualitative inquiry, where the quantity of participants is secondary to the quality of data they can provide (Cochran & Quinn-Patton, 2007). To a degree, all sampling should have a purpose and should be representative of the wider population under investigation. Within the sensitive domain, participants are identified based on their relevance to the investigation rather than employing random sampling techniques (Bryman & Bell, 2011).

- *Recruitment of participants through professional networks* – in sensitive or in hard-to-reach domains, snowball or chain referral sampling methods are particularly successful in engaging with a target audience (Atkinson & Flint, 2004). This approach relies on cumulative referrals made by those who share knowledge or interact with others at an operational level or share specific interests for the investigation (Biernacki & Waldorf, 1981). Each successive referral further expands the possible number of people reached by the researcher (Atkinson & Flint, 2004). In this way, snowball sampling increases the possible sample size and accesses participants that other techniques may not allow (Atkinson & Flint, 2001). This method is predicted to be particularly effective in the humanitarian domain where there are strong informal networks (Kuhanendran & Micheni, 2010; Schneiker, 2015). This sampling method is useful where security agencies and organisations might be reluctant to share confidential and sensitive information with those they perceive to be 'outsiders'. This method has been used in the areas of drug use and addiction research (see Sims & Iphofen, 2003a, 2003b, 2003c) where information is limited and where the snowball approach can be initiated with a personal contact or through an informant (Biernacki & Waldorf, 1981). However, one of the problems with such a method of sampling is that the eligibility of participants can be difficult to verify as investigators rely on the referral process, and the sample includes only one sub-set of the relevant user population (Biernacki & Waldorf, 1981).

- *Safeguarding participants and researchers* – perhaps one of the most obvious concerns arising from ethics in research is safeguarding participants. Whilst this is seen as a critical element of the ethics appraisal or review process, it also serves to safeguard the researcher. In this way, a robust ethics application process and a knowledgeable and facilitative ethics review committee can make informed judgements on the methodological approach being fit for purpose and the procedure being appropriate to investigate the research question. It is also important to assess any risks of the research for all those involved so that suitable measures and contingencies are in place. In order to protect the safety of the researcher, protocols for researcher safety should be used, in which the potential safety risks are assessed prior to any in-person activities (i.e. interviews) being conducted (Gregory, Paterson, & Thorne, 1999). This also extends to the safety of the researcher after the research, where the sensitive data they hold might be sought after by hostile actors. The process of conducting research on sensitive issues can also have an emotional effect on participants or researchers (Clark & Kotulic, 2004; Lee, 1993). Support networks and training in psychological first aid can be of benefit in these instances.

Discussing sensitive issues can elicit emotional responses, that participants have not previously recounted (Cowles, 1988). Therefore, it is important that researchers are prepared to deal with these situations and can assist participants in finding any further support they might require (Clarke & Johnson, 2003). Such training may allow the researcher to sensitively approach difficult topics and provide access to information that participants may not otherwise disclose (Cowles, 1988).

Ultimately, the responsibility of ethics review in research is to protect researchers and participants alike (Cowles, 1988). As Wilson (1995) states, research should be based on non-reactivity principles, such that the research should not negatively impact those involved in collecting or providing data. Whilst research activities should ensure no one is put in any danger, this limits some applications and research settings (Gregory et al., 1999). For instance, research might be extremely challenging in high-risk environments with a very real threat to life or where participants may become vulnerable simply through the activity of providing data. Extreme care is needed to safeguard those providing what might be the richest data, without compromising their safety.

Core to this, issues of privacy and confidentiality underpin many of the ethical challenges of knowledge elicitation, where investigators must ensure that:

- end-users and stakeholders are comfortable with the type of information they are sharing and how the information might be used and
- end-users are not required to breach any agreements and obligations with their employers or associated organisations.

In many ways, these ethical concerns are governed by professional codes of conduct (in the UK this would be regulated by professional bodies such as the British Psychological Society) but it is important that investigators clearly identify the purpose of an investigation and set clear and legitimate boundaries for intended usage and communication of collected data.

CONDUCTING KNOWLEDGE ELICITATION

Whilst methods exist for knowledge elicitation in the security domain, they are relatively underdeveloped (Paul, 2018). It is only recently that security aspects of interactive systems have begun to be systematically analysed (Cerone & Shaikh, 2008, chapter 25). However, little research has been published on understanding the work of security personnel and systems, which leads to the lack of case studies or guidance on how methods can be adopted or have been used in different security settings (Hancock & Hart, 2002; Kraemer, Carayon, & Sanquist, 2009). As a result, it is necessary to re-visit the fundamental issues of conducting knowledge elicitation that can then be applied to security research.

Knowledge elicitation presents several challenges to investigators, not least in recruiting representative end-users and other stakeholders upon which the whole process depends (Lawson & D'Cruz, 2011). Equally important, it is necessary to elicit and categorise/prioritise the relevant expertise and knowledge, and communicate this forward to designers and policy makers, as well as back to the end-users and other stakeholders.

One of the first steps in conducting knowledge elicitation is to understand that there can be different levels of end-users or stakeholders. Whilst the terms 'end-user' and 'stakeholder' are often confused, stakeholders are not always the end-users of a product or process, but have a particular investment or interest in the outcome and its effect on users or wider community (Mitchell, Agle, & Wood, 1997). The term 'end-user' or 'primary user' is commonly defined as someone who will make use of a particular product or process (Eason, 1987). In many cases, users and stakeholders will have different needs and often their goals or expectations of the product or process can be conflicting (Nuseibeh & Easterbrook, 2000). These distinctions and background information about users, stakeholders and specific contexts of use allow researchers to arrive at informed outcomes (Maguire & Bevan, 2002).

Whilst knowledge elicitation tends to be conducted amongst a wide range of users and stakeholders some of these domains are more restricted and challenging than others in terms of confidentiality, anonymity and privacy. These sensitive domains can include those involving children, elderly or disabled users, healthcare systems, staff/patient environments, commerce and other domains where information is often beyond public access (Gaver, Dunne, & Pacenti, 1999). In addition, some organisations restrict how much information employees can share with regard to their tasks, roles, strategies, technology use and future visions with external parties to protect commercial or competitive standpoints (Nonaka & Takeuchi, 1995). Security organisations may be particularly sensitive of any vulnerabilities that could then be perceived by the public as a lack of security awareness or exploited by competitors or aggressors for their own benefit. Security domains can also add further complications in reporting findings to support the wider understanding of user needs across this sector (Crabtree et al., 2003; Lawson, Sharples, Cobb, & Clarke, 2009), or where there are information sharing hurdles across agencies or countries (Williams & McDonald, 2018).

KNOWLEDGE ELICITATION METHODS

The human factors approach has made extensive and effective use of established social science methods such as questionnaires, surveys, interviews, focus groups, observations and ethnographic reviews and formal task or link analyses that can be used as the foundations to knowledge elicitation (Crabtree et al., 2003; Preece, Rogers, & Sharp, 2007). These methods provide different opportunities for interaction between the investigator and target audience, and hence provide different types and levels of data (Saikayasit et al., 2012). A range of complementary methods are often selected to enhance the detail of the issues explored. For example, interviews and focus groups might be employed to gain further insights or highlight problems that have been initially identified in questionnaires or surveys.

In comparison to direct interaction between the investigator and participant (e.g. interviews) indirect methods (e.g. questionnaires) can reach a larger number of respondents and are cheaper to administer but are not efficient for probing complicated issues or experience-based knowledge (Sinclair, 2005).

Focus groups can also be used, where the interviewer acts as a group organiser and facilitator to encourage discussion across several issues around pre-defined themes (Sinclair, 2005). However, focus groups can be resource intensive and difficult to arrange depending on the degree of anonymity required for the research. They are also notoriously 'hit and miss' depending on the availability of participants for particular sessions (Stedmon et al., 2013). In addition, they need effective management so that all participants have an opportunity to contribute without specific individuals dominating the interaction or people being affected by peer pressure to not voice particular issues (Friedrich & van der Poll, 2007). As with many qualitative analyses, care is also needed in how results are fed into the requirements capture. When using interactive methods, it is important that opportunities are provided for participants to express their knowledge spontaneously, rather than only responding to directed questions from the investigator. This is because there is a danger that direct questions could be biased by preconceptions that may prevent investigators exploring issues they have not already identified. On this basis, investigators should assume the role of 'learners' rather than 'hypothesis testers' (McNeese, Zaff, Citera, Brown, & Whitaker, 1995).

Observational and ethnographic methods can also be used to allow investigators to gather insights into socio-technical factors such as the impact of gate-keepers, moderators or more formal mechanisms in security. However, observation and ethnographic reviews can be intrusive, especially in sensitive domains where privacy and confidentially are important. In addition, the presence of observers can elicit behaviours that are not normal for the individual or group being viewed as they purposely follow formal procedures and act in a socially desirable manner (Crabtree et al., 2003; Stanton et al., 2005). Furthermore, this method provides a large amount of rich data, which can be time consuming to analyse. However, when used correctly, and when the investigator has a clear understanding of the domain being observed, this method can provide rich qualitative and quantitative real-world data (Sinclair, 2005).

Investigators often focus on the tasks that users perform in order to elicit tacit experience-based information or to understand the context of work (Nuseibeh & Easterbrook, 2000). Thus, the use of task analysis methods to identify problems and the influence of user interaction on system performance is a major approach within human factors (Kirwan & Ainsworth, 1992). A task analysis is defined as a study of what the user/system operation is required to do, including physical activities and cognitive processes, in order to achieve a specified goal (Kirwan & Ainsworth, 1992). Scenarios are often used to illustrate or describe typical tasks or roles in a particular context (Sutcliffe, 1998). There are generally two types of scenarios: those that represent and capture aspects of real work settings so that investigators and users can communicate their understanding of tasks to aid the development process; and those used to portray how users might envisage using a future system that is being developed (Sutcliffe, 1998). In the latter case, investigators often develop 'user personas' that represent how different classes of user might interact with the future system and/or how the system will fit into an intended context of use. This is sometimes communicated through story-board techniques either presented as scripts, link-diagrams or conceptual diagrams to illustrate processes and decision points of interest.

Whilst various methods are available for researchers trying to elicit knowledge, research methods where the researcher and participant are seen as equals trying to overcome a problem together, are often more effective for sensitive domain research (Paul, 2018). Such methods are often described as 'contrived' (Milton, 2007) and expand upon methods where the participant simply describes how they accomplish a task, such as verbal protocol analysis (Shadbolt & Smart, 2015). Contrived methods, such as those highlighted in the figure above, allow the participant and the researcher to explore the issue together, as co-investigators, helping create more open conversations (Paul, 2018). They might therefore be seen as more appropriate for sensitive domain research.

COMMUNICATING KNOWLEDGE BACK TO END-USERS AND STAKEHOLDERS

Whilst various methods assist investigators in knowledge elicitation, it is important to communicate the findings back to relevant users and stakeholders. Several techniques exist in user experience and user-centered design to communicate the vision between investigators and users. These generally include scenario-based modelling (e.g. tabular text narratives, user personas, sketches and informal media) and concept mapping (e.g. scripts, sequences of events and link and task analyses) including actions and objects during the design phase (Sutcliffe, 1998). Scenario-based modelling can be used to represent the tasks, roles, systems and how they interact and influence task goals, as well as identify connections and dependencies between the user, system and the environment (Sutcliffe, 1998). Concept mapping is a technique that represents the objects, actions, events (or even emotions and feelings) so that both the investigators and users form a common understanding in order to identify gaps in knowledge (Freeman & Jessup, 2004; McNeese et al., 1995). The visual representations of connections between events and objects in a concept map or link analysis can help identify conflicting needs, create mutual understandings and enhance recall and memory of critical events (Freeman & Jessup, 2004). Use-cases can also be used to represent typical interactions, including profiles, interests, job descriptions and skills as part of the knowledge elicitation representation (Lanfranchi & Ireson, 2009). Scenarios with personas can be used to describe how users might behave in specific situations in order to provide a richer understanding of the context of use. Personas typically provide a profile of a specific user, stakeholder or role based on information from a number of sources (e.g. a typical child using a chat-room, a parent trying to govern the safety of their child's on-line presence, a shopper and a person using a home-banking interface). What is then communicated is a composite and synthesis of key features within a single profile that can then be used as a single point of reference (e.g. Mary is an 8-year-old girl with no clear understanding of internet grooming techniques; Malcolm is a 60-year-old man with no awareness of phishing tactics). In some cases, personas are given names and background information such as age, education, recent training courses attended and even generic images/photos to make them more realistic or representative of a typical user. In other cases, personas are used anonymously in order to communicate generic characteristics that may be applicable to a wider demographic.

Knowledge elicitation with users working in sensitive domains also presents issues of personal anonymity and data confidentiality (Kavakli, Kalloniatis, & Gritzalis, 2005). In order to safeguard these, anonymity and pseudonymity can be used to disguise individuals, roles and relationships between roles (Pfitzmann & Hansen, 2005). In this way, identifying features of participants should not be associated with the data or approaches should be used that specifically use fictitious personas to illustrate and integrate observations across a number of participants. If done correctly, these personas can then be used as an effective communication tool without compromising the trust that has been built during the elicitation process.

Using a variety of human factors methods provides investigators with a clearer understanding of how security, as a process, can operate based on the perspective of socio-technical systems. Without a range of methods to employ and without picking those most suitable for a specific inquiry, there is a danger that the best data will be missed. In addition, without using the tools for communicating the findings of knowledge elicitation activities, the overall process would be incomplete and end-users and other stakeholders will miss opportunities to learn about security and/or contribute further insights into their roles. Such approaches allow investigators to develop a much better understanding of the bigger picture such as the context and wider systems, as well as more detailed understandings of specific tasks and goals.

ESTABLISHING THE TRUSTWORTHINESS OF QUALITATIVE DATA

Historically, the trustworthiness of qualitative research has always been challenged by positivist researchers. However, frameworks exist to improve the integrity, credibility and reliability of qualitative data (Lincoln, 1995; Silverman, 2011). An analytical approach to research not only increases the trustworthiness of the inquiry (Annett, 2005; Wilson, 2005) but is also necessary and useful for human factors research that sits between academia and praxis (Milton, 2012; Stanton et al., 2005). In this way, it allows an understanding of both how research contributes to the knowledge base and also its real-world application (Annett, 2005; Stanton et al., 2005).

Several authors have proposed principles for establishing trustworthiness in qualitative inquiry (Denzin & Lincoln, 2000; Given, 2008b; Guba, 1981; Lincoln, 1995; Silverman, 2011). It has become a central pillar of qualitative research, and particularly in exploratory investigations that are not guided by previous research

(Lincoln, 1995). Shenton (2004) provided a synthesis to ensure trustworthiness, which condenses four well-accepted constructs first posed by Guba (1981) and developed further by Guba and Lincoln (1985).

Credibility

Credibility is concerned with ensuring the findings are a true reflection of the research which has been conducted (Shenton, 2004). Denzin and Lincoln (2000) state that credibility is central to ensuring trustworthiness in qualitative research. Shenton (2004) proposed several constructs for credibility:

- Well-established research methods should be adopted. Less common methods may be used in conjunction to help extend the reach of the inquiry.
- Familiarity with the field under investigation is necessary, both through the researcher's professional involvement (where possible) but also through analysis of previous findings and appropriate review of existing research and knowledge.
- Where possible, purposive sampling should be employed to reduce any bias in data collection.
- Triangulation of mixed methods allows the research to be understood from multiple angles and compensates for any weaknesses inherent to certain methods.
- Methods to promote honesty should be used, including the opportunity for participants to refuse to be part of the investigation as well as the ethical basis of the research being stressed prior to data collection. This form of preventative measure reduces the possibility of participants lying or deceiving during data collection and assures them that they are in control of the data collection process. This is further supported with iterative questioning, in which the participants are asked to confirm information provided previously, and where information provided is rephrased later in the data collection session. This necessitates training and practice in the methods used but allows more transparent and honest datasets.
- Thick description has been used to provide detail for results and how they help develop knowledge and conclusions. Though this method is often lengthy, it allows readers to understand the way in which the data have been synthesised.

Transferability

The ability to transfer the interpretation of results to groups wider than the sample studied is an important aspect of both qualitative research (Silverman, 2011) as well as human factors methods, which are inherently practitioner-focussed (Wilson, 2005). In order to achieve this, thick descriptions of the results can be used that allow the reader to draw their own conclusions about how the results can be transferred (Shenton, 2004). It is also necessary, for research replication, to provide a full account of how the data were collected, and the approach taken, including inclusion criteria, the methods used to collect data, the number of sessions conducted and how long these took (Guba, 1981; Shenton, 2004).

Dependability

Whilst quantitative, positivist research is concerned with empirical reliability, or how data collection should yield the same results every time (Silverman, 2011), qualitative research is mindful that the phenomenon under investigation may change over time (Shenton, 2004). Qualitative research usually only claims to present a view at a given time when the data were collected or in relation to the context they were collected in (Shenton, 2004). Instead, qualitative research may provide a 'prototype model', allowing the same methods to be employed by other researchers, understanding that the same conclusions may not be drawn and that understandings may evolve over time (Shenton, 2004).

Confirmability

Qualitative research does not rely on objective methods used by positivists as the collection and processing of data revolve around the researcher (Shenton, 2004). Researcher subjectivity and bias can be a major challenge and influence on the trustworthiness of qualitative research (Denzin & Lincoln, 2000). The use of triangulation in data collection is an important step in reducing bias and allows other researchers to scrutinise how the data were collected and analysed (Shenton, 2004).

Using these principles, it is important that research is designed based on the selection and use of appropriate methods that safeguard those involved and also that the method of communication is equally sensitive to issues of privacy and confidentiality. These factors also help identify how human factors methods (borrowed and developed from the social sciences) are designed to not only produce academically relevant data but also data can be used to tailor practical solutions to security threats (Stanton et al., 2005). Furthermore, by providing recommendations it is possible to review the transferability and trustworthiness of research findings beyond the sample studied (Shenton, 2004).

TOWARDS AN INTEGRATED UNDERSTANDING OF ETHICAL RESEARCH IN SENSITIVE SECURITY DOMAINS

Having reviewed the concepts underpinning ethical research in sensitive security domains, it is possible to provide an integrated view of these factors (Fig. 1).

In this configuration, we see that ethics is bounded by a number of typical threats to research in relation to intrusion, sanctions and political impacts of the work. It is important to be aware of the potential effects of these factors before starting out on a particular research activity as this may later impact on the trustworthiness of the research, or prevent data being collected in the first place.

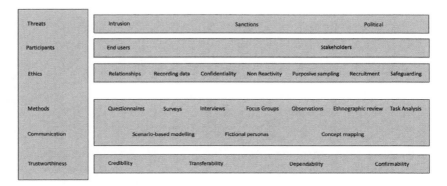

Fig. 1. Integrated Approach to Ethical Research.

With regard to knowledge elicitation as a methodological approach it is also important to understand who the end-users and stakeholders might be. We have seen already that these different actors within the problem space will have different perspectives and levels of investment in helping to find solutions.

A range of ethical issues have been introduced in this chapter which are relevant to participants (both end-users and stakeholders), embodied in the development of trusted relationships, how data may be recorded for sensitivity, confidentiality, non-reactivity, purposive sampling, recruitment of participants and safeguarding those involved.

A range of established methods from the social sciences are readily available for conducting knowledge elicitation and these need to be matched with appropriate communication techniques for sensitive data. Methods where the participant and researcher are seen as co-investigators, both exploring a solution to an issue (opposed to methods where information is being drawn out from the participant) are potentially more appropriate in sensitive domains.

Finally, the trustworthiness of the data needs to be considered prior to the research being conducted, so that responsible research is designed from the outset. This not only underpins the credibility, transferability, dependability and confirmability of research, but also fundamental concepts such as validity and reliability of what is often qualitative research.

Many of these concepts are inter-related and relevant to both end-users and stakeholders. By using this framework as a general tool for assisting with the design, conduct and communication of research in sensitive domains, it also provides a basis for reflecting on the success of different approaches so that lessons can be learned about the process of ethics as much as the conduct of ethics.

CONCLUSION

Security research usually takes an inductive approach, seeking to identify new theoretical principles through the collection of new data. In order to conduct research within sensitive domains that is equally sensitive to the needs of those involved, a user-centred approach is important for understanding security from a human factors perspective. It is also important to understand the contexts in which investigations are situated so that ethical principles are upheld throughout the research process. There are many formal and established methodologies that are of use and it is essential that the researcher considers key issues as outlined in this chapter before choosing a particular approach. Whilst various methods and tools can indeed be helpful in gaining insight into particular aspects of knowledge elicitation for security, caution must be at the forefront as a valid model for eliciting such data does not exist specifically for security research at present. At the moment, investigations rely on the experience, understanding and skill of the investigator in deciding which approach is best to adopt in order to collect robust data that can then be fed back into the system process. Alongside this, it is important to establish the trustworthiness of qualitative data based on principles of credibility, transferability, dependability and confirmability. In this way, the ethical basis of research in this domain reaches beyond the actual activity of conducting the research but also what the research contributes to the wider knowledge base and understanding. Doing so allows a more structured approach for such research to be taken in the future and provides further opportunities for other researchers to access both the humanitarian security domain, as well as other security domains in which access to information could be limited.

REFERENCES

Adams, A., & Cox, A. (2008). Questionnaires, in-depth interviews and focus groups. In P. Cairns & A. Cox (Eds.), *Research methods for human–computer interaction* (pp. 17–34). Cambridge: Cambridge University Press.

Annett, J. (2005). A note on the validity and reliability of ergonomics methods. *Theoretical Issues in Ergonomics Science, 3*, 228–232.

Atkinson, R., & Flint, J. (2001). Accessing hidden and hard-to-reach populations: Snowball research strategies. In N. Gilbert (Ed.), *Social research update* (p. 33). Guilford: University of Surrey.

Atkinson, R., & Flint, J. (2004). Snowball sampling. In A. Bryman, M. Lewis-Beck, & T. Liao (Eds.), *The SAGE encyclopaedia of social science research methods* (pp. 1043–1044). Thousand Oaks, CA: SAGE Publications, Inc.

Babbie, E. (2011). *The practice of social research*. Belmont, CA: Wadsworth, Cengage Learning.

Barnard, A., Geber, R., & McCosker, H. (2001). Undertaking sensitive research: Issues and strategies for meeting the safety needs of all participants. *Forum: Qualitative Social Research, 2*(1), 1–14. Retrieved from http://nbn-resolving.de/urn:nbn:de:0114-fqs0101220. Accessed on May 26, 2021.

Barton, K. (2015). Elicitation techniques: Getting people to talk about ideas they don't usually talk about. *Theory and Research in Social Education, 43*(2), 179–205.

Beerli, M., & Weissman, F. (2016). Humanitarian security manuals: Neutralising the human factor in humanitarian action. In M. Neuman & F. Weissman (Eds.), *Saving lives and staying alive: Humanitarian security in the age of risk management* (pp. 71–81). London: C. Hurst & Co.

Biernacki, P., & Waldorf, D. (1981). Snowball sampling. Problems and techniques of chain referral sampling. *Sociological Methods & Research, 10*(2), 141–163.

Bollentino, V. (2008). Understanding the security management practices of humanitarian organisations. *Disasters, 32*(2), 263–279.

Brewer, C. (2017). Aid workers: What overseas volunteers need to know. *Independent Nurse, 11*, 16–18.

Brewers, J. (1990). Sensitivity as a problem in field research: A study of routine policing in Northern Ireland. *American Behavioural Scientist, 33*(5), 578–593.

Brunderlein, C., & Grassmann, P. (2006). Managing risks in hazardous missions: The challenges of securing United Nations access to vulnerable groups. *Harvard Human Rights Journal, 19*(1), 63–94.

Bryman, A., & Bell, E. (2011). *Business research methods* (3rd ed.). Oxford: Oxford University Press.

Buzan, B., & Hansen, L. (2009). *The evolution of international security studies.* Cambridge: Cambridge University Press.

Cerone, A., & Shaikh, S. A. (2008). Formal analysis of security in interactive systems. In M. Gupta & R. Sharman (Eds.), *Handbook of research on social and organizational liabilities in information security* (pp. 415–432). Hershey, PA: IGI-Global.

Clark, J., & Kotulic, A. (2004). Why there aren't more information security research studies. *Information and Management, 41*, 597–607.

Clarke, J., & Johnson, B. (2003). Collecting sensitive data: The impact on researchers. *Qualitative Health Research, 13*(3), 421–434.

Cochran, M., & Quinn-Patton, M. (2007). *A guide to using qualitative research methodology.* Geneva: Medicines Sans Frontier.

Cowles, K. (1988). Issues in qualitative research on sensitive topics. *Western Journal of Nursing Research, 10*(2), 163–179.

Crabtree, A., Hemmings, T., Rodden, T., Cheverst, K., Clarke, K., Dewsbury, G., … Rouncefield, M. (2003). Designing with care: Adapting cultural probes to inform design in sensitive settings. In *Proceedings of OzCHI 2003*, University of Queensland, Brisbane Australia (pp. 4–13).

Creswell, J. (2003, November 18–26). *Research design: Qualitative, quantitative, and mixed methods approach* (2nd ed.). London: SAGE Publications Ltd.

Czwarno, M., Harmer, A., & Stoddard, A. (2017). *Aid worker security report 2017. Behind the attacks: A look at the perpetrators of violence against aid workers.* London: Humanitarian Outcomes.

Daudin, P., & Merkelbach, M. (2011). *From security management to risk management: Critical reflections on aid agency security management and the ISO risk management guidelines.* Geneva: Security Management Initiative.

Denzin, N., & Lincoln, Y. (Eds.). (2000). *The SAGE handbook of qualitative research* (2nd ed.). Thousand Oaks, CA: SAGE Publications, Inc.

Dickenson-Swift, V., James, E., & Liamputtong, P. (2007). Doing sensitive research: What challenges do qualitative researchers face?. *Qualitative Research, 7*(3), 327–353.

Eason, K. (1987). *Information technology and organizational change.* London: Taylor and Francis.

Fox, N. (2008). Induction. In L. Given (Ed.), *The SAGE encyclopaedia of qualitative research methods* (pp. 429–430). London: SAGE Publications, Ltd.

Freeman, L. A., & Jessup, L. M. (2004). The power and benefits of concept mapping: Measuring use, usefulness, ease of use, and satisfaction. *International Journal of Science Education, 26*(2), 151–169.

Friedrich, W. R., & van der Poll, J. A. (2007). Towards a methodology to elicit tacit domain knowledge from users. *Interdisciplinary Journal of Information, Knowledge and Management, 2*, 179–193.

Gaver, B., Dunne, T., & Pacenti, E. (1999). Design: Cultural probes. *Interaction, 6*(1), 21–29.

Given, L. (2008a). Emergent design. In L. Given (Ed.), *The SAGE encyclopaedia of qualitative research methods* (pp. 245–248). London: SAGE Publications, Ltd.

Given, L. (Ed.) (2008b). *The SAGE encyclopaedia of qualitative research methods.* London: SAGE Publications, Ltd.

Gregory, D., Paterson, B., & Thorne, S. (1999). A protocol for researcher safety. *Qualitative Health Research, 9*(2), 259–269.

Guba, E. (1981). Criteria for assessing the trustworthiness of naturalistic inquiries. *Educational Communication and Technology Journal, 29*, 75–91.

Guba, E., & Lincoln, Y. (1985). *Naturalistic inquiry.* Beverly Hills, CA: SAGE.

Hancock, P. A., & Hart, S. G. (2002). Defeating terrorism: What can human factors/ergonomics offer?. *Ergonomics in Design, 10*, 6–16.

Harmer, A., Haver, K., & Stoddard, A. (2010). *Good practice review 8: Operational security management in violent environments* (rev. ed.). London: Overseas Development Institute.

Harmer, A., & Schreter, L. (2013). *Delivering aid in highly insecure environments: A critical review of literature, 2002–2012.* London: Humanitarian Outcomes.

Harmer, A., Stoddard, A., & Toth, K. (2013). *Aid worker security report 2013. The new normal: Coping with the kidnapping threat.* London: Humanitarian Outcomes.

Hoffman, R. (1987). The problem of extracting the knowledge of experts from the perspective of experimental psychology. *AI Magazine, 8*(2), 53–66.

Kaiser, K. (2009). Protecting respondent confidentiality in qualitative research. *Qualitative Health Research, 19*(11), 1632–1641.

Kavakli, E., Kalloniatis, C., & Gritzalis, S. (2005). Addressing privacy: Matching user requirements to implementation techniques. In *7th Hellenic European research on computer mathematics and its applications conference (HERCMA 2005)*, Athens, Greece, 22–24 September.

Kelly, D. (2014). *The art of reasoning: An introduction to reason and critical thinking.* New York, NY: W.W. Norton & Company, Inc.

Kirwan, B., & Ainsworth, L. K. (1992). *A guide to task analysis.* Boca Raton, FL: CRC Press, Taylor & Francis Group.

Kraemer, S., Carayon, P., & Sanquist, T. F. (2009). Human and organisational factors in security screening and inspection systems: Conceptual framework and key research needs. *Cognition, Technology and Work, 11*(1), 29–41.

Kuhanendran, J., & Micheni, K. (2010). Saving lives together: A review of security collaboration between the United Nations and humanitarian actors on the ground. Retrieved from http://www.alnap.org/resource/9859 Accessed on May 26, 2021.

Lanfranchi, V., & Ireson, N. (2009, September 1–5). User requirements for a collective intelligence emergency response system. In *Proceedings of the 23rd British HCI group annual conference on people and computers: Celebrating people and technology*, Cambridge, UK (pp. 198–203).

Lawson, G., & D'Cruz, M. (2011). Ergonomics methods and the digital factory. In L. Canetta, C. Redaelli, & M. Flores (Eds.), *Intelligent manufacturing system DiFac* (pp. 23–34). London: Springer.

Lawson, G., Sharples, S., Cobb, S., & Clarke, D. (2009). Predicting the human response to an emergency. In P. D. Bust (Ed.), *Contemporary ergonomics 2009* (pp. 525–532). London: Taylor and Francis.

Lee, R. (1993). *Doing research on sensitive topics.* London: SAGE Publications, Ltd.

Lee, R., & Renzetti, C. (1990). The problems of researching sensitive topics: An overview and introduction. *American Behavioural Scientist, 33*(5), 510–528.

Lewis, P., Saunders, M., & Thornhill, A. (2009). *Research methods for business students* (5th ed.). Harlow: Pearson Education Ltd.

Lincoln, Y. (1995). Emerging criteria for quality in qualitative and interpretive research. *Qualitative Inquiry, 1*, 275–289.

Maguire, M., & Bevan, N. (2002). User requirements analysis. A review of supporting methods. In *Proceedings of IFIP 17th world computer congress*, Montereal, Canada, 25–30 August (pp. 133–148). Dordrecht: Kluwer Academic Publishers.

Martin, E., Metcalfe, V., & Pantuliano, S. (2011). *Risk in humanitarian action: Towards a common approach?.* Humanitarian Policy Group Report 39. Overseas Development Institute, London.

McNeese, M. C., Zaff, B. S., Citera, M., Brown, C. E., & Whitaker, R. (1995). AKADAM: Eliciting user knowledge to support participatory ergonomics. *International Journal of Industrial Ergonomics, 15*, 345–363.

Merriam, S., & Tisdell, E. (2016). *Qualitative research: A guide to design and implementation.* San Francisco, CA: John Wiley & Sons, Inc.

Milton, N. (2007). *Knowledge acquisition in practice: A step-by-step guide.* London: Springer-Verlag.

Milton, N. (2012). Acquiring knowledge from subject matter experts. In J. Kantola & W. Karwowski (Eds.), *Knowledge service engineering handbook* (pp. 253–278). Boca Raton, FL: CRC Press.

Mitchell, R. K., Agle, B., & Wood, D. J. (1997). Toward a theory of stakeholder identification and salience: Defining the principle of who and what really counts. *The Academy of Management Review, 22*(4), 853–886.

Nonaka, I., & Takeuchi, H. (1995). *The knowledge-creating company: How Japanese companies create the dynamics of innovation.* New York, NY: Oxford University Press, Inc.

Nuseibeh, B., & Easterbrook, S. (2000). Requirements engineering: A roadmap. In *Proceedings of international conference of software engineering (ICSE-2000)*, Limerick, Ireland, 4–11 July (pp. 37–46). New York, NY: ACM Press.

Pailthorpe, B. (2017). Emergent design. In C. Davis, J. Mattes, & R. Potter (Eds.), *The international encyclopaedia of communication research methods* (pp. 1–2) Hoboken, NJ: Wiley-Blackwell.

Paul, D. (2018). *A knowledge elicitation approach to improving security management systems in the humanitarian sector*. Unpublished Ph.D. thesis, Coventry University.

Pfitzmann, A., & Hansen, M. (2005). *Anonymity, unlinkability, unobservability, pseudonymity and identify management: A consolidated proposal for terminology*, version v0.25, December 6, 2005. Retrieved from http://dud.inf.tu-dresden.de/Anon_Terminology.shtml. Accessed May 26, 2021.

Preece, J., Rogers, Y., & Sharp, H. (2007). *Interaction design: Beyond human–computer interaction* (2nd ed.). Hoboken NJ: John Wiley & Sons Ltd.

Saikayasit, R., Stedmon, A., & Lawson, G. (2015). A macro-ergonomics perspective on security: A rail case study. In A. W. Stedmon & G. Lawson (Eds.). *Hostile intent and counter-terrorism: Human factors theory and application* (pp. 277–294). Aldershot: Ashgate Publishing Limited.

Saikayasit, R., Stedmon, A. W., Lawson, G., & Fussey, P. (2012). User requirements for security and counter-terrorism initiatives. In P. Vink (Ed.), *Advances in social and organisational factors* (pp. 256–265). Boca Raton, FL: CRC Press.

Schneiker, A. (2015). Humanitarian NGOs security networks and organisational learning: Identity matters and matters of identity. *International Journal of Voluntary and Nonprofit Organisations, 26*(1), 144.

Shadbolt, N., & Smart, P. (2015). Knowledge elicitation: Methods, tools and techniques. In S. Sharples & J. Wilson (Eds.), *Evaluation of human work* (4th ed., pp. 163–200). Boca Raton, FL: CRC Press.

Shenton, A. (2004). Strategies for ensuring trustworthiness in qualitative research projects. *Education for Information, 22*, 63–74.

Sieber, J., & Stanley, B. (1988). Ethical and professional dimensions of socially sensitive research. *The American Psychologist, 43*(1), 49–55.

Silverman, D. (2011). *Interpreting qualitative data* (4th ed.). London: SAGE Publications, Ltd.

Sims, J., & Iphofen, R. (2003a). Parental substance use and its effects on children. *The Drug and Alcohol Professional, 3*(3), 33–40.

Sims, J., & Iphofen, R. (2003b). The primary care assessment of hazardous and harmful drinkers. *Journal of Substance Use, 8*(3), 1–6.

Sims, J., & Iphofen, R. (2003c). Women and substance misuse (monograph). The British Library Catalogue Number M03/37596 Special Acquisitions.

Sinclair, M. A. (2005). Participative assessment. In J. R. Wilson & E. N. Corlett (Eds.), *Evaluation of human work: A practical ergonomics methodology* (3rd ed., pp. 83–112). London: CRC Press, Taylor & Francis Group.

Stanton, N., Salmon, P. M., Rafferty, L. A., Walker, G. H., Baber, C., & Jenkins, D. P. (2013). *Human factors methods: A practical guide for engineering and design* (2nd ed.). Boca Raton, FL: CRC Press LLC.

Stanton, N. A., Salmon, P. M., Walker, G. H., Baber, C., & Jenkins, D. P. (2005). *Human factors methods: A practical guide for engineering and design* (pp. 21–44). Aldershot: Ashgate Publishing Limited.

Stedmon, A. W., Saikayasit, R., Lawson, G., & Fussey, P. (2013). User requirements and training needs within security applications: Methods for capture and communication. In B. Akhgar & S. Yates (Eds.), *Strategic intelligence management* (pp. 120–133). Oxford: Butterworth-Heinemann.

Sutcliffe, A. (1998). Scenario-based requirements analysis. *Requirements Engineering, 3*, 48–65.

Williams, P., & McDonald, M. (Eds.). (2018). *Security studies: An introduction* (3rd ed.). Oxon: Routledge.

Wilson, J. (2010). *Essentials of business research: A guide to doing your research project*. London: SAGE Publications, Ltd.

Wilson, J. R. (1995). Ergonomics and participation. In J. R. Wilson & E. N. Corlett (Eds.), *Evaluation of human work: A practical ergonomics methodology* (2nd and rev. ed.). London: Taylor & Francis.

Wilson, J. R. (2005). Methods in the understanding of human factors. In N. Corlett & J. R. Wilson (Eds.), *Evaluation of human work: A practical ergonomics methodology* (3rd ed., pp. 1–31). London: Taylor & Francis.

CHAPTER 12

COVERT ASPECTS OF SURVEILLANCE AND THE ETHICAL ISSUES THEY RAISE

David J. Harper, Darren Ellis and Ian Tucker

ABSTRACT

This chapter focusses on the ethical issues raised by different types of surveillance and the varied ways in which surveillance can be covert. Three case studies are presented which highlight different types of surveillance and different ethical concerns. The first case concerns the use of undercover police to infiltrate political activist groups over a 40-year period in the UK. The second case study examines a joint operation by US and Australian law enforcement agencies: the FBI's operation Trojan Shield and the AFP's Operation Ironside. This involved distributing encrypted phone handsets to serious criminal organisations which included a 'backdoor' secretly sending encrypted copies of all messages to law enforcement. The third case study analyses the use of emotional artificial intelligence systems in educational digital learning platforms for children where technology companies collect, store and use intrusive personal data in an opaque manner. The authors discuss similarities and differences in the ethical questions raised by these cases, for example, the involvement of the state versus private corporations, the kinds of information gathered and how it is used.

Keywords: Ethical issues; undercover police; human rights; encryption; artificial intelligence; educational technology

Ethical Issues in Covert, Security and Surveillance Research
Advances in Research Ethics and Integrity, Volume 8, 177–197
ISSN: 2398-6018/doi:10.1108/S2398-601820210000008013

INTRODUCTION

In this chapter, we focus on the ethical issues raised by different types of surveillance and the varied ways in which surveillance can be covert. Over the last decade, we have examined the social and psychological aspects of a range of surveillance practices and technologies including how the public understand and experience them (Ellis, Harper, & Tucker, 2016; Harper, Ellis, & Tucker, 2014; Harper, Tucker, & Ellis, 2013). We have been struck by the way in which public discourse about the ethics of surveillance is very much shaped by the types of surveillance seizing the popular imagination at the time. In one of our projects, in the Summer of 2010, when Londoners were asked about surveillance, they tended to spontaneously associate it with Closed Circuit Television (CCTV) in public spaces and some needed to be prompted about other, less visible, modes of surveillance. Over a decade later and the public are more aware of the way in which electronic data from digital devices is gathered, stored and used by governments and private corporations because of media reporting about technology companies and about the Edward Snowden National Security Agency (NSA) disclosures. Yet many are still not aware of the myriad ways in which they are surveilled every day and often only a restricted range of issues – privacy, security and convenience – feature in public discourse. However, as Macnish notes in his introduction to this volume, surveillance involves a range of activities, practices and technologies that often engage distinct types of ethical concern. In this chapter, therefore, we examine three contemporary examples of covert forms of surveillance – all involving the gathering, storage and usage of information about people in a covert or hidden manner – both human and technological and involving the state or private corporations. We discuss the specific aspects of these types of surveillance which raise ethical concerns. In the concluding section, we discuss commonalities and differences in the kinds of ethical questions engaged by the case studies and suggest potential avenues worthy of further exploration by researchers and in public debate.

CASE STUDY 1 – COVERT SURVEILLANCE OF ACTIVIST GROUPS BY UNDERCOVER POLICE: THE 'SPYCOPS' SCANDAL

Analogue Surveillance in a Digital World: Covert Surveillance by Human Beings

Technological surveillance might have captured the contemporary popular imagination but surveillance by human beings – the oldest form of surveillance – is still with us. Although endemic in totalitarian societies, human surveillance by the state (as opposed to surveillance by private investigators or security companies) operates at a much smaller scale in Western liberal democracies: in the UK in 2019, there were 3,652 authorisations of 'Covert Human Intelligence Sources' (i.e. informants or undercover officers) and 8,049 authorisations for 'directed surveillance' (i.e. covert surveillance of a person in public by undercover surveillance teams). In contrast, technological surveillance is much more prevalent – for example, in the same period, there were 116,171 authorisations[1] for the use of communications data by the Metropolitan Police Service Central Intelligence Unit (Investigatory Powers Commissioner's Office, 2020). Yet, although technology-mediated surveillance is much more common, human surveillance can intrude into people's personal lives in a much more invasive and potentially harmful manner since it often involves deceptive relationships and betraying others' trust.

This case study concerns the Special Demonstration Squad (SDS), which ran from 1968–2008, and similar units like the National Public Order Intelligence Unit (NPOIU[2]), established in 1999. In 2015, following a series of revelations and official inquiries, the UK government established a judge-led investigation – the Undercover Policing Inquiry (UCPI[3]) – which began to hear evidence in November 2020.

Issues Raised During the UCPI

The SDS was established in 1968 within the London Metropolitan Police's Special Branch,[4] the policing body responsible for national security and terrorism and liaising with the Security Service (MI5). SDS officers often adopted cover identities by assuming the name of a real person who had died as a child.[5] They would change their appearance to blend in with activists, had vehicles and apartments in their cover names and would attend meetings, befriend activists and live their lives using these cover identities. In contrast to undercover police investigating crimes, these infiltrations were unusual in that they often lasted for several years, and officers did not collect evidence for criminal prosecutions. Over 1,000 groups were infiltrated (Evans, 2017). The information collected was quite intrusive. For example, the UCPI heard evidence that undercover officers:

> recorded the political activities of children as well as details of their parents' domestic lives. On one occasion, an undercover officer sent back to his supervisors the babysitting rota that had been organised by leftwing campaigners …. They also recorded the births of campaigners' children and made comments in their reports about the lives of politically active parents, such as the fact they had a child with Down's syndrome …. Some reports recorded deeply personal information, such as leftwing activists experiencing mental illness and depression or having an abortion …. Others recorded the sexuality of activists …. The police spies regularly reported on the bank accounts and jobs of campaigners, along with their home addresses. (Evans, 2021c, 12 May)

SDS officer 'Paul Gray' (HN126,[6] 1977–1982) reported extensively on young people, including children active in Hackney School Kids Against the Nazis, as well as their teachers, sending photographs to his managers (Heaven, 2021). Evans (2020a, 28 October) reports that undercover officers collected information on campaigns about police injustice (e.g. the Stephen Lawrence campaign), caused miscarriages of justice because their presence was withheld from lawyers defending activists (in 26 cases officers had been arrested along with activists) and appear to have shared data with private companies enabling them to 'blacklist' applicants for jobs (see also Lubbers, 2015).

In contrast with technical surveillance, human intelligence can give insight into the plans and intentions of targets, but it generates many ethical dilemmas. In one of the earliest discussions of the use of human intelligence sources within social movements, Marx (1974) observed that they faced a dilemma: staying on the fringes of the group gathering intelligence passively meant they had much less access to information than if they took on leadership roles. The UCPI has heard how undercover officers often rose to key administrative positions in the groups they infiltrated, passing membership lists to their headquarters who, in turn often passed them onto 'Box 500', the Security Service (MI5). However, as Marx (1974) notes, being a more active and senior member of a group increases the risk that officers significantly affect the direction of the group's activities and raises serious questions about whether they might be viewed as agent provocateurs. Marx (1974) also observes that the importance of the group and the threat is vulnerable to exaggeration:

> Further, wishful thinking, limited exposure, and selective perception may lead the agent to believe a group's own exaggerated estimates of its power and appeal and to confuse vague revolutionary rhetoric with specific plans. (p. 420)

Undercover Surveillance and Human Rights

A key concern for the activists surveilled by these officers is that their human rights were violated. Kate Wilson, an environmental activist who lived with 'Mark Stone' (in reality, NPOIU undercover officer Mark Kennedy) was deceived into a sexual relationship by this undercover police officer (Evans, 2021a, 20 April). In a landmark judgement in 2021 the Investigatory Powers Tribunal[7] upheld Wilson's complaint that several articles of the European Convention on Human Rights had been breached in her case (Wilson, 2021; Wilson v (1) Commissioner of Police of The Metropolis (2) National Police Chiefs' Council (2021, 30 September)). The articles breached were:

- Article 3: which prohibits torture and 'inhuman or degrading treatment or punishment'.
- Article 8: the right to respect for one's private and family life.
- Article 9: the right to freedom of thought, conscience and religion.
- Article 10: the right to freedom of expression.
- Article 11: the right to freedom of assembly and association.
- Article 14: Protection from discrimination

These articles are also relevant to many of the other activists surveilled by these undercover units. Some of the most serious ethical issues concern the way in which many officers invaded activists' personal lives. The UCPI is investigating the work of at least 139 undercover officers from the SDS, NPOIU and other units of whom more than 20 (i.e. over 14%) had sexual relationships with members of the groups under their cover identities (Evans, 2020a, 28 October). Many had long-term intimate relationships with activists, living with them for long periods and four fathered children with activists (Evans, 2021b, 22 April). Undercover officers often feigned mental health problems at the end of their deployment as part of an exit strategy. In 1987, animal activist 'Bob Robinson' suddenly broke contact with a female activist with whom he had had a child two years earlier. In 2012, she discovered that he was an undercover SDS officer called Bob Lambert. She subsequently received an apology and £425,000 compensation in 2015 after taking legal action alleging assault, negligence, deceit and misconduct by senior officers (Kelly & Casciani, 2014). She said that it was 'like being raped by the state. We feel that we were sexually abused because none of us gave consent' (Lewis, Evans, & Pollak, 2013).

Seven women sued the Metropolitan Police for the emotional trauma caused by such deceptive intimate relationships (some lasting up to nine years) and the subsequent apology from Martin Hewitt, an assistant commissioner at the Metropolitan Police acknowledged that their human rights had been violated:

> some officers, acting undercover whilst seeking to infiltrate protest groups, entered into long-term intimate sexual relationships with women which were abusive, deceitful, manipulative and wrong ... these relationships were a violation of the women's human rights, an abuse of police power and caused significant trauma ... relationships like these should never have happened. They were wrong and were a gross violation of personal dignity and integrity. (Evans, 2015)

Other Harms of Undercover Surveillance

Undercover work is a common policing tactic when investigating serious organised crime networks and these deployments are recognised as stressful for officers (Curran, 2021) and extreme levels of compartmentalised secrecy mean their families often cannot be told what they are doing and they live with a constant worry about getting 'burned' (exposed) or losing a target (Loftus, Goold, & Mac Giollabhuí, 2016). For those infiltrating activist groups, there are unique challenges for officers – for example, many report being violently assaulted on demonstrations by uniformed police unaware that they were working undercover (see also Marx, 1974). In some cases, officers may experience mental health breakdowns (Casciani, 2015). Their families can experience other harms and three ex-wives of SDS officers said that the deployments had caused their marriages to break down (Evans, 2020b, 4 November). At least 42 dead children's identities were stolen and the police have admitted this caused their families 'hurt and offence' (Evans, 2016).

Infiltration also harms the groups targeted. Marx (1974, p. 428) notes that the discovery of informers or undercover officers can leave groups with 'feelings of demoralization, helplessness, cynicism and immobilizing paranoia, and can serve to disintegrate a movement'. Stephens Griffin's (2020) interviews with activists who had been surveilled revealed that their conceptions of a fixed and stable external reality were fundamentally challenged – as one participant put it 'everyone was questioning everything' (p. 8) with some being diverted from environmental activism. SDS 'Officer A' told a reporter '[i]f the SDS had been in existence at the time of the Suffragettes, their campaigns would never have got off the ground and they would have been quickly forgotten' (Thompson, 2020).

There are important questions then, about balancing the state's obligation to preserve public order and its obligation to protect legitimate debate and to provide the basis for a functioning civil society. How do we weigh up the potential harms of undercover surveillance with its possible benefits? Macnish (2015) has argued that proportionality and the level of intrusiveness are important considerations.

The Proportionality of Political Intelligence Gathering by Undercover Police

Given that the work of units like the SDS involved considerable intrusion into the personal lives of some activists, was it justified by the level of threat and were there no realistic alternatives? The SDS was formed because of rising concern about a wave of protests about the Vietnam War. For example, in a March 1968 demonstration thousands of people marched on the US embassy in London, the police lost control and more than 200 people were arrested (Evans & Lewis, 2013). The police and government were concerned about the threat of revolution posed by those it saw as subversive, especially those in anarchist and Trotskyist groups. In 1975, the Home Office Minister, Lord Harris of Greenwich, defined subversive activities as those 'which threaten the safety or well-being of the state and which are intended to overthrow or undermine parliamentary democracy by political, industrial or violent means' (Security Service, n.d.).

However, over the 40 years of its existence, there does not appear to have been any detailed and regular threat assessment conducted by the SDS nor any systematic consideration of potential harms and benefits. Moreover, there is evidence of inequity in the types of groups targeted. Although the UCPI have not published a full list of groups targeted, the *Guardian* journalist Rob Evans and the Undercover Research Group have collated a list of 135 organisations (Evans, 2019). As studies in the USA have found (Marx, 1974), the groups targeted were, overwhelmingly, on the political left, suggesting that target selection was inequitable, a key issue in deciding on the ethics of surveillance (Macnish, 2015). Out of the 135 groups infiltrated, only two were right-wing: the British National Party was infiltrated by three SDS officers and Combat-18 by one (Evans, 2019). The National Front, a violent racist group which was very active in the 1970s, does not appear to have been targeted at all.

According to evidence given by HN329, a founding member of the SDS, the unit focussed on 'people who were opposed to the current political situation, or the current government' (Casciani, 2020, 12 November) which seems a broader definition of subversion than that of Lord Harris and appears to simply involve opposition to the government of the day. HN329 went on to say '[i]t may well be that a particular group is completely harmless but we would be asked to find out what their objectives were. A file would then be opened' (Casciani, 2020, 12 November).

However, evidence heard by the UCPI suggests that surveillance of many groups deemed not to pose a threat in terms of serious crime or violence continued. For example, the Anti-apartheid Movement (AAM) was infiltrated by four SDS officers. In an earlier Freedom of Information Act investigation by the BBC, the Metropolitan Police was found to have gathered, between 1969 and 1995, 30 inch-thick files on the AAM. These files included 'reports of demonstrations and pickets' consisting of 'methodical listings of the banners carried and slogans chanted' but 'the documents seen by the BBC contain no evidence of the movement having been involved in anything criminal' (Rosenbaum, 2005). Anti-apartheid activist and ex-government minister Peter Hain argued that '[t]he police, in targeting us, were putting themselves on the wrong side of history' and he asked why they were not 'targeting the agents of apartheid bombing and killing' (Casciani, 2021a, 30 April). When an SDS officer was asked whether anti-apartheid groups had sought to overthrow democracy, he stated that '[i]t was not all about overthrowing democracy but nuisance – they caused problems and dangers to the public' (Casciani, 2021b, 4 May).

The Socialist Workers Party (SWP) appears to have been a particular focus for the SDS. Although most groups seem to have been infiltrated by one or two SDS officers, the SWP was infiltrated by no fewer than 26 officers between 1970 and 2007 (Evans, 2019). For a small organisation with a membership in the low thousands with relatively little national influence, the proportionality of such surveillance seems questionable. Moreover, the SWP was already under heavy surveillance by the Security Service – Hollingsworth and Fielding (2003) report that MI5 had 25 informers in the organisation over a 30-year period whilst all 12 of its telephone lines were tapped. This level of infiltration of small groups has been seen in the USA too. Garrow (1988) reports that 17% of the Communist Party USA were FBI informants as were 11% of the US SWP even though it only had 480 members.

But, as the barrister for activists argued at the UCPI, the SDS did not appear to conduct any 'regular and thorough risk and threat assessments which fully set out and consider any alleged risk to the public and the state from both public disorder and subversion' (Heaven, 2021, p. 4). Indeed, a witness from the Security Service (MI5) was sanguine about the threat of subversion, noting that:

> It appears … that the Security Service did not consider that subversive organisations posed a particularly high priority threat, and the pressure to investigate these organisations often came from the Prime Minister and Whitehall. (Witness Z, 2021)

However, despite this, the UCPI has heard evidence that the Security Service continued to task SDS officers with gathering information for its files.

'Domestic Extremists' as the New 'Subversives'

In the twenty-first century the term 'subversive' has gone out of fashion and, instead, policy documents now refer to the similarly ambiguous term 'domestic extremism'. Schlembach (2018) observes that some definitions emphasise the risk of violence whilst others refer to 'serious criminal activity', a much broader category if it includes damage to property and public disruption rather than violence towards people. The ambiguity and apparently widespread use of this term is likely to lead to the kinds of problems seen with the similarly ambiguous term 'subversive'.

It is hard to escape the conclusion that these undercover units were used less because of the level of threat posed by activist groups but for pragmatic reasons like the fear of political embarrassment when they cause public disruption or the ease of surveillance by human rather than technological means. Garrow (1988, p. 9), for example, has argued that the FBI made extensive use of informants in political groups because human sources were more efficient than electronic surveillance 'which consumed vast quantities of agent and clerical staff time while gathering, vacuum-cleaner style, far more chaff and trivia than even the FBI wanted'. Even if we accept that the state has a legitimate interest in surveilling such organisations, it is hard to believe that, in the era of big data and the extensive use of social media by campaign groups, there are not alternative, less intrusive forms of surveillance which would avoid the risk of the kinds of abuses investigated by the UCPI.

We do not know whether there is now more rigorous assessment of the threat posed by groups and whether there are mechanisms for weighing up the potential harms and benefits of such intrusive surveillance. Evidence given to the UCPI suggests there was previously a level of disregard for the range of potential harms which bordered on the reckless. Although there might be a temptation to regard abuses as the result of a small number of 'rotten apples', the number of officers involved suggests that the failings are of a systemic nature. Given that the vast majority of undercover officers involved in sexual relationships with activists were men (as were their managers), some activists have argued that the apparent lack of guidance about sexual relationships with activists indicates the existence of institutional sexism (Evans, 2014).

In contrast to undercover political intelligence gathering, infiltration of organised crime networks by undercover officers attracts more public support. However, here too, innovative policing tactics have raised ethical dilemmas. In the next section, we discuss Operation Trojan Shield, a recent international policing operation where criminal organisations were surveilled via ΛNØM, an apparently encrypted device which, unbeknownst to the criminals, secretly sent copies of messages to the police.

CASE STUDY 2 – ΛNØM AND OPERATION TROJAN SHIELD

ANOM

In 2018, a secure messaging company called Phantom Secure was suspended and shut down as the CEO Vincent Ramos was arrested in Washington. The Canadian company had provided many international criminals, such as high-level drug traffickers and other organised crime groups, with modified secure mobile phones (Federal Bureau of Investigation, 2018). An investigation revealed that they sold the devices exclusively to members of criminal organisations, particularly targeting transnational criminal organisations (Cheviron, 2021). Ramos was asked by the FBI to insert a backdoor into the device so that the criminal communications could be surveilled but he refused. However, with the closure of Phantom Secure, organised crime networks needed secure communications and the fact that its clientele seemed to consist only of criminals meant that law enforcement agencies, assessing that the general public would not be affected, saw an ideal opportunity to target criminal networks.

An international collaboration developed between the San Diego FBI office's Operation Trojan Shield and the Australian Federal Police's (AFP) Operation Ironside to develop a next generation encrypted device and app known as ANOM (often styled as AN0M or ΛNØM).

The FBI worked with a 'Confidential Human Source' (Cheviron, 2020) to develop and distribute the devices in exchange for a reduced sentence, $120,000, and travel expenses of around $60,000. Initially ANOM was beta tested with 50 users in Australia. Cheviron suggests that this trial was a success and enabled the AFP to penetrate two of the most sophisticated criminal networks operating in Australia. Importantly, for the project's ethical viability, he adds that 'according to Australian law enforcement, 100% of Anom users in the test phase used Anom to engage in criminal activity' (Cheviron, 2020, p. 8). In other words, the technology was not being used for anything outside of crime. The operation moved on to the next phase and, by May 2021 there were about 9,000 devices in use. The devices – costing approximately £2,000 for a six-month service plan – sent and received encrypted electronic communications and stored data in encrypted form but had limited functionality. For example, users could not make normal phone calls or surf the internet. However, users were not aware that a master key was built into the device which surreptitiously attached to each message, allowing them to be instantly stored and decrypted by law enforcement. It was widely reported that over 800 people were arrested around the world, $48m in cash and cryptocurrencies and over 32 tonnes of drugs were seized, and more than 100 murder plots were counteracted. Europol reported that over 27 million messages were collected and it is expected that there will be further arrests in the future.

Privacy advocates have welcomed the fact that the operation did not involve inserting backdoors into products used by the general public, but they have also raised concerns. For example, Ashkan Soltani, previously the Chief Technologist of the Federal Trade Commission in the Division of Privacy and Identity Protection, stated that the operation showed that 'You can use good old-fashioned detective work and operations without backdooring protocols and services that consumers widely use' (Murphy, 2021). However, he went on to question the potential for the surveillance of innocent people. How many 'non-targets', he asked, were 'swept up in this operation?' (Murphy, 2021). Cheviron (2020) states that he believes 'that Anom devices are used exclusively to openly discuss criminal schemes or to maintain relationships in furtherance of those schemes' (p. 11). Presently, we can only assume that 'non-targets' were not caught up within the surveillance operation.

Concerns have also been raised about the impact of such operations on the legitimate encryption industry and about the way in which international law enforcement collaborations can enable national laws to be circumvented.

'Laundering' Surveillance

Jennifer Lynch, the Surveillance Litigation Director at the Electronic Frontier Foundation, has stated that US law enforcement was not able to monitor domestic Anom users because this would violate the Fourth Amendment and the Wiretap Act. Therefore, the USA relied upon other countries without these regulations 'to launder its surveillance' (Murphy, 2021). To circumvent US laws, the devices routed BCC encryptions of the messages to an iBot server outside of the USA, where it was decrypted, then re-encrypted with an FBI encryption code before being decrypted again for viewing (Cheviron, 2020). Around the middle of 2019, the investigators sought a third country to obtain an iBot server of its own because, although Australia's judicial order allowed for the interception of Anom communications, it was unauthorised to share the information with foreign partners (Cheviron, 2020, p. 8, footnote 6). The mass raids and arrests took place on 8 June 2021, the day after the expiration of the court order allowing the third country to supply Anom server data to the FBI and this was probably no coincidence.

Greg Barns SC from the Australian Lawyers Alliance suggested that Australia was likely chosen as a partner in the operation because of its 'very weak privacy protections'. He went on to state:

> Often with these operations you go to the country with the weakest laws, as it were, so that you can obtain more evidence more easily and run less of a risk of evidence being obtained illegally. (Swanston, 2021)

Barns has argued that this is a form of entrapment wherein people are induced into committing a crime – entrapment is allowed in Australia but not in the USA.

Varying legal regimes mean that such international law enforcement collaborations provide potential societal benefits in terms of increased flexibility in mounting operations against well-funded targets but potential societal harms by undermining legal protections within each jurisdiction. This international operation has also reignited the debate about the legitimacy of public access to encryption.

The Rights and Wrongs of Encryption and Decryption

The US Department of Justice has made it clear that a goal of the operation was to target encryption. Randy Grossman, the acting US attorney said:

> Hardened encryption devices usually provide an impenetrable shield against law enforcement surveillance detection. The supreme irony here is that the very devices that these criminals were using to hide from law enforcement were actually beacons for law enforcement. We aim to shatter any confidence in the hardened encrypted device industry with our indictment and announcement that this platform was run by the FBI. (United States Department of Justice, 2021)

Wired reports that the US Department of Justice and other law enforcement agencies have long lobbied for access to 'end-to-end' encrypted data from, for example, social media and other communication platforms (Newman, 2021). Since data are kept scrambled by companies so that they remain undecipherable along their journey across the internet, law enforcement agencies do not have access to their content, a problem they refer to as 'going dark'. However, *Wired* argue that the FBI and, of course other agencies, have had continued success in finding creative ways of developing workarounds by, for example, targeting the devices rather than the encryption protocols themselves.

Some might argue that, given the success of operations like this, backdoors should be built into all apps. For example, in 2019 the UK's Government Communications Headquarters (GCHQ) proposed that communication systems should be designed to include a silent, unseen participant like another member of the group chat, enabling government agencies to access them. However, there was a storm of reaction against this, not only from human rights groups but also from the Big Tech companies. Indeed, many of these companies introduced end-to-end encryption in the first place because of public reaction to the activities of the US and UK governments. Edward Snowden disclosed that, under the NSA's PRISM programme, technology companies passed internet data to the NSA and that, under the MUSCULAR programme, GCHQ and the NSA had hacked into the main communications links connecting the data centres run by Yahoo! and Google without their knowledge. PRISM threatened public trust in technology companies whereas MUSCULAR threatened the companies' trust in the US and UK governments. End-to-end encryption appeared to them to provide a solution to both problems.

Research suggests that, whilst there is wide public support for overt surveillance like CCTV, there is less support for covert and digital surveillance. The 34th British Social Attitudes (BSA) Survey reported that, although 80% of the public supported the use of video surveillance in public areas, 60% supported the collection of 'information about anyone living in Britain without their knowledge' and only 50% supported the monitoring of emails and other internet activity (Clery, Curtice, & Harding, 2016). Although Operation Trojan Shield will in the future be seen as a very successful method of counteracting serious organised crime, it will also serve to remind us that our online lives are always in danger of being covertly surveilled.

Operation Trojan Shield threw up some unique challenges. For example, the FBI needed to ensure both that the general public was not affected and that the fake encrypted phone company's cover was maintained. Andrew Young, a partner in the Litigation Department in law firm Barnes and Thornburg stated 'We can't just run a good investigation; we have to run a good company' (Cox, 2021). This included ensuring both that the marketing of the company was done correctly, and that the fake company was credible. In order to gain and maintain good customer service and satisfaction they had to provide technical support and deal with hackers. Importantly, they had to make sure that it did not become mainstream – they could not allow it to get into the hands of the public because of the ethical issues related to surveilling non-targets. Hence, distribution needed to happen within the criminal circles. A key unwitting distributor was Hakan Ayik who had long standing connections with Australian biker gangs and was an alleged drug lord. Ayik is currently an international fugitive, wanted not only by the authorities but, presumably, by previous customers who hold him responsible for their predicament (BBC News online, 2021).

Operation Trojan Shield is a good example of surveillance through data and digital technologies. Indeed, the capture, processing and categorisation of data has unsurprisingly become a significant part of surveillance studies and raises significant ethical challenges (Harper et al., 2013; Tucker, 2013; Van Dijck, 2014). Another key area, outside of law enforcement, in which data capture and processing is a growing concern is in relation to children's learning in schools, and the associated role of forms of education technology (so-called 'EdTech'). The use of digital learning platforms, and associated technologies in schools, has risen significantly during the Covid-19 pandemic. However, it is not clear that governance structures have kept pace with their increased use, or with the new technological developments on the horizon (e.g. use of artificial intelligence, AI). The next section focusses on some of the ethical concerns of EdTech, with a specific focus on the UK context.

CASE STUDY 3 – SURVEILLANCE, EDUCATION AND EMOTIONAL AI

The use of large scale digital learning platforms, such as Google Classroom, has increased significantly over the past decade. Many schools have welcomed the possibility to use platforms that can streamline key learning processes, and often these are free of charge. For instance, Google Classroom allows teachers to set work for children, to mark and feedback, and to communicate updates via Classroom or linked Google platforms, such as via Gmail. The fact that Google's digital learning platform is free to use, makes it an attractive option for many schools, particularly given significant pressure on school budgets in many countries. The use of platforms such as Google Classroom has risen markedly during the Covid-19 pandemic, with registered users rising from 40 to 150 million worldwide during this period (Williamson, 2021). The advantages of using the platform in terms of delivering learning mean that it is likely that many schools will continue to use it after Covid-19 'lockdowns' imposed by many countries, which meant children accessed the learning remotely from home. Furthermore, Google, as the main provider of free digital learning platforms in primary and secondary education has sought to further strengthen its position through integration with other of its products and services, for example, providing low-cost Google Chromebooks to schools, that integrate seamlessly with its education ecosystem; examples include Classroom, Meet and Gmail.

Concerns have been raised about the increased presence of large data companies in education – with reference to children's privacy, and the extent of data generation from children's learning activity. For instance, the Electronic Frontier Foundation filed an official complaint with the Federal Trade Commission about data mining of children's personal information by Google's Workspace for Education (Williamson, 2021). Google's reply to such concerns is to stress the robustness of its privacy policy, in terms of not sharing personalised data. However, what is missing is transparency regarding how Google uses the data. Concerns have been raised that education technologies effectively become surveillance technologies because of the mass data processing involved in Edtech (Williamson, Potter, & Eynon, 2019). And furthermore, that the growing presence of education technologies in public education systems 'intensifies and normalises the surveillance of students' (Manolev, Sullivan, & Slee, 2019). We argue that the surveillance elements of education technologies are, in essence, covert, because (a) such technologies are not 'surveillance by design' and (b) children are highly unlikely to recognise them as forms of surveillance.

Governance of Education Technology in Schools

Children are, by definition, classed as a vulnerable group, and yet there is significant opacity regarding the governance of the use of education-focussed technologies such as Google Classroom in UK schools. This point is a key message from a recent Digital Futures Commission report (Day, 2021), which undertook a detailed analysis of the data-related legislation, and associated governance processes (at government and school level), in relation to the use of what they refer to as 'EdTech'. Whilst there are clear legislative frameworks for data processing, such as GDPR, there is no specific legislation focussing on the use of EdTech in schools, which given that its use, and therefore the role of the private sector, has increased significantly in recent years, is somewhat of a surprise. This lack of a legislative framework creates a governance vacuum, as schools and local education authorities (LEAs) do not have clear legislation upon which to develop and implement their local governance practices. The current system also places significant responsibility on schools to manage governance, as policies allow and encourage schools to identify their own EdTech systems, meaning that different schools can use different platforms (although the 'free to use' policies of big players such as Google Classroom means that certain platforms are coming to dominate).

The fact that legislation lags behind the data generating and processing practices of EdTech makes it difficult to identify the entirety of the ethical concerns in relation to children's data in schools. With children having to attend school by law (unless they have a home-schooling agreement with their LEA), they have no choice but to engage with any EdTech used by their school. This makes the use of EdTech such an important ethical issue, because children cannot avoid it. The opacity regarding the governance of data processing activity means that forms of covert surveillance emerge. For instance, does a child understand that if they opt-in to an associated product/service provided by their EdTech provider, they could be consenting to the company to use their data for marketing purposes – and that such activity involves a direct contract between child and digital platform, outside of any school policy (Day, 2021)?

AI and EdTech

Concerns about the potential for surveillance of children's learning are broadening in relation to new developments involving the use of forms of AI in digital learning platforms. This step potentially signifies a move towards automated forms of learning, whereby children can ask an AI-driven conversational agent questions related to learning. Google CEO, Sundar Pichai, recently announced its foray in this area, an AI-driven system called LaMDA (Language Model for Dialogue Applications), which is a natural language processor-based conversational agent that children can ask questions of and subsequently receive responses in a conversational format (Williamson, 2021). We know that such systems rely on 'learning' from the data gathered from previous interactions, so will involve mass aggregation of data related to children's learning, and as such, involve widespread surveillance of engagement with digital learning platforms.

Given the fact that AI and data mining are dependent on having large amounts of data, there is significant incentive to expand aggressively into new domains like education. In addition to major technologies and data companies such as Google moving into large scale data mining in education, there are also smaller technology firms drawn to education and the development of AI-driven tools to capture and categorise children's learning.

One example is the use of AI-based emotion detection systems, for example, http://www.4littletrees.com/ which has been used in secondary education in Hong Kong (Murgia, 2021). 4 Little Trees is an AI-driven system that is designed to identify and monitor children's emotional responses and activity during online lessons. The aim is to provide feedback to teacher and schools about when students lose attention, and whether this informs as to the effectiveness of teaching practices and allow for teachers to respond to children's learning in 'real time': for example, if 4 Little Trees suggests a child is losing attention a teacher can ask a question to that child to re-engage them. 4 Little Trees is based on facial recognition systems that have been used by law enforcement and border control agencies in recent years. 4 Little Trees extends the 'recognition' capabilities of such systems through claiming to be able to identify not the person's identity, but their emotions, feelings, sentiments. The growth of emotion-related facial recognition systems, which have been named 'emotional-AI' has been significant in recent years (McStay, 2018, 2020). The attraction to advertisers of being able to identify individuals' emotional responses to adverts is a major one and is driving the industry. Its use in education is at the embryonic stage, but there is no reason to think that education will be naturally immune to the desire and push to automate that AI-driven systems offer.

There are important points to note regarding emotion-AI systems such as 4 Little Trees. Firstly, that the data collected from children are of an intrusive nature (e.g. emotional state, videos of children in their homes and so on). Secondly, it is not entirely transparent how the data will be used, both by the private sector (i.e. 4 Little Tress) and by schools. Whilst 4 Little Trees states that data collected by authority figures (i.e. teachers) will be used to make decisions about children's engagement with learning, it is not clear how it might be used in the future. Finally, the universal model of emotion that such technologies are developed from (i.e. that a core set of emotions exist with largely universal modes of expression) has been extensively critiqued (Barrett, 2018; Barrett, Adolphs, Marsella, Martinez, & Pollak, 2019; Ellis & Tucker, 2020). The implication of these critiques is that the categorisation of the emotional states of children cannot reliably be taken as accurate. If we cannot rely on interpretations of systems such as 4 Little Trees, it is problematic to base elements of children's education on them. An expression of inattention could relate to a child reflecting on a problem relating to their learning, rather than inattention per se. Furthermore, if a child is deemed to be inattentive and unengaged, despite previous warnings, would this lead to punishments?

The real time monitoring, tracking and categorising of children's facial expressions during online learning is an example of an emerging form of surveillance. Whilst it resonates with traditional notions of top-down power, in the form of powerful organisations (such as technology companies and schools) initiating and undertaking the surveillance, its operation is closer to what Isin and Ruppert (2020) refer to as *sensory power,* which involves 'data that tracks and traces people in their movements, sentiments, needs and desires' (p. 2). In the case of 4 Little Trees, it is the tracking and categorising of facial expressions in terms of emotion, mood and attention. Isin and Ruppert claim sensory power is a new form of power that is distinguished from traditional notions of sovereign, disciplinary and regulatory power. Data tracking technologies such as emotion-AI systems have made possible more sophisticated forms of surveillance in terms of focussing down on specific psycho-physiological activity, such as with micro-facial expressions. Others forms of tracking have also emerged, such as fitness trackers that can capture and categorise heart rate, skin conductance and so on.

The ethical challenges of EdTech are only going to continue to grow as with increased use of AI in digital learning platforms. To date, much of the data under focus has involved things such as children's IP addresses, time spent engaging with platforms, wider patterns of use and such like. The advent of tools such as 4 Little Trees adds an additional layer because it generates different kinds of data about children. The processing of descriptive data about patterns of use (such as location, duration) is added to data interpreting and categorising children's faces directly in relation to emotion and attentional state. This is a more sophisticated level of data, which is seen as attractive due to its potential to inform regarding the effectiveness of different forms of online learning. However, its categorising of facial expressions as informing of emotional states, based on problematic emotion science, makes it both intrusive and potentially inaccurate due to not being scientifically valid.

Allowing private companies to develop and use facial recognition technologies in children's learning environments presents major ethical challenges, from concerns regarding data protection through to allowing private companies access to videos of children's engagement in 'real time' learning in their homes. This is an emerging area of concern, for which new forms of governance are required. Whilst the 4 Little Trees system is not currently in use in the UK, it is indicative of one direction that EdTech is taking, and as such it is an important example of the considerations for governance processes. As the Digital Futures Commission Report notes:

> [G]iven the lack of data governance or data analytics expertise in schools, putting the responsibility on schools to negotiate these contracts puts a large amount of power in the hands of EdTech companies to interpret and apply data protection laws in a way that suits their own commercial purposes, without any oversight. (Day, 2021, p. 46)

In relation to the current use of EdTech in UK schools, the system's positioning of responsibility at the level of schools, which can often lack the detailed technical knowledge to map sophisticated data generating and processing practices onto existing governance, is not an optimal strategy to ensure transparent and ethical governance structures. Legislation and governance structures are required to be developed and implemented at the level of government and given the significant increase in the use of EdTech during the Covid-19 pandemic, the need is significant and pressing (Day, 2021).

DISCUSSION

The three case studies we have presented raise some common and some different ethical concerns. All involved the gathering of data on individuals but the nature of the information varied. In the 'spycops' and AI EdTech cases the data were potentially of a very personal nature whereas ΛNØM appeared to gather data mainly about criminal activity. Both the 'spycops' and ΛNØM cases involved intentional deception whereas, in the case of AI EdTech the nature of the data gathering was opaque rather than deceptive. The data in the ΛNØM case were gathered to support criminal prosecutions whereas, in the 'Spycops' and AI EdTech cases the future use of the data, and thus consequences for the individuals, was unclear. Similarly, in the latter two cases, the information was potentially inaccurate. The cases differed also in respect of whether the information was gathered by the state or by private corporations. In the two cases of state surveillance, deception was also involved. Key concerns here include proportionality and whether the targeting was discriminate. In the ΛNØM case, the target group appeared to be clearly defined but, although undercover infiltration might be regarded as proportionate in relation to the threat posed by serious organised crime networks, there are questions about the benefit versus harm calculus. For example, it is unclear whether the operation will have unintended long-term consequences like weakening public trust in commercial encryption products. In the 'spycops' case, there was little evidence of a rigorous threat assessment and deliberation of harms and benefits, the targeting seemed to lack discrimination and there was significant collateral intrusion and breaches of human rights.

In the case of AI EdTech, the involvement of large private corporations gathering data raises some different ethical questions not only about the datafication of children who have not been able to give consent and the commercialisation of education but also about what Zuboff (2019) has termed 'surveillance capitalism'. The motto of surveillance capitalism can be summarised, in Bruce Schneier's (2015) memorable phrase, as '[i]f something is free, you're not the customer; you're the product' (p. 83). It has been argued that many private corporations now hold more personal information on the public than governments. Whilst, in principle, governments can be held accountable by their citizens, corporations are only accountable to their shareholders and the law (which is notoriously weak in this area, especially in the USA). This gives technology companies considerable leeway in how they use data gathered from their users. An investigation by ProPublica (https://www.propublica.org/) revealed that Facebook uses over 52,000 unique attributes – including categories like 'affinity', with different ethnic groups, 'pretending to text in awkward situations' and 'breastfeeding in public' – to classify its users which they market to advertisers (Angwin, Mattu, & Parris, 2016). ProPublica have reported on how some advertisers have used this information in a discriminatory fashion, for instance, only advertising housing to white people. This is an example of how information collected in an opaque fashion can be utilised in a way that users are unaware of and thus this raises concern about how data collected on children might be used in the future.

Our review of these three cases demonstrates that, although covert aspects of surveillance prompt some common ethical concerns (e.g. privacy, lack of transparency, etc.), some questions arise from the specificity of the type of surveillance, who is employing it (e.g. the state or private corporations) and for what purpose. As a result, it is important in public discussion of ethics not to treat surveillance as a set of homogenous practices.

There is clearly a need for a more informed public debate about covert aspects of surveillance and further research is warranted on how the public understand and weigh up competing moral imperatives. For example, in relation to the 'spy-cops' case, what level of surveillance is publicly acceptable to prevent non-violent public disorder by activists compared with, say, people actively engaging in violent acts of terrorism? And, in either case, what degree of certainty do we have in the intelligence gathered? The 34th BSA Survey did not investigate these more intrusive types of surveillance though, interestingly, it found that two-thirds of the population supported the rights of groups to hold demonstrations and 50% supported this right even if the groups wanted to overthrow the government by revolution (Clery et al., 2016).

One of the challenges in public discourse about the ethics of surveillance is that, as we have noted, only a selected number of ethical issues are discussed and often those associated with particular types of surveillance. For example, state surveillance via CCTV and collection of digital communications engages questions of privacy but not the kinds of deception required in undercover operations. As a result, it can be helpful to utilise frameworks which prompt us to consider a broad range of ethical questions. One such framework is the 'ethical grid' developed by David Seedhouse (2009). Although there is not enough space to discuss the grid in detail, for the present discussion it is sufficient to understand that Seedhouse views good ethical decision-making as involving four different 'layers': a concern for individuals (which broadly engages concerns about human rights like respecting and creating autonomy, respecting persons equally; and serving needs first); a deontological layer (concerning moral duties like telling the truth, minimising harm, keeping promises and seeking to do the most positive good); a consequentialist layer (concerning the consequences of actions like what would deliver the most beneficial outcome for oneself, the individual, a particular group and/or society); and a layer of external considerations (such as laws, codes of practice, risks, the wishes of others, resources available, the effectiveness and efficiency of action, disputed facts and the degree of certainty of the evidence on which action is taken).

Since Seedhouse developed the ethical grid for use by healthcare professionals, it requires adaptation when considering the covert aspects of surveillance. But the notion that ethical decision-making requires attending to human rights, moral duties and the consequences of actions as well as a range of external considerations is a useful one and could help to guide future discussions. For example, there are obviously tensions within and between human rights and deontological and consequentialist concerns. We might wish to create and respect autonomy and equality for children, but society is prepared to accept restrictions on the autonomy of members of organised crime networks to minimise the harms caused by serious crime. External considerations are also important – for example, what degree of certainty do we have that the information gathered (such as in relation to children's emotional state) is accurate? Hopefully the use of such frameworks might lead researchers to address a broader set of ethical questions and might inform a more comprehensive public debate. Given the secrecy and lack of transparency inherent in covert surveillance, such public debate is important.

NOTES

1. Some of these authorisations may be 'thematic'– that is, covering organisations.

2. This unit was subsumed into different organisations: the National Domestic Extremism Unit (2011–2013) and the National Domestic Extremism and Disorder Intelligence Unit (2013–2016). Domestic extremism now seems to be managed, along with national counter terrorism, by the National Police Chiefs' Council's Counter Terrorism Coordination Committee through the National Counter Terrorism Policing Headquarters.

3. The inquiry's extensive website (https://www.ucpi.org.uk/) provides access to hearing transcripts and evidential documents (over 1,000 at the time of writing). When hearings are being held summaries of each day's evidence can also be found on an activist website: http://campaignopposingpolicesurveillance.com/.

4. In 2006, the Metropolitan Police's Special Branch was subsumed under Counter Terrorism Command (SO15).

5. This tactic was popularised by Frederick Forsyth's 1971 novel *The Day of the Jackal*.

6. Names in inverted commas are cover identities rather than officers' real names. In the UCPI many officers are referred to by a code beginning with the letters 'HN'.

7. The Investigatory Powers Tribunal was established by the Regulation of Investigatory Powers Act 2000 in order to deal with complaints about their use.

REFERENCES

Angwin, K., Mattu, S. & Parris Jr., T. (2016, 27 December). Facebook doesn't tell users everything it really knows about them. Retrieved from https://www.propublica.org/article/facebook-doesnt-tell-users-everything-it-really-knows-about-them

Barrett, L. F. (2018). *How emotions are made: The secret life of the brain*. London: PAN Books.

Barrett, L. F., Adolphs, R., Marsella, S., Martinez, A. M., & Pollak, S. D. (2019). Emotional expressions reconsidered: Challenges to inferring emotion from human facial movements. *Psychological Science in the Public Interest, 20*(1), 1–68. https://doi.org/10.1177/1529100619832930

BBC News Online. (2021). Hakan Ayik: The man who accidentally helped FBI get in criminals' pockets. *BBC News Online*. Retrieved from https://www.bbc.co.uk/news/world-57397779

Casciani, D. (2015). Undercover policing inquiry: Why it matters. BBC News Online. Retrieved from https://www.bbc.co.uk/news/uk-33682769

Casciani, D. (2020, 12 November). Undercover officer targeted 'anti-establishment' left. BBC News online. Retrieved from https://www.bbc.co.uk/news/uk-54924071

Casciani, D. (2021, 30 April). Undercover police on wrong side of history, says ex-cabinet minister Lord Hain. BBC News Online. Retrieved from https://www.bbc.co.uk/news/uk-56948404

Casciani, D. (2021, 4 May). Undercover policing: Officer defends spying on anti-apartheid movement. BBC News Online. Retrieved from https://www.bbc.co.uk/news/uk-56988040

Cheviron, N. (2021). Affidavit in support of application for search warrant. Case 3:21-mj-01948-MSB Document 1 Filed 05/18/21 PageID.45 Page 2 of 33. Retrieved from https://web.archive.org/web/20210609190720/https://www.justice.gov/usao-sdca/press-release/file/1402426/download

Clery, E., Curtice, J., & Harding R. (2016). *British social attitudes: The 34th report*. London: NatCen Social Research. Retrieved from www.bsa.natcen.ac.uk

Cox, J. (2021, 10 June). 'We have to run a good company': How the FBI sold its encryption honeypot. *Vice*. Retrieved from https://www.vice.com/en/article/m7e733/anom-fbi-andrew-young-encryption-honeypot

Curran, L. S. (2021). An exploration of well-being in former covert and undercover police officers. *Journal of Police and Criminal Psychology, 36*, 256–267. https://doi.org/10.1007/s11896-020-09406-x

Day, E. (2021). *Governance of data for children's learning in UK state schools*. Digital Futures Commission, 5Rights Foundation. Retrieved from https://digitalfuturescommission.org.uk/wp-content/uploads/2021/06/Governance-of-data-for-children-learning-Final.pdf

Ellis, D., Harper, D. & Tucker, I. (2016). The psychology of surveillance: Experiencing the 'Surveillance Society'. *The Psychologist*. 29 (September), 682–685. Retrieved from https://thepsychologist.bps.org.uk/volume-29/september/experiencing-surveillance-society

Ellis, D., & Tucker, I. (2020). *Emotion in the digital age: Technologies, data and psychosocial life*. London, UK: Routledge.

Evans, R. (2014). Police spies still get free rein to have sexual liaisons, say women suing Met. *The Guardian*. Retrieved from https://www.theguardian.com/uk-news/2014/mar/28/police-spies-sexual-liaisons-women-suing-met

Evans, R. (2015). Police apologise to women who had relationships with undercover officers. *The Guardian*. Retrieved from https://www.theguardian.com/uk-news/2015/nov/20/met-police-apologise-women-had-relationships-with-undercover-officers

Evans, R. (2016). Met to apologise to woman after admitting officer stole dead son's identity. *The Guardian*. Retrieved from https://www.theguardian.com/uk-news/2016/dec/15/met-police-barbara-shaw-rod-richardson-anti-capitalist

Evans, R. (2017). Undercover police spied on more than 1,000 political groups in UK. *The Guardian*. Retrieved from https://amp.theguardian.com/uk-news/2017/jul/27/undercover-police-spied-on-more-than-1000-political-groups-in-uk

Evans, R. (2019). UK political groups spied on by undercover police – search the list. *The Guardian*. Retrieved from https://www.theguardian.com/uk-news/ng-interactive/2018/oct/15/uk-political-groups-spied-on-undercover-police-list

Evans, R. (2020, 28 October). Secrets and lies: Untangling the UK 'spy cops' scandal. *The Guardian*. Retrieved from https://www.theguardian.com/uk-news/2020/oct/28/secrets-and-lies-untangling-the-uk-spy-cops-scandal

Evans, R. (2020, 4 November). Ex-wives of undercover police tell of marriages 'based on lies'. *The Guardian*. Retrieved from https://www.theguardian.com/uk-news/2020/nov/04/ex-wives-undercover-police-inquiry-marriages-based-lies

Evans, R. (2021, 20 April). Police spy's bosses knew activist was being duped into sexual relationship, court told. *The Guardian*. Retrieved from https://www.theguardian.com/uk-news/2021/apr/20/police-spys-bosses-knew-activist-was-being-duped-into-sexual-relationship-court-told

Evans, R. (2021, 22 April). Fourth officer allegedly fathered child after meeting woman undercover. *The Guardian*. Retrieved from https://www.theguardian.com/uk-news/2021/apr/22/fourth-officer-allegedly-fathered-child-after-meeting-woman-undercover

Evans, R. (2021, 12 May). Undercover police frequently spied on children, inquiry hears. *The Guardian*. Retrieved from https://www.theguardian.com/uk-news/2021/may/12/undercover-police-frequently-spied-on-children-inquiry-hears

Evans, R. & Lewis, P. (2013). *Undercover: The true story of Britain's secret police*. London, UK: Guardian/Faber & Faber.

Federal Bureau of Investigation (2018, 16 March). International criminal communication service dismantled phantom secure helped drug traffickers, organized crime worldwide. Retrieved from https://www.fbi.gov/news/stories/phantom-secure-takedown-031618

Garrow, D. J. (1988). FBI political harassment and FBI historiography: Analyzing informants and measuring the effects. *The Public Historian, 10*(4), 5–18. https://doi.org/10.2307/3377831

Harper, D. J., Ellis, D. & Tucker, I. (2014). Surveillance. In T. Teo (ed) *Encyclopedia of critical psychology* (pp. 1887–1892). New York: Springer. https://doi.org/10.1007/978-1-4614-5583-7_305

Harper, D., Tucker, I. & Ellis, D. (2013). Surveillance and subjectivity: Everyday experiences of surveillance practices. In K.S. Ball & L. Snider (eds) *The surveillance-industrial complex: A political economy of surveillance* (pp.175–190). London, UK: Routledge.

Heaven, K. (2021, 15 April). Opening statement for tranche one phase two on behalf of the co-operating group of co-operating non-state, non-police core participants. (2021). Undercover Policing Inquiry. Retrieved from https://www.ucpi.org.uk/publications/opening-statement-from-richard-chessum-and-mary-for-tranche-1-phase-2/

Hollingsworth, M. & Fielding, N. (2003). *Defending the realm: Inside MI5 and the war on terrorism.* New edition. London, UK: André Deutsch.

Investigatory Powers Commissioner's Office (2020). *Annual Report of the Investigatory Powers Commissioner 2019* (HC 1039). London: Author. Retrieved from https://hansard.parliament.uk/commons/2020-12-15/debates/20121549000015/InvestigatoryPowersCommissionerAnnualReport2019

Isin, E., & Ruppert, E. (2020). The birth of sensory power: How a pandemic made it visible?. *Big Data & Society, 7*(2). https://doi.org/10.1177/2053951720969208

Kelly, J. & Casciani, D. (2014, 24 October). Met pays £425,000 to mother of undercover policeman's child. BBC News online. Retrieved from https://www.bbc.co.uk/news/uk-29743646

Lewis, P., Evans, R. & Pollak, S. (2013, 24 June). Trauma of spy's girlfriend: 'like being raped by the state'. *The Guardian.* Retrieved from https://www.theguardian.com/uk/2013/jun/24/undercover-police-spy-girlfriend-child

Loftus, B., Goold, B. & Mac Giollabhuí, S. (2016). From a visible spectacle to an invisible presence: The working culture of covert policing, *British Journal of Criminology, 56*(4), 629–645. https://doi.org/10.1093/bjc/azv076

Lubbers, E. (2015). Undercover research: Corporate and police spying on activists. An introduction to activist intelligence as a new field of surveillance. *Surveillance & Society, 13*(3/4), 338–353. https://doi.org/10.24908/ss.v13i3/4.5371

McStay, A. (2018). *Emotional AI: The rise of empathic media.* London, UK: SAGE Publications.

McStay, A. (2020). Emotional AI, soft biometrics and the surveillance of emotional life: An unusual consensus on privacy. *Big Data & Society, 7*(1), 205395172090438. https://doi.org/10.1177/2053951720904386

Macnish, K.N.J. (2015). An eye for an eye: Proportionality and surveillance. *Ethical Theory and Moral Practice, 18*(3), 529–548. https://doi.org/10.1007/s10677-014-9537-5

Manolev, J., Sullivan, A., & Slee, R. (2019). The datafication of discipline: ClassDojo, surveillance and a performative classroom culture. *Learning, Media and Technology, 44*(1), 36–51. https://doi.org/10.1080/17439884.2018.1558237

Marx, G. T. (1974). Thoughts on a neglected category of social movement participant: The agent provocateur and the informant. *American Journal of Sociology, 80*(2), 402–442. https://doi.org/10.1086/225807

Murgia, M. (2021, 12 May). Emotion recognition: Can AI detect human feelings from a face? *Financial Times.* Retrieved from https://www.ft.com/content/c0b03d1d-f72f-48a8-b342-b4a926109452?shareType=nongift

Murphy, H. (2021, 9 June). How the FBI's Trojan Shield operation exposed a criminal underworld. *Financial Times.* Retrieved from https://www.ft.com/content/65ed6eb5-4968-4636-99bc-27a516d089dd

Newman, L. (2021, 11 June). The FBI's Anom stunt rattles the encryption debate. *Wired.* Retrieved from https://www.wired.com/story/fbi-anom-phone-network-encryption-debate/

Rosenbaum, M. (2005). Tracking the anti-apartheid groups. BBC News online. Retrieved from http://news.bbc.co.uk/1/hi/uk_politics/4285964.stm

Schlembach, R. (2018). Undercover policing and the spectre of 'domestic extremism': the covert surveillance of environmental activism in Britain. *Social Movement Studies, 17*(5), 491–506. https://doi.org/10.1080/14742837.2018.1480934

Schneier, B. (2015). *Data and Goliath: The hidden battles to collect your data and control your world.* New York, US: W.W. Norton.

Security Service (undated). FAQs about MI5: Does MI5 investigate trade unions and pressure groups? Retrieved from https://www.mi5.gov.uk/faq/what-is-the-difference-between-mi5-and-mi6-sis

Seedhouse, D. (2009). *Ethics: The heart of health care.* Third edition. Chichester, UK: Wiley.

Stephens Griffin, N. (2020). 'Everyone was questioning everything': Understanding the derailing impact of undercover policing on the lives of UK environmentalists. *Social Movement Studies,* 1–19. Advance online publication. https://doi.org/10.1080/14742837.2020.1770073

Swanston, T. (2021, 9 June). Australia's 'very weak' privacy protection may be behind key role in global operation against organised crime. ABC News. Retrieved from https://www.abc.net.au/news/2021-06-10/nsw-operation-ironside-privacy-in-wake-of-afp-raids/100202924

Thompson, T. (2010, 14 March). Inside the lonely and violent world of the Yard's elite undercover unit. *The Guardian*. Retrieved from https://www.theguardian.com/uk/2010/mar/14/undercover-police-far-left-secret

Tucker, I. (2013). Bodies and surveillance: Simondon, information and affect. *Distinktion: Scandinavian Journal of Social Theory*, *14*(1), 37–41. https://doi.org/10.1080/1600910X.2013.766225

United States Department of Justice (2021, 8 June). FBI's encrypted phone platform infiltrated hundreds of criminal syndicates; Result is massive worldwide takedown. Retrieved from https://www.justice.gov/usao-sdca/pr/fbi-s-encrypted-phone-platform-infiltrated-hundreds-criminal-syndicates-result-massive

Van Dijck, J. (2014). Datafication, dataism and dataveillance: Big Data between scientific paradigm and ideology. *Surveillance & Society*, *12*(2), 197–208. https://doi.org/10.24908/ss.v12i2.4776

Williamson, B., Potter, J., & Eynon, R. (2019). New research problems and agendas in learning, media and technology: The editors' wishlist. *Learning, Media and Technology*, *44*(2), 87–91. https://doi.org/10.1080/17439884.2019.1614953

Williamson, B., (2021, May 28). *Google's plans to bring AI to education make its dominance in classrooms more alarming*. Fast Company. Retrieved from https://www.fastcompany.com/90641049/google-education-classroom-ai

Wilson, K. (2021). Kate Wilson: After spy cops case the Met is beyond redemption. *The Guardian*. Retrieved from https://www.theguardian.com/uk-news/2021/sep/30/kate-wilson-after-spy-cops-case-the-met-is-beyond-redemption

Wilson v (1) Commissioner of Police of The Metropolis (2) National Police Chiefs' Council (2021, 30 September). IPT/11/167/H. Retrieved from https://www.ipt-uk.com/judgments.asp?id=61

Witness, Z. (2021, 22 March). First witness statement of Security Service Witness Z. Undercover Policing Inquiry. Retrieved from https://www.ucpi.org.uk/publications/first-witness-statement-of-security-service-witness-z/

Zuboff, S. (2019). *The age of surveillance capitalism: The fight for a human future at the new frontier of power*. New York, US: Public Affairs.

GUIDANCE NOTES FOR REVIEWERS AND POLICYMAKERS ON COVERT, DECEPTIVE AND SURVEILLANCE RESEARCH

Ron Iphofen, Simon E. Kolstoe, Kevin Macnish, Paul Spicker and Dónal O'Mathúna

PREAMBLE

Covert research is research which has not been declared to research participants or subjects. *Surveillance* research is a form of covert research which involves undeclared monitoring of a subject's actions and/or their data which may or may not be personal. *Deceptive* research is research whose nature has been misrepresented to the subject; it may be covert, but more usually it is not. Deception may form an element in any research approach. Covert, surveillance and deceptive research are often treated as raising similar ethical concerns, but they are different kinds of activity. Each category of research includes variable forms of data gathering, analysis and reporting, and therefore raises a variety of ethical issues, some distinct and some overlapping.

Care must be taken with a great deal of existing guidance and advice on these types of research. Some guidance can include misunderstandings of the nature of covert, surveillance and deceptive research, and should not be endorsed. For example, much advice suggests that these forms of enquiry are rare, have always been rare and that alternative methods should always be preferred. This is not the case. Most of the chapters in this volume contain some degree of challenge to that

Ethical Issues in Covert, Security and Surveillance Research
Advances in Research Ethics and Integrity, Volume 8, 199–209

ISSN: 2398-6018/doi:10.1108/S2398-601820210000008014

sort of advice. A great deal of research, particularly in the humanities and social sciences, has benefitted from either one or a combination of these approaches. A lengthy tradition, going back at least to the 1940s, uses these kinds of approaches. Indeed, it might be said that ALL public research has some undisclosed elements.

Research proposals which include methods that do not disclose that research is being done, or do not obtain full informed consent from participants, often raise ethical concerns for reviewers. Equally policymakers and their advisors may have concerns about either using or commissioning evidence from surveillance, covert or deceptive research. The following points are provided as a concise summary of the issues addressed in greater detail throughout the open access volume within which these notes are first produced (Iphofen, R., & O'Mathúna, D., (Eds.). (2022). *Ethical issues in covert, security and surveillance research* (Advances in Research Ethics and Integrity, Vol. 8). Bingley: Emerald Publishing). These considerations were written with a broad set of reviewers in mind, including those reviewing proposals under consideration for funding, ethics 'approval', ethics 'opinion' or publication. We do not provide simple categorisations of specific research methods as either ethical or unethical, but offer these considerations as prompts to facilitate further reflection and consideration of the details of each proposal that will allow more complete assessments of the proposed research.

PART A

Guidance for Reviewers on Covert, Surveillance and/or Deceptive Research

(1) Do Not Assume These Research Approaches to be Inherently Unethical
For the reasons discussed throughout this collection and for those summarised below, these approaches to research cannot be assumed to be inherently unethical. The ethical principles by which research must be judged depend on answers to a range of questions such as:

(a) Who has a right to know the information that is being obtained?
(b) Who has a right to control access to that information?
(c) Whose interests must be protected and why?

It cannot be assumed that all information is the private property of the individual from whom it is obtained. In some circumstances, the information is public, and withholding information about it may be unethical in itself.

The use of deception in research is widely thought to be problematic. The very word 'deception' implies an intention deliberately to mislead people who are participating in research. Many writers have supposed that covert research is intrinsically deceptive. Covert research is simply research which is not fully disclosed, and there are many situations where complete disclosure will not take place. That is not necessarily 'deceptive'. Several chapters in this open access volume have discussed compelling ethical reasons why full disclosure is not ethically required for particular types of research. Those who assume covert research to be deceptive have generally been influenced by a particular class of sociological research, covert participant observation, which has at times led into illegal, unethical or at least ethically questionable activities. The examples they cite have included participation in sexual activity in public toilets, football hooliganism, neo-fascist political organisations and gang culture. The researchers producing such evidence needed to offer compelling reasons for why some elements of deception and covert work were necessary in these situations.

(2) Do Not Treat Covert, Deceptive and/or Surveillance Research 'Approaches' as a Set of Homogeneous Practices

Covertly observing people in private may be a breach of their rights, although there may be cases where this is justified. Observing people in public is less controversial, although still may impinge on people's reasonable expectations of privacy. Surveillance is not covert when 'consented' to by individuals seeking to purchase goods and services. And if the 'purposes' of surveillance are fully conveyed to those being surveilled it cannot be seen as deceptive. For these reasons, the details of what researchers plan to do and how they plan to do it have to be examined. Surveillance activities which are not necessary to the research should be removed, and efforts taken in all cases (covert, surveillance and deceptive) to mitigate potential harms which could arise. This may include, for example, pixelating faces of people when monitoring CCTV for learning about footfall patterns in public areas.

Deception has been widely used in research and in many different ways. Just as the term has a range of meaning in general conversation, it means different things in research contexts. Examples include the following:

- A medical treatment trial divides people into two groups, half of which *unknowingly* receive a placebo. For example, everyone might be told that they are receiving an experimental drug and then one group is given a placebo.
- A psychologist tells research subjects that the research is being done to examine one psychological trait, when in fact it is being done to examine another one. Subjects might be told they are experimenters, while accomplices may pose as subjects.
- An experiment is set up in which the naïve subject is thrust into interactions with the researcher's accomplices, people who are party to the deception.
- A journalist secures an interview with a politician on the understanding that it will be used for a profile, when the actual intention is to subject the politician to public criticism.
- A researcher poses as a member of the public to discover how people are treated by an agency.

Only in the medical case is research being undertaken in the private sphere. It is possible to find examples of journalism which intrude on private life – for example, 'blagging', or pretending to celebrities' service providers that they are authorised to get personal information – but such practices are unquestionably unethical. Furthermore, in deceptive cases, the research subjects should be informed of the truth after the research has taken place.

(3) Consider the Vital Role of 'Context'

The ethical considerations to be applied to covert and/or surveillance research as well as any research involving deception must be assessed in terms of the context in which the research is conducted. This refers to the concepts of 'situated ethics' (where the ethical values and principles accepted in a specific situation or context must be given due consideration in any overall ethical assessment) and what is known as 'researcher positionality' (where the motives, intentions and skills of the individual researchers or organisations must be taken into consideration).

Most professional codes of guidance identify at least four main areas of ethical concern. These include:

(1) the 'research relationship', which is the responsibility to the research's funders or sponsors;
(2) the relationship of the researcher to the research participants or to human subjects;
(3) responsibilities to the researcher's profession and to other researchers; and
(4) responsibilities to the wider society.

The objections to these research approaches are mainly focussed on the second and third of these, but some stretch to the fourth. At the same time, justifications for covert research (including surveillance research) may well be given in the context of the fourth. In all cases of deception in research, the consequences in these four domains must be considered and assessed.

(4) Engage in a Full Examination of the Approach

Surveillance and/or covert research or any element of deception should be assessed in terms of: who is doing what to whom, in what situation and for what purpose? This is a way of expanding the context of the research actions being assessed. In all research, there is a possibility that the actions of the researcher will change the behaviour of the research subject or participant, and a process of full disclosure may defeat the object of the research. The effect of revealing one's status as a researcher might be to alter the behaviour of the people being observed, and that would be self-defeating.

The presence of a researcher as participant might, for example, indicate in itself a level of support for the activity being researched (whether the other participants are aware of this researcher or not), such as acting as encouragement to anti-social behaviour (arising from a larger supportive group reducing inhibitions of the participants). None of those risks, serious as they are, is directly attributable to deceit as such.

Circumstances may arise where researchers mislead people innocently: for example, telling them that the research will be used to examine one problem, when it may turn out to be used for another; that the research will be uniquely part of one research project, when often data are recycled into others; or that the research will be used to improve treatment when it turns out that it does not do so. These are less ethically problematic than cases of deliberate deception, but proportionate efforts should be made to make the truth known to the research participants once the research concludes.

(5) Be Aware of the 'Methods' Available to Engage in Covert and/or Surveillance Research

The techniques available to conduct covert research or surveillance as well as ways of using forms of deception are developing all the time as the technologies develop. The ethical considerations to be borne in mind when using new technologies must keep up with developments in technology. Ethics appraisal must take into account the specific way that data are being gathered and the nature of those data. Some covert methods of data gathering include: a researcher directly observing the actions of subjects; a researcher indirectly observing the actions of subjects (such as via CCTV or the use of audio recording devices); a researcher participating in a group, community or organisation primarily to conduct research and not disclosing their research role to the members of the community; a researcher deliberately concealing some or all elements of the research (i.e., not 'fully informing' the subjects/participants under study); automated data gathering and analysis that is controlled by an algorithm. While remaining aware of these methods, also be aware of their limitations and realistic alternatives to the proposed research methods.

(6) Consider How the Growth of Data Analytics Has Implications for the Degree of Covert and/or Surveillance Research Made Possible

Assessing the ethical implications for covert actions requires reviewers to remain up-to-date with the rapid growth and increasing technological sophistication of Big Data. While making possible increasingly global coverage, the potential for drilling down to specific individuals and/or their communities is also enhanced. Public and political tolerance of such innovations will depend upon the uses to which they are put and that should assist with any ethics appraisal. Reviewers should consider the potential for misuse of any piece of research and ensure that researchers are aware of and have taken steps to mitigate these concerns in their work.

(7) Consider the Range of Advice and Guidance Available to Help in Assessing the Ethics of Any Proposal Containing Covert and/or Surveillance Research

Both surveillance and covert study might violate a principle of 'prior' informed consent – in which case it might be possible to seek consent from observed subjects/participants retrospectively. This might prove difficult with surveillance research that is supposed to be anonymous. This would require identifying and finding the people surveilled, or who contributed the data. Informed consent, however, is only requisite when the information being obtained is private; it is neither ethically required, nor ethical to require it, when such information is neither private nor reasonably expected to be such, for example, in the evaluation of the conduct of government. As with all methods, every effort should be made to ensure people's dignity and autonomy are promoted, and risks to subjects, researchers, the research community and society in general are minimised. In all cases, to protect researchers and research agencies, national and international law should be respected.

(8) Consider in Detail How 'Standard' Ethical Research Principles, Such As Anonymity, Confidentiality and Consent, Are To Be Managed

Anonymity and confidentiality are sometimes used as methods to protect the interests of research subjects. In some contexts, research subjects are not identifiable, and seeking informed consent would compromise the integrity of that anonymity. In cases where the participants are known to the researcher, researchers might not have total control over anonymity – especially when participants themselves engage in disclosure acts, or given modern data analytics technologies which enable personal identification to take place. Similarly, when researchers receive information about illegal acts 'in confidence', to retain that confidence might require the researcher to contravene a law and may violate the rights of others.

People cannot give prior informed consent if they do not know what they are consenting to, and the whole point of deception is to ensure that they do not know what is going on at the time when it is happening. The question is whether the research is of such a character that prior informed consent is required. Public policy research includes many circumstances where the consent of the subject is not required: they include some actions in the public domain, actions to make governments accountable or aspects of organisational research.

This does not address the criticism that the absence of consent fails to treat people with respect. If the person affected has no right to consent, part of the objection to deception falls – but the remaining part, that this is not treating people with respect, is difficult to avoid. Deceiving people about the purpose of research, and enlightening them afterwards, treats them as 'naïve subjects'.

If people do not know what is happening, they cannot exercise a meaningful choice about it which is a challenge to their autonomy. But a restriction on liberty is not the primary concern. It is that sometimes research inflicts costs and harms on research subjects, for example, by the deliberate infliction of stress or anxiety, and the right to consent afterwards is not much consolation.

Deception certainly betrays trust. Whenever researchers negotiate the terms of a contract with a research participant, they make undertakings, explicitly or implicitly: engaging in deception about their role is a breach of the particular rights and duties that are created in the process. However, reasons exist (discussed fully in Iphofen & O'Mathúna, 2022) to ethically justify doing so, even while such research remains risky and must be very carefully reviewed. Where deception has occurred, the correct information, and the reasons for the deception, should be made explicit to the participants when their involvement finishes.

(9) Consider the Public Interest

A major justification often given for covert and/or surveillance research is that it offers the only way of gathering data that may be in the public interest. The reviewer's role is to assess, in as much detail as possible, whether the proposed research engagement can be considered truly 'in the public interest'. Note that what is in the public interest is not always the same as what the public finds interesting.

Some (like Homan, R. (1991). *The ethics of social research.* London: Macmillan) argue that deception raises legitimate concerns over the professional responsibilities of researchers:

- deception may 'pollute the research environment', leading people to be suspicious of researchers;
- deception is bad for the reputation of research and researchers; and
- use of deception may legitimate deception to be more widely used.

Additionally, there is the risk that:

- the habit of deception may infect the researcher's behaviour – it could 'become a way of life' and
- the strain of maintaining a deception may be damaging to the researcher.

It is not in the public interest for trust in research and researchers to be undermined. Therefore, deception in research must be justified, carefully reviewed and disclosed to participants when their participation concludes.

(10) Ensure You Are as Informed as Possible by the Available Literature and Illustrative Case Studies So That You Can Give Careful Consideration to the 'Promises' Made By Any Research That Is Covert, That Requires Surveillance and/ or Entails Significant and Ethically 'Risky' Deception

Thoroughly examine any research proposal that appears (implicitly or explicitly) to require deceptive, covert and/or surveillance practices. Information about the ethical risks entailed in these research approaches is clear and easily available. A recommended source is the open access volume for which this guidance was developed and is cited in the Preamble.

PART B

Guidance for Policymakers on Covert, Deceptive and Surveillance Research

Policymakers and those who advise and directly influence them should be informed by evidence from research that has been conducted with rigour and integrity. Some research is so completely ethically tainted that widespread consensus agrees it should not have been conducted and the evidence obtained should not be used (the classic example is experimentation conducted in Nazi concentration camps). Other research is so methodologically flawed that it should not be used in policymaking. The chapters in this open access volume (see below) examined some challenging research methods in depth, and provided detailed discussions about when such methods can be ethically justified and when they might not be. The types of research explored involve covert, deceptive and/or surveillance methods. These were defined briefly in the Preamble to these guidance notes, and here we provide a concise summary in the form of guidance notes for policymakers. These considerations were written with a broad set of policymakers in mind, and those providing guidance to policymakers, such as advisors and think tanks. We do not provide simple categorisations of specific research methods as ethical or unethical, but offer these considerations as prompts to facilitate further reflection and consideration of the details of each piece of research to allow more complete assessments of whether or not the research findings should influence policy. The following points are provided as a concise summary of the issues addressed in greater detail throughout the open access volume in which these notes were first produced (Iphofen & O'Mathúna, 2022).

(1) Do Not Assume Covert, Deceptive and/or Surveillance Research To Be Inherently Unethical
For the reasons discussed throughout this collection and for those summarised below, these research approaches cannot be assumed to be inherently unethical. Policies based on such research can be ethically justified. The ethical principles by which this form of research must be judged depend on answers to a range of questions such as:

(a) Who has a right to know the information that is being obtained?
(b) Who has a right to control access to that information?
(c) Whose interests must be protected and why?

These questions have been considered in greater depth throughout the open access volume within which this guidance is contained. It cannot be assumed that all information is the private property of the individual from whom it is obtained. In some circumstances, the information is public and should be used to inform public policy. Not allowing public information to inform public policy may be unethical in itself.

(2) Do Not Treat Covert, Deceptive and/or Surveillance Research 'Approaches' as a Set of Homogeneous Practices
Covertly observing people in private may be a breach of their rights, although there may be cases where this is justified. Observing people in public is less controversial, although still may impinge on people's reasonable expectations of privacy. Surveillance is not covert when 'consented' to by individuals seeking to purchase goods and services. And if the 'purposes' of surveillance are fully conveyed to those being surveilled it cannot be seen as deceptive. For these reasons, the details of what researchers plan to do and how they plan to do it have to be examined. Surveillance activities which are not necessary to the research should be removed, and efforts taken in all cases (covert, surveillance and deceptive) to mitigate potential harms which could arise. This may include, for example, pixelating faces of people when monitoring CCTV for learning about footfall patterns in public areas.

(3) Deceptive Research Practices Cover a Variety of Approaches That Must Be Understood before Deciding to Use or Not Use Such Results

Deception has been widely used in research and in many different ways. Just as the term has a range of meaning in general conversation, it means different things in research contexts. Examples include:

- A medical treatment trial divides people into two groups, half of which *unknowingly* receive a placebo. For example, everyone might be told they are receiving an experimental drug and then one group is given a placebo.
- A psychologist tells research subjects that the research is being done to examine one psychological trait, when in fact it is being done to examine another one.
- An experiment is set up in which the naïve subject is thrust into interactions with the researcher's accomplices, people who are party to the deception. Subjects might be told they are experimenters, while accomplices may pose as subjects.
- A journalist secures an interview with a politician on the understanding that it will be used for a profile, when the actual intention is to subject the politician to public criticism.
- A researcher poses as a member of the public to discover how people are treated by an agency.

Using deception in research is 'risky' as it can lead to various types of harms, and often has negative connotations, which should be taken into account by policymakers. Despite this, these approaches can be ethically justified if the knowledge gained from such research is important, especially for public policy, and if the harms involved are not excessive and mitigated against as much as reasonably possible. Research involving deception must be carefully and thoroughly examined to determine whether the deception was justified in order to decide whether or not to use its findings in policymaking.

(4) Policymakers Should Consider the Vital Role of 'Context'

The ethical considerations to be applied to research involving covert, deceptive and surveillance methods must be assessed in terms of the context in which the research is conducted. These factors include the importance of culture and history, and how this impacts the assessment of research. This refers to the concepts of 'situated ethics' (where the ethical values and principles accepted in a specific situation or context must be given due consideration in any overall ethical assessment) and what is known as 'researcher positionality' (where the motives, intentions and skills of the individual researchers or organisations must be taken into consideration).

(5) Engage in a Full Examination of the Detailed Approach Used in the Research

Research with covert, deceptive and surveillance methods should be assessed in terms of: who is doing what to whom, in what situation and for what purpose?

This is a way of expanding the context of the research actions being assessed. In all research, there is a possibility that the actions of the researcher will change the behaviour of the research subjects or participants, and a process of full disclosure may defeat the object of the research. These assessments require advisors with requisite skills and may take some time, which should be taken into account when planning policy development.

(6) Be Open and Transparent If Research Using Covert, Deceptive or Surveillance Methods Was Used to Inform Policy

The use of these methods should be acknowledged when describing the studies that were used to inform policy. Attempts to hide or ignore dimensions of a study that might be seen by some as raising ethical questions are likely to generate further controversy beyond that of the research itself. Not disclosing such aspects of studies might lead some to question or even distrust the integrity of the policymaking process. Transparency and open discussion about the studies used to inform policy, along with addressing questions some might have about them, will help to offset such controversies.

(7) Provide a Clear Rationale to Explain How Research Using Covert, Deceptive or Surveillance Methods Was Determined as Suitable to Inform Policy

If covert, deceptive or surveillance research is used to inform policy, the process and criteria by which such assessments were made should be openly available. This both helps to inform users of the policy about how specific studies were included or excluded, and helps to provide information to the public on how such assessments can and should be made. Such a process should be determined and put in place ahead of time for those making and influencing policy that is likely to be informed by research using these methods.

(8) Data Analytics May Be Used to Inform Policy, But They Must Be Used Carefully and Transparently

Big Data raises a number of relatively new ethical quandaries which are only just starting to be carefully and thoroughly evaluated. This open access volume provides some such detailed assessments. Policymakers should develop guidelines and regulations that ensure data are used ethically and appropriately. In turn, policy should be developed on the basis of ethically justified Big Data research, especially when they have been collected using covert, deceptive or surveillance methods. Much further work needs to be carried out in this area to ensure data are an asset and not a liability for society.

(9) Policymakers Should Seek Community Input on Acceptable Research Practices

Communities and cultures will differ in their evaluation of the acceptability of covert, deceptive and surveillance methods in research. Policymakers should seek input from the communities impacted by their policies ('stakeholders') so that these views are taken into account. This will also help to ensure that policies may be more likely to be seen as acceptable by the community. Since these views may change over time, especially following prominent events related to these forms of research, this input should be sought on a regular basis. The mechanisms used for gathering this input can also be used by policymakers to explain their rationale in using or not using such types of research.

(10) Ensure You Are as Informed as Possible by the Available Literature and Take Account of Illustrative Case Studies
Information about the ethical risks entailed in these research approaches is clear and easily available. As recommended above, see Iphofen and O'Mathúna (2022).

SUGGESTIONS FOR ADDING TO AND/OR IMPROVING THIS GUIDANCE SHOULD BE SENT TO: https://prores-project.eu/contact-us/

INDEX